The Health Care Revolution

CALIFORNIA/MILBANK BOOKS ON HEALTH AND THE PUBLIC

1. *The Corporate Practice of Medicine: Competition and Innovation in Health Care,* by James C. Robinson
2. *Experiencing Politics: A Legislator's Stories of Government and Health Care,* by John E. McDonough
3. *Public Health Law: Power, Duty, Restraint,* by Lawrence O. Gostin
4. *Public Health Law and Ethics: A Reader,* edited by Lawrence O. Gostin
5. *Big Doctoring in America: Profiles in Primary Care,* by Fitzhugh Mullan, M.D.
6. *Deceit and Denial: The Deadly Politics of Industrial Pollution,* by Gerald Markowitz and David Rosner
7. *Death Is That Man Taking Names: Intersections of American Medicine, Law, and Culture,* by Robert A. Burt
8. *When Walking Fails: Mobility Problems of Adults with Chronic Conditions,* by Lisa I. Iezzoni
9. *What Price Better Health? Hazards of the Research Imperative,* by Daniel Callahan
10. *Sick to Death and Not Going to Take It Anymore! Reforming Health Care for the Last Years of Life,* by Joanne Lynn
11. *The Employee Retirement Income Security Act of 1974: A Political History,* by James A. Wooten
12. *Evidence-Based Medicine and the Search for a Science of Clinical Care,* by Jeanne Daly
13. *Disease and Democracy: The Industrialized World Faces AIDS,* by Peter Baldwin
14. *Medicare Matters: What Geriatric Medicine Can Teach American Health Care,* by Christine K. Cassel
15. *Are We Ready? Public Health since 9/11,* by David Rosner and Gerald Markowitz
16. *State of Immunity: The Politics of Vaccination in Twentieth-Century America,* by James Colgrove
17. *Low Income, Social Growth, and Good Health: A History of Twelve Countries,* by James C. Riley
18. *Searching Eyes: Privacy, the State, and Disease Surveillance in America,* by Amy L. Fairchild, Ronald Bayer, and James Colgrove
19. *The Health Care Revolution: From Medical Monopoly to Market Competition,* by Carl F. Ameringer

The Health Care Revolution

From Medical Monopoly to Market Competition

CARL F. AMERINGER

University of California Press

BERKELEY LOS ANGELES LONDON

Milbank Memorial Fund

NEW YORK

University of California Press, one of the most distinguished university presses in the United States, enriches lives around the world by advancing scholarship in the humanities, social sciences, and natural sciences. Its activities are supported by the UC Press Foundation and by philanthropic contributions from individuals and institutions. For more information, visit www.ucpress.edu.

The Milbank Memorial Fund is an endowed operating foundation that engages in nonpartisan analysis, study, research, and communication on significant issues in health policy. In the Fund's own publications, in reports or books it publishes with other organizations, and in articles it commissions for publication by other organizations, the Fund endeavors to maintain the highest standards for accuracy and fairness. Statements by individual authors, however, do not necessarily reflect opinions or factual determinations of the Fund. For more information, visit www.milbank.org.

University of California Press
Berkeley and Los Angeles, California

University of California Press, Ltd.
London, England

Library of Congress Cataloging-in-Publication Data

Ameringer, Carl F.
The health care revolution : from medical monopoly to market competition / Carl F. Ameringer.
p. ; cm. — (California/Milbank books on health and the public ; 19)
Includes bibliographical references and index.
ISBN: 978-0-520-25480-0 (cloth : alk. paper)
1. Health care reform—United States—History—20th century. 2. American Medical Association—History—20th century. 3. Medical care—United States—Finance—History—20th century. 4. United States. Federal Trade Commission—History—20th century. I. Milbank Memorial Fund. II. Title. III. Series.
[DNLM: 1. United States. Federal Trade Commission. 2. American Medical Association. 3. Health Care Reform—history—United States. 4. Antitrust Laws—history—United States. 5. Economic Competition—history—United States. 6. Health Policy—history—United States. 7. History, 20th Century—United States. WA 11 AA1 A512h 2008]

RA395.A3A5974 2008
362.1'0425—dc22 2007016244

Manufactured in the United States of America

17 16 15 14 13 12 11 10 09 08
10 9 8 7 6 5 4 3 2 1

This book is printed on New Leaf EcoBook 50, a 100% recycled fiber of which 50% is de-inked post-consumer waste, processed chlorine-free. EcoBook 50 is acid-free and meets the minimum requirements of ANSI/ASTM D5634-01 (*Permanence of Paper*).

For Caroline and Katie

The first and most urgent necessity in the area of government policy is the elimination of those measures which directly support monopoly.

MILTON FRIEDMAN, *Capitalism and Freedom*

Contents

Foreword

The Milbank Memorial Fund is an endowed operating foundation that works to improve health by helping decision makers in the public and private sectors acquire and use the best available evidence to inform policy for health care and population health. The Fund has engaged in nonpartisan analysis, study, research, and communication about significant issues in health policy since its inception in 1905.

The Health Care Revolution: From Medical Monopoly to Market Competition is the nineteenth of the California/Milbank Books on Health and the Public. The publishing partnership between the Fund and the University of California Press encourages the synthesis and communication of findings from research and experience that could contribute to more effective health policy.

Carl Ameringer describes as revolutionary a "shift from a professional to a market regime" in health care as a result of the application of federal antitrust laws to the behavior of physicians since the 1970s. This revolution and what he calls the "counteroffensive" against it by organizations of physicians have had a profound influence on policy making that affects not only access to health care, but also the quality and cost of that care.

Ameringer writes the history of the revolution and evaluates its significance for policy. His research draws on skills and experience he acquired as a lawyer and former assistant attorney general of Maryland and as a political scientist. An example of the unusual perspective he brings to this book is his observation that "in addition to being the only Western industrialized nation that lacks a government-run or government-financed health care system, the United States is also unique in its enduring adherence to an antitrust tradition." This tradition, according to Ameringer, has been a "significant factor in the decision of policy makers to pursue markets rather than budgets to contain costs and to allocate resources."

At the end of the book Ameringer assesses the effects of the incomplete revolution and its implications for policy in the future. The history Ameringer presents has shifted considerable power from the suppliers of health services, and especially from physicians, to the demand side of the market for care, and particularly to government and employer purchasers and the health plans and insurers who are their agents. Purchasers, Ameringer concludes, "are just beginning to mine the fruits of this alignment." The partial triumph of the market over professional monopoly could, for example, induce purchasers to act collectively to remedy market failure.

Carmen Hooker Odom, President
Daniel M. Fox, President Emeritus
Samuel L. Milbank, Chairman

Preface

Most nations of the world share similar goals concerning the provision of health care to their citizens—broad access, low costs, and high quality. But the means for achieving these goals can differ, particularly in the United States, where a market-based approach as opposed to a more centralized, government-run system prevails.

Many historians and political scientists have written about the failure of the United States to achieve universal health coverage. In so doing, they often decry the role of the medical profession, which, for much of the twentieth century, resisted government intervention. But in focusing almost exclusively on the repudiation of a government-based system, historians and political scientists frequently neglect the U.S. path toward market competition. Many economists and legal scholars, on the other hand, have written about the virtues of free markets to enhance consumer welfare and economic efficiency. They note the use of antitrust laws during the 1970s and 1980s to increase competition by wresting control of the health care industry from organized medicine. The result is that two distinct accounts have emerged to relate the trajectory of U.S. health policy. These accounts have been informed by the particular line of inquiry, policy preferences, and methodology of certain scholarly disciplines. This book seeks to synthesize and narrow the gap between these competing accounts and perspectives. It also seeks to tell a story that few have told about the efforts of market proponents to overcome the hegemony of the medical profession.

I began my journey in 1999 when I presented a paper on the Federal Trade Commission and the American Medical Association at the *Journal of Policy History* Conference, typically held in St. Louis once every two years. The policy history conference provides a unique opportunity for historians and political scientists to come together to discuss their research pursuits. I was most fortunate in my first outing to be on a panel with Paul Quirk. Thanks to Quirk's keen insights, I was able to hone my analysis for publication in the *Journal of Policy History*.

While attending the policy history conference on another occasion, this time in 2002, I had the good fortune to meet Dan Fox. Having read my first book on the state medical boards, Fox expressed interest in my research. When I told Fox of my desire to write a book on the confrontation between professionalism and capitalism, he invited me to submit a proposal. With encouragement from Fox and Lynne Withey of the University of California Press, an offer of a book contract was made. The Milbank Memorial Fund generously provided me with a travel allowance, making it possible for me to interview numerous individuals and to spend several days at a time conducting research in Chicago, Washington, D.C., and Durham, North Carolina. A faculty development grant and a one-semester sabbatical from teaching also jump-started my book project.

Early in my research, I met David Hyman, then special counsel to the FTC, and Donald Palmisano, president of the AMA, at a conference at Northwestern University. Hyman expressed interest in my work and, in the succeeding months and years, facilitated access to important documents and individuals. With Palmisano's assistance, I eventually came into contact with Ross Rubin, the head of legislative affairs at the AMA. Rubin provided important information about the medical association, including pertinent correspondence between AMA and government officials and published reports of the association's House of Delegates. Absent the support of Hyman and Rubin, the story that I tell would be vastly incomplete. I owe much to their extraordinary assistance.

In addition to Hyman, Rubin, and Palmisano, I want to thank several other persons who generously gave of their time during the research phase of this book. These include B. J. Anderson, Ernest Barnes, Jack Bierig, Barry Costilo, H. E. Frech, Thomas Greaney, Clark Havighurst, William Kovacic, Art Lerner, Timothy Muris, Alan Palmer, and Dan Schwartz.

Thanks in no small part to my former colleagues at the University of Wisconsin–Oshkosh and a one-year reduction in my teaching load after my sabbatical, I was able to complete a first draft of the manuscript by the end of 2005. That would mark the beginning of a remarkable and undeniably intense review process. Rather than send the manuscript to a few individuals for blind review, the Fund and the press assembled a large group of diverse scholars and practitioners for face-to-face interaction. These included Jim Bentley, Ed Berkowitz, Bob Dickler, Clark Havighurst, David Hyman, Art Lerner, Dan Schwartz, and Rosemary Stevens. Each read the manuscript in its entirety, and each offered comprehensive and helpful advice. The meeting that took place in Washington, D.C., and lasted almost two full days was an occasion that I will always remember. I cannot thank the participants enough for their efforts and the Fund and the press for sponsoring the event. But for the intensity of the vetting process, coupled with the helpful prodding and probing of Dan Fox, the flaws in my story would have been far more apparent. I, of course, take full responsibility for those that remain.

Finally, I would like to thank my wife, Suzanne, my parents, Charles and Jean, and my mother-in-law, Mary. They provided me with much love and support throughout. This book is dedicated to my daughters, Caroline and Katie. Over the years, they stoically endured my dinner-table ramblings on health policy.

Introduction

This book is about the health care revolution of the 1970s, which ended the medical monopoly in the United States and made a market-based health policy politically thinkable for the first time. It relates the events leading up to the revolution and the use of federal antitrust laws to help bring it about. It examines the revolution's trajectory and discerns its consequences and aftershocks. Finally, it brings to light the efforts of the medical profession in the 1990s to alter the revolution's course.

As is true of most revolutions, a conflict transpired between those who sought to maintain the status quo and those who sought to reform the system. In this story, the proponents of market competition, led by the Federal Trade Commission, overthrew the medical monopoly, led by the American Medical Association. The initial confrontations between these two adversaries took place in legal forums where the FTC held the advantage. But as the competition for hegemony expanded to include additional players, the economic principles that reformers propounded became diluted in the face of special interests.

In the process of telling this story, I seek to answer some important questions about the acquisition, control, and loss of political and economic power in the United States. How do policy regimes, such as the medical monopoly, come about? What are the underpinnings of their authority? Under what circumstances do new regimes rise to take their place? What is the process for shifting power from one regime to another? What happens once a change in regimes occurs?

A BRIEF SYNOPSIS

In the late 1970s in the United States, a profound shift in government policy occurred. Simply stated, the federal government abandoned the notion, held since the beginning of the twentieth century, that regulation was good, that it served the public interest. Instead, policy makers adopted the economic theory of regulation which held that most regulation benefited interest groups. Suddenly, it seemed the responsibilities of government agencies, such as those that oversaw the trucking, telecommunications, or airlines industries, were terminated or greatly diminished. Policy makers now lauded the strengths of competition rather than proclaiming its weaknesses.

Federal policy to promote competition transformed the health care industry. As in other industries, policy makers moved to deregulate health care, but their approach was different. Unlike the trucking, telecommunications, or airlines industries, in which onerous governmental regulations discouraged new competitors from entering the field, the medical profession, not government, restricted competition through myriad rules, ethical pronouncements, and anticompetitive practices. Thus, rather than pull back, the federal government moved forward, using the antitrust laws to promote competition.

Before the 1970s, the application of the antitrust laws to the medical profession was sporadic at best. Attorneys from the U.S. Department of Justice rarely pursued physicians and their associations, in part because federal courts lacked jurisdiction over local or intrastate matters. In addition, members of the legal community believed that the antitrust laws, which prevented restraints of "trade" or "commerce," did not apply to professional practice. Professionals, they said, were not engaged in business pursuits. Moreover, economists, such as Kenneth Arrow, perceived that certain practices of the medical profession, even if anticompetitive, were necessary to overcome imperfections in the market for health care services. These imperfections, Arrow said, stemmed from "the existence of uncertainty in the incidence of disease and in the efficacy of treatment" (1963:947). Arrow's analysis tracked the public-interest approach to regulation.

Several things changed over the course of the twentieth century to make the application of the antitrust laws to the medical profession more feasible. First, the practice of medicine evolved from an enterprise that was largely isolated and independent to one that was dependent upon colleagues, hospitals, and expensive technology for the diagnosis and treatment of disease. Physicians increasingly specialized in a particular area of medicine, worked in a hospital or other institutional setting, and relied on third parties or insurance companies to pay their fees. Second, the federal government in the 1960s became a major purchaser of health care. For the first time, the interests of government in containing costs opposed those of physicians who sought to maximize their returns. Professional associations, now bargainers on behalf of physicians, clashed with public agencies over pay and workplace control. Third, the dispiriting events of the Vietnam War and the Watergate scandal, combined with the civil rights, women's rights, and the consumer movements in the 1960s and 1970s, undermined traditional institutions and entrenched practices. The "learned professions"—among them medicine, law, dentistry, and engineering—lost standing and prestige. Fourth, during the 1970s the country experienced economic turmoil in addition to political unrest. An oil crisis, high unemployment, and runaway inflation precipitated two recessions. Policy makers and politicians searched for fresh ideas and new insights that would stem the recessionary tide.

Laissez faire economics—the policy of relying on competitive markets to guide economic development and protect consumer interests—was not a new idea, but its reformulation by Milton Friedman and other disciples of the Chicago school challenged the approach of New Dealers who favored government "command and control." In the highly charged political, social, and economic atmosphere of the 1970s, the ideas of market proponents took hold and grew. By the end of the decade, most politicians, influenced by the "new" economics, supported deregulation, privatization, and tax relief.

The principles of market theory spilled over to the health care arena, where spending had rapidly increased, primarily because of the availability of federal funds following enactment of the Medicare and Medicaid programs. To stem costs, government officials first tried health planning and other forms of regulation, but the initial results were disappointing. Financial incentives to decrease spending did not exist, and the system for delivering health care remained largely fragmented and inefficient. Most physicians practiced by themselves or in pairs and accepted payment only on a fee-for-service basis; there was little, if any, coordination of general and specialty practice (see Stevens 1971).

Physician Paul Ellwood and economist Alain Enthoven, early pioneers of market reform, favored the reorganization of the health care industry. Ellwood spearheaded the integration of finance and delivery, coining the term *health maintenance organization,* or HMO; Enthoven, for his part, advanced prepaid group practice and the independent practice association, or IPA. Both individuals envisioned an environment that required doctors in competing groups "to work together to manage quality and cost of care for their voluntarily enrolled populations" (Enthoven 1999). Legal scholar Clark Havighurst also favored the HMO model and prepaid group practice but believed that the resistance of physicians and their professional associations would hinder their development. Seeking to open the market to "a wide range of health care and delivery options," Havighurst advocated the use of the antitrust laws to free the health care industry from professional domination (Agrawal and Veit 2002:27).

In the mid-1970s, the Federal Trade Commission moved to implement Havighurst's ideas. Lawyers at the FTC banned restrictions on advertising, solicitation, and contract practice; prohibited professional associations from organizing boycotts of insurance carriers; and curtailed physician oversight of competitors and their activities. Unshackled, HMOs and other organizations that "managed care" emerged in the 1980s. Managed care organizations used several techniques to control spending and rationalize health care delivery. These techniques included utilization review, preauthorization for certain diagnostic procedures and treatment modalities, the use of primary care providers as gatekeepers, and a new mechanism for paying physicians, known as capitation, that represented a big change from the customary method, known as fee-for service.

But neither staff-model HMOs, which integrated finance and delivery, nor prepaid group practices developed and flourished as Ellwood and Enthoven had hoped and envisioned. Instead, commercial insurers, responding to the demands of large employers, formed extensive provider networks and sold comprehensive insurance coverage; physicians, for their part, "contract[ed] with as many carriers as possible to protect their patient volumes" (Agrawal and Veit 2002:36). Few players, carriers and physicians alike, assumed dual responsibility for controlling costs and for improving quality. The segregation of delivery and finance persisted.

Physicians' frustration with managed care and market competition precipitated a counterrevolution in the 1990s. The principal organizers of the counterrevolution, the AMA and its component state and local medical societies, attacked managed care in Congress, state legislatures, the courts, and the media. Responding to the complaints of physicians as well as those of their patients, legislators in all fifty states enacted hundreds of laws and regulations ostensibly for reasons of consumer protection. The resulting mix of professional, industry, and government oversight and regulation increased the complexity of an already complex system. The politics of health care—as fragmented, polarized, and perplexing as the industry itself—stifled the original goals of the market proponents.

CONFLICTING REGIMES AND IDEOLOGIES

The story of the health care industry in the United States is a story of conflicting regimes and their accompanying ideologies. For the first seventy-five years of the twentieth century, the professional regime prevailed. Since the overthrow of professional authority in the late 1970s, the market regime has taken hold. The professional regime and the market regime are creatures of historical context: the public-interest theory of regulation, nurtured during the Progressive and New Deal eras, bolstered professional ideology; the economic theory of regulation, which gained traction in the 1970s, augured market competition. Both regimes utilized important organizing tools: the AMA Code of Medical Ethics supported professional authority; federal antitrust laws sustained market theory. And both regimes formed political coalitions to advance their objectives: the professional coalition, spearheaded by the AMA, furthered the interests of physicians and their professional associations; the managed care coalition, comprised of purchasers and payers of health care, promoted the interests of government and insurers.

I proceed from the premise that powerful ideas are central to the overthrow and replacement of a policy regime or monopoly. Policy makers turn to ideas to make sense of the world in times of social unrest, economic crisis, or political uncertainty. Ideas aid policy makers in building coalitions and make collective action possible. They are "weapons" in the overthrow and "blueprints" in the design of new regimes and institutions (Blyth 2002:252–259).

Though I recognize the important role of interest groups in the formation of public policy, I assert that individual motivations are highly complex and do not readily lend themselves to a single approach or theory. Public policy is not the product of self-interest alone, as some advocates of rational choice or public choice theory have asserted (see Downs 1985; Stigler 1988; Feldstein 1988); rather, the policy process reflects the interaction of both ideas and interests.

I claim that powerful ideas prevail over interests when change is nonincremental, but that interests prevail over ideas once a new regime emerges. More specifically, I argue that market theory prompted the health care revolution, including the antitrust strategy of the Federal Trade Commission. Once market thinking gained a foothold, special interests turned market principles to their economic and political advantage.

This approach has much support in the literature. Political scientist Mark Blyth, for instance, demonstrated that economic ideas underlie two "great transformations" in American public policy in the twentieth century, the first in the 1930s and the second in the 1970s. "What is critically important in understanding agents' behaviors," Blyth wrote, "are the ideas held by agents, not their structurally derived interests" (2002:34). Policy analyst John McDonough showed that market theory led to the demise of hospital rate-setting in several states. According to McDonough, "Regulatory schemes are borne out of explosive crises when old ideas no longer work and the status quo no longer meets current needs; after a period of seeming stability and equilibrium as the new idea evolves, the new system inevitably confronts a new crisis leading to a new replacement policy idea and structure" (1997:214). Writing over a decade before Blyth and McDonough, political scientists Martha Derthick and Paul Quirk asked why special interests were unable to stop the deregulation of the airlines, trucking, and telecommunications industries. "Most certainly, the regulated industries in our three cases did not ask to be deregulated," Derthick and Quirk asserted (1985:21). "Our cases demonstrate the role that disinterested economic analysis can play in the formation of public policy" (Derthick and Quirk 1985:246).

The similarities among these three studies and the one described in this book are obvious and compelling. Each links the sea change in the intellectual climate of the 1970s to a specific transformation in government policy, whether lower taxes, hospital rate-setting, deregulation, or the overthrow of the professional monopoly. Each notes several preconditions to the application of market theory, such as changes in government finance (the Medicare and Medicaid programs), the social environment (civil rights, women's rights, and consumer movements), and science and technology. And each recognizes the important but secondary role of special interests when change is nonincremental.

Once a new policy regime assumes control, special interests compete for political and economic advantage within the confines of the new legal order. This is the stage where "ideas take a back seat" and pressure groups prevail (McDonough 1997:215). Individuals who successfully push their ideas in policy circles typically must wait and see how things unfold. Few can predict the direction that a new policy regime will take and the outcomes, often unintended, that may result (see Kingdon 1995:177–178).

The work of political scientists Paul Sabatier and Hank Jenkins-Smith on "advocacy coalitions" or policy elites informs this part of the analysis (1993; 1999). Advocacy coalitions comprise individuals with shared beliefs. Stated another way, shared beliefs are the "glue" that hold advocacy coalitions together. Coalitions compete within a policy subsystem by pursuing their objectives in diverse public forums (courts, agencies, and legislatures) and at all levels of government (local, state, and national). Public policy, according to Sabatier and Jenkins-Smith, reflects the interaction of competing coalitions.

In the 1980s and 1990s, two advocacy coalitions emerged to dominate the health care subsystem. These were the professional coalition spearheaded by the AMA and the managed care coalition comprised of payers and purchasers of health care (insurers, health plans, large employers, and government agencies). The trajectory of the health care industry during the 1980s and 1990s has reflected, to a significant degree, the outcomes of numerous contests between these two coalitions. At times, professional associations and corporate health plans clashed over purely monetary matters: reimbursement rates and the like; at other times, they clashed over core beliefs, such as the nature and extent of professional self-regulation, clinical autonomy, and the freedom of patients to choose their own physicians.

Managed care, as it developed, threatened physicians' core beliefs. HMOs, preferred provider organizations (PPOs), and other corporate forms and arrangements often required administrators (nonphysicians as well as physicians) to devise clinical standards and to oversee doctors' work. These practices infringed on professional self-regulation. In addition, the techniques that HMOs and PPOs adopted to control costs—capitation, gatekeeping, preauthorization, and utilization review—undercut clinical autonomy. Finally, HMOs and PPOs entered into contracts with physicians for reasons related to the quality and efficiency of their performance rather than simply their willingness to undertake the work. These tactics, known as selective contracting and closed panels, offended the principle of free choice of physician.

Despite growing differences during the 1980s and 1990s among doctors in background, philosophy, and specialization, the profession's core beliefs—self-regulation, autonomy, and free choice of physician—remained a steady source of pride and solidarity. An important feature of core beliefs is that they resonate and remain active even when a group loses power or structural change occurs. Groups will fight to uphold their core beliefs and will rally around them in times of uncertainty or stress (see Sabatier and Jenkins-Smith 1993; 1999). So it was with the medical profession. Exploiting certain exceptions to the antitrust statutes, the AMA-led coalition lobbied state legislatures to pass anti–managed care laws, euphemistically called "patient protection legislation." There was very little that the FTC and Department of Justice could do about it other than respond in the political arena. Though the managed care coalition prevailed in Congress, professional associations won over state legislatures. By the late 1990s, political and legal conflicts between the professional and the managed care coalitions had produced a cacophony of court opinions, decrees, and legislative enactments that, taken as a whole, eviscerated many of managed care's techniques for lowering the costs of health care services.

A SHORT PRIMER ON THE ANTITRUST LAWS

The purpose of this section is to ease the reader's understanding of the events depicted in this narrative. Though challenging and complex, antitrust law does not encompass numerous rules and regulations. Rather, the antitrust statutes—the Sherman Act of 1890 and the Clayton and Federal Trade Commission Acts of 1914—are relatively short and few. Like the U.S. Constitution, they contain several open-ended words and phrases and, like the U.S. Constitution, the Supreme Court has shown a keen interest in their interpretation. "The central institution in making the antitrust laws has been the Supreme Court," Robert Bork has written (Bork 1978:409). "That is true," he said, "because the antitrust laws are so open-textured, leave so much to be filled in by the judiciary, that the Court plays in antitrust almost as unconstrained a role as it does in constitutional law" (1978:409). Consequently, one must look to Supreme Court opinions and the economic philosophy that such opinions embody in order to discern the past and current trajectory of antitrust policy in the United States.

The following statutory provisions and legal concepts contained in Supreme Court opinions are central to a proper understanding of the events detailed in this book.

Section 1 of the Sherman Act

There is perhaps no clearer example of an "open-textured" law than section 1 of the Sherman Act (hereafter "section 1"), the provision at issue in the majority of cases involving the medical profession. Section 1 states as follows: "Every contract, combination in the form of trust or otherwise, or conspiracy, in restraint of trade or commerce among the several States, or with foreign nations, is hereby declared to be illegal." Did the framers of section 1 mean to imply that every contract or combination that limited competition was illegal or only those that were socially objectionable?

The Rule of Reason

Seeking to clarify the meaning of section 1, the Supreme Court developed the "rule of reason." The rule of reason, the Court said, was for use in determining a restraint's "impact on competitive conditions" (*National Society of Professional Engineers v. United States,* 435 U.S. 679, 688 [1978]). Did the restraint in question, the Court asked, "merely regulate and perhaps thereby promote competition," or did it "suppress or even destroy competition"? (*Chicago Board of Trade v. United States,* 246 U.S. 231, 238 [1918]). The rule of reason had nothing to do with the price of a particular good or the "special characteristics of a particular industry" (*Professional Engineers*, 435 U.S. at 689). Rather, it centered on the concerted efforts of private parties to destroy competition. Several factors entered into the Court's "reasonableness" inquiry. These factors included "the *purpose* of the particular agreement, the *market power* of the parties, whether a *less restrictive alternative* [was] available, and the agreement's procompetitive and anticompetitive *effects*" (Havighurst, Blumstein, and Brennan 1998:519, emphasis in original).

The Per Se Rule

Notwithstanding the Court's refined interpretation of section 1, proving a restraint of trade under the rule of reason could be very time consuming, difficult, and expensive. According to law professor Thomas Greaney, "It is no secret that rule of reason, as currently interpreted, has become a defendant's paradise. Few, if any, plaintiffs can shoulder the burden of proving markets, market power, absence of likely entry, likelihood of collusion, and the myriad of other requirements entailing highly speculative evidence that have been heaped upon them" (Greaney 1996:140). Responding to such concerns and for purposes of "clarity and ease of enforcement," the Court developed certain per se rules or shortcuts in instances where agreements, on their face, lacked "any redeeming virtue" (*Northern Pac. Ry. Co. v. United States*, 356 U.S. 1, 5 [1958]). Price-fixing was a classic example. According to the Court, "price is the 'central nervous system of the economy,' and an agreement that 'interfere[s] with the setting of price by free market forces' is illegal on its face" (*Professional Engineers*, 435 U.S. at 692). Other similarly objectionable forms of conduct included division of markets, group boycotts, and "tying arrangements." A case-by-case inquiry into the actual effects of such agreements or conduct was unnecessary.

Many of the cases involving the guild aspects of the medical profession in the late 1970s and early 1980s involved price-fixing or group boycotts of competitors and insurers. To the lawyers who prosecuted these cases on behalf of the federal government, the violations themselves seemed readily apparent. Yet many judges hesitated when applying the per se rule to the conduct in question. Most often, they paused to consider the reasons why physicians and their professional associations acted in an anticompetitive manner. Rather than engage in a lengthy inquiry or detailed industry analysis, however, these judges employed a "quick look" rule of reason approach, an intermediate step, to evaluate restraints that were "inherently suspect" (see *F.T.C. v. Indiana Federation of Dentists*, 476 U.S. 447 [1986]).

The Learned Professions Exemption

Section 1 of the Sherman Act refers to restraints on "trade" or "commerce." Until 1975, lawyers, doctors, and other professionals successfully claimed that they were not involved in trade or commerce and thus could not restrain it. Support for the "learned professions" exemption, as it came to be known, seemed rather thin. Justice Joseph Story, in a case that predated the antitrust statutes, distinguished between "trade" and "profession." He wrote: "Wherever any occupation, employment, or business is carried on for the purposes of profit, or gain, or a livelihood, not in the liberal arts or in the learned professions, it is constantly called a *trade*" (as quoted in *Goldfarb v. Virginia State Bar,* 497 F.2d 1, 13 n. 35 [4th Cir. 1974], emphasis in original). Early Supreme Court interpretations of the antitrust laws quoted Story with approval (see *Atlantic Cleaners & Dyers, Inc. v. United States,* 286 U.S. 427, 436 [1932]). The justices seemed convinced that "one engaged in the practice of a profession 'follows a profession and not a trade' and that such 'personal effort, not related to production, is not a subject of commerce'" (see *Goldfarb,* 497 F.2d at 13).

Footnote 17

The 1975 ruling of the U.S. Supreme Court in *Goldfarb v. Virginia State Bar* (421 U.S. 773 [1975]) overturned the learned professions exemption, making clear, once and for all, that the professions were not immune from the antitrust laws—that occupation itself was irrelevant. "The nature of an occupation, standing alone, does not provide sanctuary from the Sherman Act," the Court declared (*Goldfarb,* 421 U.S. at 787). Yet the Court refused to fully equate the professions with business and commercial interests. In footnote 17 (hereafter "footnote 17") of its unanimous opinion, the Court stated: "It would be unrealistic to view the practice of professions as interchangeable with other business activities, and automatically to apply to the professions antitrust concepts which originated in other areas. The public service aspect, and other features of the professions may require that a particular practice, which could properly be viewed as a violation of the Sherman Act in another context be treated differently" (*Goldfarb,* 421 U.S. at 788–789). Under what circumstances should professions "be treated differently"?

The "Worthy Purpose" Defense

Footnote 17 signaled special treatment for the professions but provided no clear guidance for its future application. Professional associations sought to make the most of the Court's meager concession. They claimed that the antitrust laws should accommodate anticompetitive practices that had a worthy purpose or that advanced important public concerns, such as quality and safety. In *Professional Engineers*, for instance, the defendant engineering society asserted that an ethical ban on competitive bidding was needed to prevent shoddy and deceptive practices. While the society's argument was appealing, it had the potential to undermine the foundation of a public policy based on competition. Should those who collude to restrain competition be able to defend their actions by claiming they had a worthy purpose? And if so, how should courts decide what is worthy and what isn't? Writing for the Court in *Professional Engineers*, Justice John Paul Stevens held that neither the Sherman Act nor *Goldfarb* countenanced "a defense based on the assumption that competition itself is unreasonable" (435 U.S. at 696). Ethical norms, Stevens wrote, could police deception, but they could not restrict competition. Stevens's analysis shows why it is the process, not the outcome, that is most important.

The Interstate Commerce Requirement

Congress has the power under the U.S. Constitution to regulate commerce "among the several states." The effect of the commerce clause on the scope of federal laws, such as the Sherman Act, has encouraged much litigation. There must be a "demonstrable nexus," the Supreme Court has said, between the behavior that Congress seeks to regulate (restraint of trade, for instance) and commerce that is between or among different states (see *McLain v. Real Estate Bd. of New Orleans, Inc.*, 444 U.S. 232, 246 [1980]).

When Congress passed the Sherman Act in 1890, the United States was primarily a rural and agricultural society. Urbanization, immigration, and industrialization occurring near the end of the nineteenth century changed the country's profile. Advancements in science, technology, and communication broadened the sale and distribution of goods and services. What occurred in one region of the country now affected another. As disparities among regions of the country diminished and commercial interests converged in the early 1900s, policy makers sought to increase the capacity of the federal government to regulate local markets. Perhaps the greatest expansion of federal power took place in the New Deal Era when the Supreme Court in 1937 ruled that Congress could regulate any activity, even a local activity, which had a "substantial effect" on interstate commerce (*N.L.R.B. v. Jones & Laughlin Steel Corp.*, 301 U.S. 1 [1937]). Subsequent Court decisions, many in the 1960s, made it relatively easy to show that an activity had a "substantial effect." Local hotels and restaurants, for example, came within the purview of federal legislation on civil rights (see *Heart of Atlanta Motel v. United States*, 379 U.S. 241 [1964]; *Katzenbach v. McClung*, 379 U.S. 294 [1964]). By the time the Court addressed the anticompetitive practices of professionals in the 1970s, the interstate commerce requirement no longer was a major obstacle to the law enforcement efforts of federal agencies (see *Goldfarb; Hospital Bldg. Co. v. Trustees of Rex Hospital*, 425 U.S. 738 [1976]).

State-Action Immunity

The state-action doctrine, announced by the Supreme Court in *Parker v. Brown* (317 U.S. 341 [1943]), shields state-supported activity, even if anticompetitive, from the federal antitrust laws. Physicians who sit on state licensing boards, for example, typically receive the doctrine's protection.

The Court's decision in *Parker* was a product of the New Deal Era—a time when most scholars and policy makers professed that government regulation of private markets was in the public interest (Wiley 1986; Easterbrook 1984). But a shift in thinking during the 1950s and 1960s eroded the "public interest" rationale. By the 1970s, many scholars had come to believe that state regulation was the result of interest-group bargaining. Economist Mancur Olson demonstrated, for instance, that organized groups of self-interested individuals, such as physicians, excessively influenced the regulatory process (Olson 1965). Responding to this change in outlook, the Supreme Court circumscribed state-action immunity. *Goldfarb* was an early example of the Court's refined exegesis. In 1980, the Court established a two-pronged test that narrowed its holding in *Parker*. The regulatory restraint, the Court said, had to be "clearly articulated and affirmatively expressed as state policy," and the policy had to be "actively supervised" by the state itself (*California Retail Liquor Dealers Ass'n v. Midcal Aluminum, Inc.*, 445 U.S. 97 [1980]).

Section 5 of the FTC Act

Section 5 of the Federal Trade Commission Act (hereafter "section 5") prohibits "unfair methods of competition in commerce and unfair or deceptive acts or practices in commerce." This provision was the principal basis for the efforts of the Federal Trade Commission to end the anticompetitive practices of the medical profession. Like section 1 of the Sherman Act, section 5 was "open-textured." What did the framers of section 5 mean by "unfair methods of competition" or "unfair or deceptive acts or practices in commerce"?

Though the wording of section 5 was broad and expansive, early decisions of the Supreme Court circumscribed the commission's powers (see

F.T.C. v. Gratz, 253 U.S. 421 [1920]). It was not until the 1960s that the Supreme Court affirmed the authority of the FTC to regulate trade and commerce beyond the scope of the Sherman and Clayton Acts (see Kovacic 1982:616–617). When the FTC began its investigation of the medical monopoly in the mid-1970s, it possessed extensive powers. The agency's authority to prosecute anticompetitive conduct under section 5 was coextensive with and exceeded section 1 of Sherman (see *F.T.C. v. Sperry & Hutchinson Co.,* 405 U.S. 233 [1972]).

THE CAST OF PRINCIPAL PLAYERS

Several entities and individuals participated in the health care revolution. This section will introduce three of them—the American Medical Association, the Federal Trade Commission, and the U.S. Supreme Court. As leaders of their respective coalitions, the AMA and the FTC embodied the values and beliefs of the professional and market regimes. The rise and fall of the professional regime and its replacement in the late 1970s and early 1980s by the market regime mirrored the fortunes and failures of the AMA and the FTC. Various other organizations and entities (the U.S. Department of Justice, for example) played less prominent roles and are not detailed here. I will introduce significant individuals (certain legal scholars and AMA leaders) in the main narrative.

The Federal Trade Commission

The FTC (sometimes referred to as the commission or the agency) is a five-member regulatory commission established in 1914 to administer the antitrust and trade regulation laws. As an independent regulatory commission, the FTC has extensive rule making and adjudicatory powers. Rule making is a quasi-legislative process that allows the FTC to issue regulations that govern the economic conduct of individuals and corporations that fall within its jurisdiction. Adjudication is a trial-like process in which the FTC acts through cease and desist orders, consent decrees, and informal bargaining to regulate a particular industry. Whether the commission proceeds by rule making or adjudication to discourage anticompetitive conduct is within its discretion.

If the FTC decides to proceed by rule making, it must follow certain procedures. At minimum, these include public notice of the rules that the agency seeks to issue and an opportunity for interested parties to comment on them. Fashioning rules that apply to an entire industry can be exceedingly difficult and complex. Differences among local markets, for instance, often entail several exceptions, making a "one-size-fits-all" approach impractical in many situations. Unlike adjudication, which often targets an unpopular defendant, rule making can incur almost universal opposition. As Commissioner Robert Pitofsky explained in a 1979 speech: "When the FTC brought a case against one of five leading companies in an industry, its action, of course, rarely met with approval by the company sued. On the other hand, the other four companies—often murmuring *sotto voce* that the targeted firm was a bad actor and deserved it—became quiet allies of the Commission's action. Now when the Commission proposes a significant competitive limitation on an entire industry, in effect it helps organize the political opposition of that industry to the rule" (*FTC:Watch* 9 March 1979:16).

If the FTC decides to proceed by adjudication, it also must follow certain procedures. Unlike court trials, however, adjudications before administrative agencies provide a distinct "home court" advantage. After conducting an investigation, FTC attorneys may prepare a complaint, or statement of charges based on the reasonable belief that there has been a violation of the FTC Act. If the commissioners agree that a violation has occurred and that the proceeding is in the public interest, they will vote to issue formal charges against the offending party, or respondent. Unless the respondent enters into a consent agreement (in essence, an agreement to cease and desist) with the agency at this time, a hearing will take place before an administrative law judge. After the hearing, the administrative law judge will make a recommended decision that the commissioners who issued the charges in the first place will review. The commissioners can agree or disagree in whole or in part with the recommended decision of the administrative law judge. If the commissioners render a final decision that is adverse to the respondent, the respondent can appeal to a federal circuit court. In most instances, the circuit court will uphold the agency's decision. This is because courts will not overturn an agency decision unless the agency has abused its discretion or its findings are unsupported by substantial evidence.

Though its powers appear immense, the commission is constrained by the political environment in which it operates. The legislative branch sets the agency's budget and, through hearings, monitors its operations; the executive branch appoints members to the commission, including its chair, and influences the allocation of resources; finally, the judicial branch reviews agency decisions and oversees the enforcement of its rules and regulations.

For much of the twentieth century, the constitutional branches of government constrained the FTC's original mandate. Indeed, over two decades after the commission's founding, policy makers still debated the merits of competition. When the antitrust laws finally emerged as tools of a procompetitive national policy near the end of the 1930s, the Department of Justice, not the FTC, became their lead enforcer (see Wells 2002; Kovacic 1982). It was not until the 1960s and 1970s that the consumer movement in the United States thrust the FTC into the national limelight. Following harsh criticism of the agency by consumer advocates for its lack of direction and poor management, commission chairs beginning in 1970 initiated a series of reform measures. These measures included a "major shift in personnel" and the reorganization of staff to emphasize antitrust and consumer protection (Clarkson and Muris 1981:4). By mid-decade nearly one-third of the agency's employees had been replaced and the commission's budget had doubled (Clarkson and Muris 1981:5–6, 14; Federal Trade Commission, *Annual Reports*, 1974 and 1975). At the peak of the FTC's investigation of the medical profession in the late 1970s, the agency, according to the *Washington Post*, was "the second most powerful legislative body in the United States" (Carper 1977).

But as quickly as the FTC's stock rose, so it dropped to its former levels. Loss of congressional support following the 1976 presidential election combined with recriminations from powerful interests it had pursued led to budgetary and programmatic retrenchment. Some members of Congress were so unhappy with the agency's performance that they severely restricted appropriations, forcing it to shut down for two days in 1980 (Kovacic 1982:653, 664–667; Reigel 1981:449–451). Members of the Reagan administration, also dissatisfied with the agency's record, reduced the number of employees by almost 25 percent in the early 1980s (U.S. Congress, House, 1984:18 [Report of Michael Pertschuk]). But general discontent with the FTC did not adversely affect efforts of the commission to investigate and prosecute anticompetitive activities of organized medicine. Indeed, the Reagan administration gave the commission the resources it needed to pursue these particular endeavors (see Eisner 1991:222).

The American Medical Association

Unlike the FTC, whose reputation before the 1970s was that of a weak and overly cautious government agency, the AMA (sometimes referred to as the "association") was a bold and muscular organization. Until 1965, the AMA defeated virtually every piece of congressional legislation that it opposed. According to a 1952 editorial in the *New York Times*: "Some rather expert observers of the art of lobbying as practiced in Washington assert that the AMA is the only organization in the country that could marshal 140 votes in Congress between sundown Friday night and noon on Monday. Performances of this sort have led some to describe the AMA lobby as the most powerful in the country" (Huston 1952).

Before the health care revolution, the AMA and its component state and local medical societies (sometimes referred to collectively as "organized medicine" or simply "medicine") were standard-bearers of traditional medical practice, that is, the independent practitioner, fee-for-service form. Most physicians belonged to the AMA or, at the very least, their state society and adhered to the Code of Medical Ethics (the code) which the AMA promulgated, administered, interpreted, and enforced. The AMA enacted the code in 1847 and revised it on five more occasions (1903, 1912, 1949, 1957, and 1980), often in response to antitrust activities of federal and state governments (see Campion 1984; King 1983; Burrow 1977; Berlant 1975). As currently composed, the code consists of the *Principles of Medical Ethics* (the *Principles*), Current Opinions with Annotations of the Judicial Council, Fundamental Elements of the Patient-Physician Relationship, and the Reports of the Judicial Council. Periodically, the Judicial Council, a standing committee of the AMA, publishes the *Principles* together with their interpretations, known as the *Opinions and Reports* (Johnson and Jones 1993:105–107).

Though professional associations could sanction physicians for code violations of an economic nature (advertising, for instance), this was a rare occurrence. Because membership in state and local societies provided access to referrals, consultations, malpractice insurance, hospital privileges, teaching positions, and specialty ratings, physicians seldom deviated from ethical standards. The threat of professional ostracism was enough to guarantee conformity in the conduct of medical practice (see *Yale Law Journal* 1954:949).

Conformity also characterized medical politics at the AMA for much of the twentieth century. Observers in the 1950s noted that the nominating and electoral processes guaranteed that a "self-perpetuating minority" remained in control of organized medicine (see *Yale Law Journal* 1954:947). Those holding prominent positions at the county level appointed a nominating committee that selected the officers and delegates for state office. This process repeated itself at the state level, making "reelection of delegates" for local, state, and national office a "common" occurrence (*Yale Law Journal* 1954:945).

Though clashes over policy occurred, sometimes vociferously, throughout the AMA's existence, they most often transpired in the House of Delegates, the association's policy-making body, which has met and still meets only twice each year. True operational power resides and has resided in a Board of Trustees, an executive vice president, and various councils and committees, such as the Council on Medical Education, the Council on Constitution and Bylaws, the Council on Long Range Planning and Development, the Council on Legislation, and the Judicial Council. Most individuals who occupy and have occupied positions of power within the AMA rose through the ranks. Once at the AMA, they act as "corporate directors" (*Yale Law Journal* 1954:943). Economist Elton Rayack noted, for instance, that members of the Board of Trustees in the 1960s "approve[d] all AMA expenditures, nominate[d] members [of] key standing committees, appoint[ed] the editors for all AMA publications . . . and determine[d] . . . editorial polic[y]" (1967:3).

It was not until 1977 that the association granted fifty slots in the House of Delegates to the major specialty societies. Before then, only state societies elected representatives to the association. While far short of parity (one delegate per one thousand members of the AMA), the addition of fifty delegates from the specialty societies constituted, in Frank Campion's words, "a change of major dimensions" (1984:88). In 1996, the House added twenty-five more members from the specialty societies, and in 2000, special societies achieved parity with state societies (Walt 1997; Krieger 1998).

With the emergence of managed care and the attenuation of ethics provisions in the wake of the health care revolution, the number of physicians who joined the AMA dropped precipitously. Being a "personal value" membership organization (that is, members join for the "direct economic or social benefits" that they incur), the AMA as well as many state and local societies lost their allure when HMOs and specialty societies became the predominant sources for patient referrals, colleague consultations, and even malpractice insurance (see Lowi and Ginsberg 1994:506). One does not need to belong to a particular organization to receive the benefits of political representation of the type that the AMA offers; moreover, physicians often look to their specialty societies, not the AMA, for scientific and educational advancement.

The United States Supreme Court

Courts serve as forums for disputes over public policy. Complex cases, such as those involving antitrust or health policy, start from a simple complaint but grow exponentially as they proceed from investigation to trial, from trial to initial decision, and from initial decision to final ruling on appeal. Throughout this time-consuming and expensive process, the opposing parties and their lawyers dominate the proceedings. They conduct the investigations, frame the issues, and provide the evidence for the record at trial. Courts do not choose the cases that come before them. In the federal system, only the Supreme Court controls its own agenda (see O'Brien 1990:194).

Few cases ever reach the Supreme Court, and the Court decides relatively few of those that do. Of more than four thousand cases on the Court's docket in 1981, about one hundred sixty (less than 5 percent) received its full attention (O'Brien 1990:193–194, 233). The Court only considers cases having "national importance for public law and policy" (O'Brien 1990:321). During the 1980s, 47 percent of the Court's cases involved constitutional principles; about 38 percent concerned the interpretation of federal statutes (O'Brien 1990:245). Issues concerning antitrust law were of the second type.

The open-textured nature of the antitrust laws has placed a premium on judicial philosophy as the justices have struggled to reconcile professional practice with commercial pursuits. Two opposing camps emerged after the Court's ruling in *Goldfarb.* On one side were those justices who adhered to the "professional ideal" and were likely to "accept public service claims of professional organizations" (Kissam 1983:28). On the other side were those who were skeptical of such claims, particularly if they implicated the "economic behavior of professionals" (Kissam 1983:20). The latter camp, which favored a narrow interpretation of footnote 17, prevailed in the 1980s by a slim margin.

Because the two camps were close in size, small changes in Court composition could alter voting patterns and case deliberations (see Segal and Spaeth 1993:18). Appointments to the Supreme Court are infrequent (about one every twenty-two months) (O'Brien 1990:369), but recusals or lack of participation for various (often unknown) reasons are quite common. There were about two hundred recusals in the 1987–1988 term, for instance, or about one for every fifteen cases that the Court decided (O'Brien 1990:213). Recusals undoubtedly influenced the course of antitrust jurisprudence, even in instances where the final vote was certain. Justice Lewis Powell (a strong advocate of professionalism) recused himself in *Goldfarb;* Justice William Brennan failed to participate in *Professional Engineers;* Justice Harry Blackmun recused himself in *American Medical Ass'n v. F.T.C.* (455 U.S. 676 [1982] [the *AMA* case]), a 4–4 split decision that ended ethical restrictions on advertising, solicitation, and contract practice; and Justices Blackmun and O'Connor did not participate in *Arizona v. Maricopa County Medical Soc.* (457 U.S. 332 [1982]), a 4–3 decision that circumscribed the role of medical societies in economic competition. The *AMA* and *Maricopa* cases appear fortuitous given the number of recusals, three in those two cases alone.

The Court's impact on health policy in the United States has been substantial. Its decision in *Goldfarb,* followed by *AMA* and *Maricopa,* influenced the trajectory of the health care industry. With "one stroke of the . . . pen," law professor Clark Havighurst observed, the Supreme Court in *Goldfarb* "changed the basic legal regime governing professional services, opening the door for procompetitive private innovations that the medical profession had previously been able to suppress" (2000:91).

SUMMARY AND CHAPTER OUTLINE

The events depicted in this book reflect the complex interplay between conflicting regimes and their accompanying ideologies. Ideas have been central to the emergence of the professional regime and the market regime, as chapters 1 and 3 detail. Chapter 1 begins with an assessment of progressive ideology and its connection to professionalism and the public interest theory of regulation. The medical profession's efforts at the turn of the twentieth century to advance a code of ethics, to license practitioners of medicine, and to reform medical education fit the progressive mold. In subsequent years, however, professional ideals based on the pursuit of science and education gave way to the economic interests of physicians and their professional associations, leading to numerous anticompetitive practices.

Chapter 2 examines the post–World War II years, when the professional regime began to unravel. In the 1960s, medicine's protectionist stance confronted a changing cultural perspective. This changing worldview supported greater access to health care and the advancement of consumer interests. Government programs, in particular Medicare and Medicaid, expanded the patient population, creating new demands and spurring a rise in the cost of health care services.

Fresh approaches were needed to curtail costs and jump-start the nation's economy. As outlined in chapter 3, economists of the Chicago school asserted that market competition was the answer. Economists advanced several policies to overcome high unemployment and high inflation, including deregulation, privatization, and lower taxation. Their working proposition was that government regulation was the product of certain groups who sought to protect their own interests to the detriment of consumers.

The health care industry differed from most other industries in one important respect—the medical profession, not government, regulated price and entry. Consequently, the remedy that economists prescribed was to curtail the anticompetitive practices of the AMA and its component state and local medical societies. The fusion of antitrust law with neoclassical economic theory heralded the demise of the professional monopoly. Legal scholars, such as Clark Havighurst, who subscribed to the economic theory of regulation, persuaded courts and federal agencies that the antitrust laws should apply to the "learned professions."

Chapters 4 through 7 relate the struggles that began in the mid-1970s between the AMA and the Federal Trade Commission. Chapter 4 sets the stage for the three chapters that follow. It explains how and why the commission took the lead in the health care revolution. Chapters 5 and 6 detail the central confrontation—the *AMA* case—including the administrative hearing and the lengthy appeal process. In addition, chapter 6 relates the attempt by medical societies to have Congress strip the FTC of jurisdiction over the learned professions. Finally, chapter 7 discerns the limits of antitrust enforcement concerning professional activities. It examines efforts of the FTC, some aborted and some pursued, to curtail medicine's oversight of physician education, credentialing, and hospital accreditation.

Chapters 8 and 9 depict medicine's transition from arbiter of the health care industry to advocate for independent physicians. As the health care industry consolidated during the 1980s and 1990s and hospitals and insurers became more powerful, solo and small-group practitioners searched for ways to regain their collective authority. Frustrated with perceived disparities in bargaining power, they turned to medical societies. Chapter 8 depicts the AMA's search for a special exemption from the antitrust laws for collective bargaining purposes and the relaxation of enforcement guidelines for physician joint ventures. Chapter 9 relates the association's efforts in the 1990s to demonize the managed care industry in order to aid passage of anti–managed care legislation and to influence court decisions.

Lastly, the conclusion evaluates the context for the health care revolution—the competing regimes, their core beliefs, and their opposing philosophies. It raises the question "Why market competition and not government regulation"? Thus, it relates the instant discussion, more specifically America's antitrust tradition, to the rejection of a government-run or government-financed health care system. In addition, the conclusion explores the revolution's current and future trajectory in light of the concepts and approaches that this book utilizes and advances.

1 The Professional Regime

This chapter traces the evolution of the medical profession from the late 1800s to the mid-twentieth century. Three questions frame the discussion: What factors gave rise to medicine's professional regime? How did the regime exercise its authority? What role did the antitrust laws play in the acquisition and retention of economic and political power?

In discerning the answers to these questions, this chapter stresses the importance of ideas to the development of a profession's identity, its institutions, its internal culture, and its legal authority. Scientific progress in the late 1800s augured progressive reforms; progressive ideology, in turn, advanced the economic interests of physicians and their professional associations. Medicine's success—economic, political, and social—lay in nurturing professional authority vis-à-vis physicians, patients, insurers, governments, competitors, and institutional providers. Professional norms and beliefs, not force, secured physician unity and channeled dissent; legal rules and regulations in support of norms and beliefs aided medicine's domination of the health care industry.

PROGRESSIVISM AND THE MEDICAL PROFESSION

The ideas of progressive reformers were central to medicine's rise to power in the early years of the twentieth century. Progressivism's roots lay in the natural sciences (biology, physics, and chemistry, for example) and the rational, scientific approach to solving problems that these various disciplines employed. Scientific achievement gave rise to numerous inventions—the electric motor, the telephone, the phonograph, and incandescent lighting, to name a few. Medicine benefited as well. Discoveries by scientists and physicians led to sterilization techniques, bacteriology, and X-ray technology.

These advances separated allopathic medicine (which employed conventional means, such as concentrated doses of drugs, to combat disease) from unschooled, self-described healers.

Scientific achievement stimulated social reform. Many progressives believed that poor working conditions, political corruption, and abusive business practices, all of which intensified during America's Industrial Revolution, were, in part, the product of excess competition. In the words of Philander Chase Knox, President Theodore Roosevelt's attorney general, "Uncontrolled competition, like unregulated liberty, is not really free" (as quoted in Morris 2002:88). Government regulation was the antidote. Among the reforms that progressives prescribed were railroad regulation, child labor laws, occupational licensing, and antitrust legislation.

The idea of "regulating" competition in the "public interest," based on scientific principles and standards formulated by experts, linked the ideas of progressives to the interests of physicians. Professionalism was a response to the perceived chaos of the nineteenth century, in which quacks, pretenders, and poorly trained practitioners proliferated for lack of educational standards and government regulation. Medical licensing, which took hold in the late 1800s, was a prime example. On the one hand, politicians gained from having professionals solve societal problems without having to expand the size of government; on the other, professionals furthered their own interests by wielding governmental authority to control competition. "From the perspective of those steeped in America's antistatist culture," historian Brian Balogh observed, "the hierarchy and self-governing mechanisms of the myriad professionalizing organizations were not unlike state and local governments: they dealt with problems without requiring the expansion of the centralized state" (1991:6).

A major tenet common to both progressivism and professionalism was the belief that scientific knowledge was the principal domain of experts. Progressives believed that science was too complex for public consumption, that only experts with advanced education and technical training could grasp its features, and that only experts could apply scientific principles to public problems in an objective and orderly fashion (see Starr 1982:140). These perceptions elevated the status of physicians and distinguished medical work from commercial and business pursuits. Self-regulation was a logical outgrowth of progressive ideas. Because of their advanced knowledge and training, physicians were presumed to be the only ones capable of determining their own technical standards. A unanimous decision of the U.S. Supreme Court, announced in 1888, captured progressives' point of view. "Comparatively few," Justice Stephen Field wrote, could comprehend the "subtle and mysterious" nature of medical work (*Dent v. State of West Virginia,* 129 U.S. 114, 122–123 [1888]). By 1901, all states had delegated authority to the medical profession to set standards and to police itself (Starr 1982:104).

For medicine, as well as for professions such as law and dentistry, codes of ethics were the principal means of regulating competition in the professional realm. The AMA Code of Medical Ethics, first enacted in 1847, "drew heavily" on the work of Thomas Percival, an English physician who in his 1803 book *Medical Ethics* emphasized professional courtesy and harmony, including the "self-silencing of criticism" (Brennan 1991:32; Berlant 1975:73; Fishbein 1947:36). According to medical ethicist Troyen Brennan, "Many of [Percival's] admonitions were meant to contain intraprofessional strife and to develop self-regulation" (Brennan 1991:32). By way of example, the code banned advertising and solicitation of patients, both widely perceived by physicians as divisive forms of behavior. Rules governing professional conduct, however, did not extend to practitioners outside the profession. Indeed, the code encouraged physicians "to bear emphatic testimony against quackery in all its forms." Homeopaths, eclectics, Christian Scientists, and later osteopaths and chiropractors became targets of physicians and their medical societies.

Enacted in 1890 near the height of the populist movement, the Sherman Act reflected America's suspicion of concentrated power (Hofstadter 1991; Bickel 1983). Progressives, such as Presidents Theodore Roosevelt and Woodrow Wilson, objected to huge combinations, particularly large oil companies and railroad conglomerates owned by John D. Rockefeller, J. P. Morgan, and other business tycoons. Yet, despite the occasional action against a megacorporation, early Sherman Act enforcement efforts more often affected small companies. The simple reason was that cases against small companies were easier to win (McCraw 1984:115). Louis Brandeis, who was Wilson's chief economic advisor from 1912 to 1916, sought to correct this situation. Brandeis believed that small producers were more efficient than large ones. He criticized *Dr. Miles Medical Co. v. John D. Park & Sons Co.* (220 U.S. 373 [1911]), a Supreme Court decision that held that a manufacturer's pricing agreement with several retail outlets constituted price-fixing. Brandeis's central concern was that manufacturers would seek to integrate forward into wholesale and retail trade in order to control prices (McCraw 1984:102). Such "combinations," Brandeis claimed, would destroy rather than enhance competition (McCraw 1984:97; Strum 1993:81).

The philosophy of Brandeis and other progressives underlay passage of the Federal Trade Commission Act in 1914. Brandeis viewed the act as central to Wilson's New Freedom initiative, which targeted the "great trusts." The Federal Trade Commission, Brandeis proclaimed, should investigate big business and help the Department of Justice enforce compliance with the Sherman Act. It also should provide information to small businesses seeking a level playing field in their battles with large corporations (McCraw 1984:111–112; Mason 1956:403). But the fanfare that accompanied the FTC's inauguration did not last very long. An adverse ruling of the Supreme Court in 1920, coupled with weak appointments to the commission by President Wilson, doomed the agency to second-class status for the next several decades (McCraw 1984:122–128).

Efforts of the AMA to curtail competition were unaffected, for the most part, by the antitrust laws. Indeed, the association revised the code in 1903 to regulate physicians' fees and to prohibit contract practice (Berlant 1975:101, 106). Though the AMA again revised the code in 1912, this time to eliminate "all recommendations for setting fees" (Berlant 1975:102), the change did not undercut the profession's fee-setting capabilities. A major reorganization of the AMA in 1901 had created a policy-making body, the House of Delegates, which comprised representatives from state and local medical societies (Johnson and Jones 1993:6, 42–43). State and local societies could regulate fees just as well as the AMA, if not more effectively. Although some societies faced prosecution under state antitrust laws, the threat was minimal. "Neither the threat of antitrust prosecution nor the constitutional provisions against price-fixing prevented the profession from framing fee schedules in most states," historian James Burrow noted (1977:107). Attorneys general in some states, such as Kansas, pursued price-fixing litigation against physicians, but authorities in other states, Texas and Iowa among them, determined that state laws did not prohibit fee schedules (Burrow 1977:108).

ABRAHAM FLEXNER AND THE REFORM OF MEDICAL EDUCATION

Undoubtedly the most significant achievement of the medical profession during the Progressive Era was reform of medical education. Many physicians believed that efforts to improve standards through rigorous training and a comprehensive, science-based curriculum would end "inordinate competition and all the evils of an unstable market" (Rosen 1983:64). By making it harder for individuals to enter the profession, medical schools would produce fewer doctors, and those doctors that schools did produce would be more highly trained and competent than in the past.

To be sure, Abraham Flexner's "muckraking" report of 1910, prepared for the Carnegie Foundation for the Advancement of Technology, advanced medicine's cause. But Flexner was not the first to assess the profession's educational status. The AMA had initiated inspections of medical schools before 1910 through its Council on Medical Education. The council conducted three tours of inspection, the first two between 1906 and 1910. Based on a rating scale devised to assess such things as the quality of clinical instruction, curriculum, admission requirements, and facilities, the council targeted for closure all schools that fell below a 50 percent rating (the equivalent of an F; Dodson 1919). Morris Fishbein, the powerful editor of the *Journal of the American Medical Association* (*JAMA*), reported the results of the council's inspections: "There were 160 medical schools; 82 had been rated above 70, 46 between 50 and 70 and 32 below 50. The Council condemned medical schools conducted solely for profit, night schools, schools designed to prepare students to pass state board examinations, quiz courses and many others" (Fishbein 1947:250). The AMA's early efforts were productive. According to Fishbein (p. 268), "The Council on Medical Education reported a reduction in medical colleges from 166 in 1904 to 129 in 1911."

Flexner, who began his inspection tour of medical schools in December 1908, "capitalized" on the work of the Council on Medical Education (Rosen 1983:63). Lacking formal training in medicine, Flexner received advice from leading physicians and faculty of the Johns Hopkins School of Medicine. Indeed, the Hopkins model, which stressed scientific research and clinical instruction, became the benchmark for Flexner's evaluation.

Flexner called upon medical schools to tighten their admission standards so that candidates "would begin their professional training with adequate basic preparation, particularly in science" (Rosen 1983:64). Medical schools, Flexner said, should also require hospital affiliation to assure "effective teaching of clinical medicine" (Rosen 1983:64). Proprietary schools and those "poorly financed and equipped" failed the Hopkins test (Rosen 1983:64). According to James Johnson and Walter Jones, Flexner's report "was a classic case of research gaining influence through release at the right time, into the right hands. States responded to the report's scandalous findings with a wave of regulation that implemented the unified education model that the AMA and others advocated" (1993:6).

Flexner's report accelerated a trend in school closures that had begun with the reinstitution of state licensure and the work of the Council on Medical Education. State licensing boards, under the control of professional associations, refused to license graduates from medical schools that the boards had not approved. In order to make the "approved" list, schools had to satisfy the AMA's standards, an expensive undertaking that forced proprietary institutions to upgrade their facilities and to extend the period of time for training prospective physicians. Because proprietary schools depended on tuition and fees to finance their operations, incoming students had to offset these new expenses. Many students lacked the means and the additional time required for medical training. Enrollments decreased, and the weaker schools closed (Starr 1982:118–119). In 1910, the year Flexner's report came out, there were 131 schools; twelve years later, there were only 81 schools of medicine (Rosen 1983:65).

Progressive reform of medical education gave professional associations the ability and the opportunity to restrict the supply of physicians. The Council on Medical Education became, in effect, an arm of the state used for determining which schools made the "approved" list. "Even though no legislative body ever set up the Federation of State Medical Boards or the Council on Medical Education, their decisions came to have the force of law," Paul Starr suggested (1982:121). The creation of a private entity to perform a public function had important implications. Once formed, such an entity could monitor and control the flow of information between the public and the private sectors.

AMA control of medical school enrollments spilled over to graduate medical education. Though professional organizations comprised of medical specialists developed separately from the AMA in the 1920s, by the late 1930s, the AMA had achieved a prominent role in specialty education, including internship and residency training. Again, the Council on Medical Education became the central mechanism for approval of specialty boards, their standards, and their practices (Stevens 1971:213–214). In addition, the council, almost by default, assumed responsibility for the inspection and recognition of hospitals for internships and residencies. To be sure, the AMA wanted it this way, but no other suitors existed. Medical schools lacked the required resources, and the Advisory Board for Medical Specialties formed in 1933 was, as its name suggested, "advisory" in nature (Stevens 1971:212–215, 260–263).

CONTRACT PRACTICE AND THE AMA'S TEN PRINCIPLES

Contract practice originated in the railroad, mining, and logging industries of the late nineteenth century. Physicians provided medical services to groups of patients for a fixed fee, unlike the traditional fee-for-service model. Industrial corporations, indemnity companies, benevolent and fraternal orders, farm cooperatives, and hospital associations were among the entities that engaged physicians at discount prices. Competition among physicians was so intense and incomes so low that many doctors readily accepted the discount rates (U.S. Congress, Senate, 1974:1598 [Treatise by L. S. Helland, Re: Structure of Health Care Delivery]; Burrow 1977:15, 119–132). Contract practice touched any area of the country where low-income farm workers and industrial laborers congregated.

The medical profession opposed contract practice and its counterpart, the corporate practice of medicine. Contract practice concerned physicians who sold their services to organizations or entities for a fixed fee; "corporate practice of medicine" referred to those organizations that marketed physicians' services. There are at least three reasons why medicine opposed contract and corporate practice: first, independent practitioners viewed most organizations that provided health care, such as dispensaries, clinics, or hospital associations, as potential competitors; second, physicians feared that if such organizations gained a foothold, they would dictate the terms of payment; third, practitioners believed that corporate intermediaries would interfere with their clinical autonomy (Starr 1982:25, 215–218; Rosen 1983:97–108). While the profession could invoke medical ethics to prohibit doctors from undertaking contract practice, it needed states to enact laws to prevent companies from pursuing the corporate practice of medicine.

Resistance to contract practice hardened during the Progressive and New Deal eras. In 1913, the Judicial Council "recommended definite action toward the elimination of the abuse of so-called lodge practice" (Fishbein 1947:277). For a brief period, contract practice diminished as educational reforms that reduced physician supply lessened competition (Burrow 1977:119–132). But reliance on contract practice as a source of income increased again in the late 1920s as economic conditions worsened with the onset of the Great Depression (U.S. Congress, Senate, 1974:1599 [Treatise by L. S. Helland, Re: Structure of Health Care Delivery]; Rosen 1983:70). Several prepaid health plans associated with hospitals or clinics emerged, including ones attached to Baylor University Hospital in Dallas and the Ross-Loos and Palo Alto Clinics in California (Kessel 1958:40–41; Weller 1984:1361). According to Charles Weller, there were at least fifty-eight plans at the height of the movement in 1933, representing "an exciting diversity of innovative, competitive, and pluralistic market free choice plans" (1984:1361, 1363).

Physician Michael Shadid, a Syrian immigrant, established the first cooperative hospital in the United States in Elk City, Oklahoma, in 1929 (Shadid 1939:15). Combining principles of group practice with those of periodic payment, consumer control, and preventive medicine, Shadid sought to improve medical delivery in rural communities during hard times. "In the large cities," Shadid wrote, "the doctor can send his patients to one of the many specialists available, but in the villages and small towns, of which our country is in the main composed, this is impossible" (1939:108–109). Improved access to quality care motivated Shadid's design. "I looked into the history of the many privately owned clinics that had been established. Most of them had gone out of existence. There are a few outstanding exceptions, such as the Mayo Clinic in Rochester, Minnesota, which is first-rate and highly successful. But they are so expensive that only the rich can afford them. And there lay the chief flaw in the clinic plan, as far as I was concerned. Operated on a profit basis, the rates are beyond the reach of all but a small percentage of the population" (Shadid 1939:110–111).

Shadid's attempts to create a clinic in Elk City encountered professional resistance (Shadid 1939:254). Fearing "a reduction in their individual incomes," local doctors took steps to revoke Shadid's license, to oust him from the local medical society, to cancel his medical malpractice insurance, to undercut the price of his medical services, to interfere in his recruiting of out-of-state physicians, and to form competing (sham) cooperatives (Shadid 1939:115, 124, 133–142, 152–157). Even the AMA entered the fray. AMA officials successfully pressured the federal government to end federal aid to low-income farm workers seeking care at Shadid's hospital on the grounds that the hospital did not operate "in accordance with the Principles of Medical Ethics" (Shadid 1939:161–163).

Intense opposition to contract practice reflected a change in the AMA's leadership and philosophy once the association secured political power and authority. In the early 1900s, the AMA "tended to favor physicians prominent in education, research, or clinical practice for the presidency [of the AMA]," but during the 1930s, "politically-oriented conservatives" assumed control (Campion 1984:102–103). "An increasingly wealthy part of the medical Establishment . . . moved to the right politically," Johnson and Jones observed (1993:64). Urban specialists came to dominate the association's councils and committees (Garceau 1941). Michael Shadid lamented the transformation. He wrote:

> Like so many political parties, [the AMA] originated as a forward-looking association that fought for much-needed improvements, only to degenerate into a bureaucracy upholding the status quo. Many years ago the A.M.A. forced out of existence the "diploma mills" and raised standards of medical schools throughout the country; it brought about an increase in the amount of training required of physicians; it combated the spread of quacks, false cures, and patent medicines making misleading claims. It

> established a code of ethics that was originally drawn up for the protection of the public against unscrupulous doctors but which now is twisted so as to serve for the protection of unscrupulous physicians against the public. (Shadid 1939:203)

Morris Fishbein led medicine's conservative vanguard from 1924 until his ouster from the AMA in 1949. The association did not collect dues from its members during Fishbein's tenure, making advertising and subscription sales of *JAMA,* which Fishbein edited, the primary source of revenue. Consequently, the AMA was "financially dependent on Fishbein . . . to a great degree" (Campion 1984:114). Association bylaws provided that Fishbein could attend meetings of the Board of Trustees, "and from 1924 on, for a quarter of a century [he] did so," becoming, in Frank Campion's words, "an imposing figure, the almost permanent nature of his presence there adding weight to the vigorously argued opinions he had to offer" (Campion 1984:114).

Fishbein railed against contract practice and "socialized medicine" in the boardroom and in numerous editorials. Perhaps his most famous (if not infamous) editorial, published in 1932, attacked the recommendations of the Committee on the Costs of Medical Care (CCMC). The CCMC, composed of several respected and influential members of the health care community, produced a series of reports between 1927 and 1932 that detailed certain deficiencies in the delivery and financing of health care. The CCMC urged reform. Among the reforms the CCMC recommended was prepaid group practice (Starr 1982:261–266; Weller 1984:1361; Brennan 1991:41).

Despite the "prestigious" composition of the committee, Fishbein vigorously and unceremoniously attacked the committee's recommendations (Campion 1984:117). An editorial he wrote for *JAMA* compared group practice to "medical care by . . . medical soviets" and "public health officialdom" to "socialism and communism" (Fishbein 1932:1950–1952). From Fishbein's perspective, prepaid group practice and government-run medicine were virtually the same. Though Fishbein's rhetoric seemed extreme, he had the support of medicine's rank and file (see Fox 1986). Indeed, a strong cohort of physicians on the CCMC, mostly those in private practice, opposed the findings of the majority. These physicians prepared a minority report. "The evils of contract practice are widespread and pernicious," they wrote. "[We] recommend that the corporate practice of medicine, financed through intermediary agencies, be vigorously and persistently opposed" (Fishbein 1947:398).

In 1934, the Bureau of Medical Economics of the AMA, at Fishbein's urging, prepared a study on contract practice, group practice, and "sickness insurance" (Fishbein 1947:1066–1067). The report contained ten principles for the formation of private health plans. These ten principles were as follows:

- *First:* All features of medical service in any method of medical practice should be under the control of the medical profession. No other body or individual is legally or educationally equipped to exercise such control.
- *Second:* No third party must be permitted to come between the patient and his physician in any medical relation. All responsibility for the character of medical services must be borne by the profession.
- *Third:* Patients must have absolute freedom to choose a legally qualified doctor of medicine who will serve them from among all those qualified to practice and who are willing to give service.
- *Fourth:* The method of giving service must retain a permanent, confidential relation between the patient and the family physician. This relation must be the fundamental and dominating feature of any system.
- *Fifth:* All medical phases of all institutions involved in the medical service should be under professional control, it being understood that hospital service and medical service should be considered separately. These institutions are but expansions of the equipment of the physician. He is the only one whom the laws of all nations recognize as competent to use them in the delivery of service. The medical profession alone can determine the adequacy and character of such institutions. The value depends on their operation according to medical standards.
- *Sixth:* However the cost of medical service may be distributed, the immediate cost should be borne by the patient if able to pay at the time the service is rendered.
- *Seventh:* Medical service must have no connection with any cash benefits.
- *Eighth:* Any form of medical service should include within its scope all legally qualified doctors of medicine of the locality covered by its operation who wish to give service under the conditions established.
- *Ninth:* Systems for the relief of low income classes should be limited strictly to those below the comfort level standard of incomes.
- *Tenth:* There should be no restrictions on treatment or prescribing not formulated and enforced by the organized medical profession. (from Rayack 1967:164–165)

The AMA House of Delegates approved the ten principles in full. Boiled down, the ten principles fell into three main categories, or core beliefs, of the medical profession: *self-regulation, clinical autonomy,* and *free choice of physician.* Self-regulation underlay principles 1, 5, and 10. Clinical autonomy conflated principles 2, 4, 6, and 7. Free choice of physician underscored principles 3, 8, and 9. Once issued, the ten principles became, for the next several decades, the template for the delivery and finance of health care in the United States.

Professional associations were quite serious about enforcing the ten principles, and they used several means to gain compliance with their terms. To bolster enforcement efforts, the House of Delegates passed the Mundt Resolution in 1934. Mundt tied medical staff membership in the AMA to formal approval of hospitals for internship training (Fishbein 1947:408). Recalcitrant physicians now faced a variety of disciplinary sanctions, including license revocation, loss of hospital privileges, and expulsion from state and local medical societies. By way of example, professional societies targeted physicians affiliated with the Dallas Medical and Surgical Clinic and International Harvester in Wisconsin (Fishbein 1947:408–409; Weller 1984:1367). Medical societies also led boycotts of hospital associations, group clinics, and nonconforming insurers, that is, any entity that failed to operate as they decreed.

These tactics raised questions about the extent of medicine's powers. How far could medical societies go to gain conformance with independent, fee-for-service practice? Did medicine have carte blanche to regulate the health care industry? Did the antitrust laws even apply? In 1938, the Department of Justice served notice that the AMA had gone too far.

THURMAN ARNOLD AND THE GROUP HEALTH CASE

The events leading to the indictment of the AMA by the Department of Justice in 1938 for conspiring to "impair or destroy" the business of the Group Health Association, a Washington, D.C., cooperative formed to provide medical services to certain government employees, revealed as much about the "ambiguous" state of antitrust policy as they did about the growing power of the medical profession (Gressley 1977:40). Harsh economic times at home and abroad in the 1920s and 1930s raised questions about the efficacy of competition, which, many complained, harmed small producers and brought about large fluctuations in the economy.

International cartels or combinations of independent enterprises designed to limit competition gained traction from policy makers seeking to overcome economic disruptions. Advocates claimed that cooperation among rivals had the potential to stabilize prices and prevent overproduction. The League of Nations endorsed cartels, as did many European countries, such as Great Britain, in order to "rationalize" the production of goods and services, particularly in "depressed industries like textiles and steel" (Wells 2002:11). Opposition to cartels was strongest in the United States, but the Great Depression altered beliefs about industry collusion and government regulation. Recognizing the need for American companies to compete on more favorable terms in export markets, Congress passed the Webb-Pomerene Act in 1918. Webb-Pomerene exempted U.S. firms from the antitrust laws so long as they confined their operations to foreign markets (Wells 2002:17, 33).

During the 1920s, the "associationalist" movement gained popularity among policy makers in the United States (Kovacic 1982:607). Advocates of associationalism believed that self-regulation and cooperation between business and government did more to stimulate the economy than market competition. Associationalist policies reached their height in the early years of the New Deal. The short-lived National Industrial Recovery Act (NIRA), which Congress passed in 1933 and the Supreme Court struck down in 1935, was the leading example of these policies. NIRA suspended the antitrust laws and called upon government, business, and labor leaders to draft "codes of conduct" for entire industries. "Desperate to halt the downward spiral of the economy," historian Wyatt Wells observed, "Americans seemed willing to abandon the antitrust tradition" (2002:36).

AMA leaders, such as Morris Fishbein, grasped the significance of New Deal economic policy. A 1935 publication of the AMA contained the following endorsement: "Recent national legislation [NIRA] proposes to extend the functions of such trade associations much further and to give them a very extensive control over the various industries and to hold them responsible for the amount of production, for prices and for the competitive relations of their members. These are functions closely analogous to those long conducted by professional associations and would seem to indicate that industry is finding it desirable to follow professional models rather than the reverse" (as quoted in Weller 1984:1355 n. 23). Fishbein and other medical leaders apparently had concluded that collusion among physicians through their medical societies was permissible and that government policy promoted the practice.

As the economy continued to sputter, however, associationalism and cartelization lost support. Following another steep recession in 1937, members of Congress and the academic community spoke out against industrial concentration, causing Roosevelt to reverse course (Gressley 1977:42). President Roosevelt, Wells wrote, "embraced antitrust out of desperation" (2002:38). In 1938, Roosevelt appointed Thurman Arnold, an opponent of cartels, to head the Antitrust Division of the Department of Justice. Under Arnold's direction, the Department of Justice took action against the petroleum, chemical, and other large industries for their collusive practices. Representing an even further break from the past, Arnold also targeted the AMA, which in 1938 comprised 110,000 out of 145,000 American physicians.

Thurman Arnold's antitrust philosophy reflected his Western roots and his teaching experience at Yale University, where the "legal realist" school was in vogue. Although distrustful of big business, Arnold was "less doctrinaire than Brandeis" (Wells 2002:41). "The test is efficiency and service—not size," Arnold wrote (as quoted in Wells 2002:41). Despite some grounding in law and economics, Arnold was not an economic practitioner. According to his biographer, Gene Gressley, Arnold "had an innate skepticism of 'preachers' with manufactured economic panaceas" (1977:43). A litigator, not a theoretician, Arnold fashioned "a pliable policy molded to the necessities of the individual prosecutions" (Gressley 1977:47).

Notwithstanding Arnold's skepticism of economic theory, his writings augured the chief tenets of what would be called the Chicago school—consumer welfare and economic efficiency. "The idea of antitrust laws is to create a situation in which competition compels the passing on to the consumers the savings of mass distribution and production," Arnold wrote (as quoted in Gressley 1977:54). "The only purpose [of the antitrust laws]," he noted, "is to see that corporate growth results from efficiency—not the elimination of competition by aggression or merger" (p. 463). In a letter penned in 1966, Arnold asserted that antitrust enforcement during the Roosevelt administration marked a turning point in the trend "toward a European cartel system" (as quoted in Gressley 1977:464). "Had Roosevelt not decided to attack such combinations," Arnold claimed, "we would have ended up in a few years with a legally approved cartel system" (pp. 462–463).

Arnold's case against the AMA involved a conspiracy to induce physicians and hospitals to boycott Group Health, the aforementioned Washington, D.C., cooperative. The alleged co-conspirators threatened to expel (and in a couple instances did expel) from their local medical societies physicians who either joined the medical staff of Group Health or consulted with staff physicians. They circulated "white lists" of approved organizations, groups, and individuals, omitting the name of Group Health. And they invoked the Mundt Resolution to intimidate Washington hospitals that admitted Group Health doctors to their medical staffs. Coercion of hospitals, according to the Department of Justice, constituted "the most serious interference with the activities of Group Health. Conceivably, the association might have functioned without medical society doctors and without the benefit of their consultations. But under present-day conditions it could not offer provisions for health services of value, without [access to] hospitals" (Brief for the United States 1939:88).*

True to their personalities, Fishbein and Arnold emerged as the lead combatants in the Group Health case. Arnold struck first, naming Fishbein a co-conspirator along with several other individuals and professional entities, including the AMA and the District of Columbia Medical Society. According to Fishbein, Arnold "delicately timed" the indictments on a Sunday afternoon "for Monday morning newspapers" (Fishbein 1947:534). In truth, Arnold had released two previous statements concerning the matter and, as Fishbein admitted, had given the AMA the "opportunity to avoid trial by agreeing to consent decrees which would assure the cooperation of the [AMA] in the operation of cooperative clinics" (1947:534). But Fishbein was not interested. The *JAMA* editor responded to Arnold's indictment in his inimitable fashion: "The statement by the assistant attorney general is in accord with the point of view which he has held for some time in relationship to our government," Fishbein wrote (1947:534). "Apparently it remains to be determined whether or not the federal administration can use the laws and the courts to mold the people of the United States to its beliefs in every phase of life and living" (1947:534).

Opinions, not surprisingly, differed. Several newspapers criticized Arnold for attacking the medical profession. The *New York Daily Mirror* complained that "Arnold's system is a brutal combination of the Star Chamber and Nazi bureaucracy." "The doctors of America should unite," the newspaper said, "in this fight against a system which jeopardizes the liberties of every citizen" (as quoted in Fishbein 1947:537). H. L. Mencken, the acerbic columnist for the *Baltimore Sun,* was equally vociferous. According to Arnold, Mencken was "very much annoyed with me for my prosecution of the [AMA] . . . he thought that Dr. Fishbein was a very great man indeed, and in my investigation of the AMA files during the prosecution I found a note from Mencken urging Fishbein not to be intimidated by these New Deal 'goons'" (as quoted in Gressley 1977:453–454). Years later, Arnold retorted: "It has been my experience that any group, whether from labor or industry or the profession, which gets itself in a position where it thinks it has special privileges will fight for them with complete intolerance and that John L. Lewis and Dr. Fishbein are brothers under the same skin" (as quoted in Gressley 1977:383).

Although the facts favored Arnold, a legal issue emerged that jeopardized the prosecution's case. Section 1 of the Sherman Act "prohibit[ed] contracts,

*Harold C. Havighurst, Clark Havighurst's father, was a special assistant to Thurman Arnold in the Group Health case (see Brief for the United States 1939:88).

combinations and conspiracies that unreasonably restrain[ed] *trade*" (emphasis added). Did the practice of medicine constitute a trade for purposes of the Sherman Act? Relying on Supreme Court precedent, the U.S. district court for the District of Columbia held that the word "trade" excluded the "learned professions" (*United States v. American Medical Ass'n,* 28 F.Supp. 752, 755 [D.D.C. 1939]). Exuberant, Fishbein wrote: "The [court's] opinion . . . lends encouragement and is an inspiration to continuous effort in behalf of a free profession. The medical profession of this country will not be coerced, threatened, abused, or otherwise maltreated, and it will fight to the finish when its high traditions demand a righteous resistance" (1947:541).

But Fishbein's exuberance was short-lived. The United States Court of Appeals for the District of Columbia reversed, holding that the word "trade" embraced medical practice as well as ordinary commercial activity (*United States v. American Medical Ass'n,* 110 F.2d 703, 711 [D.C. Cir. 1940]). Having ruled against the AMA, the appeals court remanded the case to the district court for trial. Following a lengthy hearing, a jury acquitted the individual defendants but held against the AMA and the District of Columbia Medical Society. Thereafter, the trial judge fined the AMA and the medical society in the amounts of $2500 and $1500, respectively.

Despite the meager fines, the AMA filed a petition for a writ of certiorari to the U.S. Supreme Court. Although the Court agreed to hear the case, it failed to decide the "trade" issue (*American Medical Ass'n v. United States,* 317 U.S. 519 [1943]). In an opinion by Justice Owen Roberts, the Court reasoned that the government only had to show that defendants had conspired to restrain the business of Group Health, "a membership corporation engaged in business or trade." It was unnecessary, the Court determined, to decide "the question whether a physician's practice of his profession constitutes trade under [Sherman]" (*American Medical Ass'n,* 317 U.S. at 528). Having skirted the "trade" issue, the Court upheld the AMA's conviction.

Although this ruling was a defeat for the AMA, the reach of the Group Health case was limited. Because the Court did not decide whether "trade" and "profession" were coterminous, the de facto "learned professions" exemption was still viable. Moreover, future prosecutions, if they were outside Washington, D.C., would have to satisfy the commerce clause of the U.S. Constitution. Because the commerce clause restricted federal authority to commerce "among the several states," antitrust enforcers would have to show that any conspiracy to restrain trade would have a "substantial effect" on interstate commerce. This was a difficult undertaking. Most members of the legal community considered the practice of medicine to be wholly intrastate.

Other barriers to prosecution existed as well. The most important of these was the doctrine of state-action immunity that the Supreme Court announced in 1943, the same year it decided the Group Health case. In *Parker v. Brown,* the Court held that the Sherman Act applied to "individual and not state action." The Court reasoned that "in a dual system of government in which . . . the states are sovereign," state regulation trumped federal antitrust policy (*Parker,* 317 U.S. at 351). By creating an exemption for state-supported activity, the Court encouraged medical societies to lobby state legislatures for antitrust protection. Various state enactments that barred the formation of lay-controlled plans or required all plans to provide free choice of physician were protected from the reach of the Sherman Act. The "corporate practice of medicine doctrine," a product of state court rulings, also fell within *Parker*'s zone of protection. Based on flimsy analysis, the corporate practice of medicine doctrine prohibited corporations from retaining physicians to treat patients on a prepaid basis. Because corporations could not obtain a license to practice medicine, judges reasoned, they also could not employ or in certain circumstances engage licensed physicians to do it for them (see *People v. United Medical Services, Inc.,* 200 N.E. 157 [Ill. 1936]; *Parker v. Board of Dental Examiners,* 14 P.2d 67 [Cal. 1932]; see also Chase-Lubitz 1987:464–467). Rather than enhance prepaid group practice, as the Group Health case signaled, the Court's ruling in *Parker* undercut the formation and development of alternative delivery systems.

Nonetheless, the decision in the Group Health case had more than symbolic effect. The case was the first attempt by the Department of Justice to apply the antitrust laws to the medical profession. Several prepayment plans, including Kaiser Permanente, the Health Insurance Plan of New York, and Group Health Cooperative of Puget Sound, emerged in the 1940s, at or near the end of the Group Health case. Kaiser and other plans succeeded largely because some state courts (mostly on the West Coast) upheld lay-controlled plans (Starr 1982:324). In addition, many of the tactics that professional associations had employed in the Group Health case became suspect, forcing societies to adopt new strategies to eliminate competition. One such strategy, employed by medical societies against a prepayment plan located in Oregon, piqued the interest of the Department of Justice in the late 1940s.

THE *OSMS* CASE

Lay-controlled prepayment plans were most prominent in states on the West Coast, such as Oregon, where several "hospital associations" provided health care for a fixed price to workers in the lumber, railroad, and mining industries (Goldberg and Greenberg 1977:50). Oregon's state legislature fostered the hospital-association movement when it passed a law that expressly permitted the corporate practice of medicine. Hospital associations flourished in Oregon, and by 1935, they financed 60 percent of all insurance disbursements (Goldberg and Greenberg 1977:51).

The hospital associations aggressively sought to contain costs, using many of the tactics later employed by managed care, such as preauthorization, utilization review, and fixed payments for certain medical procedures. State and local medical societies in Oregon objected to these cost-containment measures, declared them "unethical," and threatened expulsion and disciplinary action against physicians who cooperated with the hospital associations. Unlike the situation in the Group Health case, however, these tactics proved unsuccessful. In 1941, soon after the federal circuit court held against the AMA in the Group Health case, medical societies in Oregon formed their own prepaid health plan, known as the Oregon Physicians Service, or OPS.

The "prospect of wide enrollment, of assured payment for services, of noninterference in clinical decisions, and of increased professional solidarity" attracted physicians to OPS (Goldberg and Greenberg 1977:58). By 1943, OPS dominated the market for health insurance, achieving a 60 percent share. But Oregon's medical societies were not content to let the matter rest. Employing some of their former tactics, the medical societies made noncooperation with the hospital associations a condition of joining OPS. They also discouraged physicians from "taking tickets" from patients who were members of hospital associations. Direct reimbursement of physicians through their patients' "tickets" was the primary mechanism that hospital associations used to curtail costs. Combined with the large number of physicians who joined OPS (85 percent of all licensed physicians in the first year), such tactics proved fatal to the hospital associations. Those few hospital associations that survived agreed to abandon their cost-containment efforts, including utilization and fee review. In 1946, OPS became part of an emerging network of Blue Shield plans (Goldberg and Greenberg 1977:58–62).

Seven years after the founding of OPS, the Department of Justice brought action against the Oregon State Medical Society, several local societies, and certain individual physicians for injunctive relief. Specifically, the Department of Justice claimed that defendants had attempted to monopolize prepaid medical care. Following a lengthy trial, the federal district judge who heard the case held that the Department failed to prove its case against the physicians and their medical societies (*United States v. Oregon State*

Medical Society, 95 F.Supp. 103 [D. Or. 1950] [hereafter *OSMS*]). He determined that OPS was "not a conspiracy but, rather, an entirely legal and legitimate effort by the profession to meet the demands of the times for broadened medical and hospital service" (*OSMS,* 95 F.Supp. at 105).

On appeal, the U.S. Supreme Court, in an opinion by Justice Robert Jackson, affirmed the lower court's decision (*United States v. Oregon State Medical Society,* 343 U.S. 326, 330 [1952]). Jackson agreed with the district judge that the evidence against the defendants was deficient. That should have ended the matter. But Jackson, in a statement unnecessary to the Court's holding (known as *dictum*), signaled that the antitrust laws weakly applied to the "ethical standards" of the medical profession. Jackson declared: "We might observe in passing, however, that there are ethical considerations where the historic direct relationship between patient and physician is involved which are quite different than the usual considerations prevailing in ordinary commercial matters. This Court has recognized that forms of competition usual in the business world may be demoralizing to the ethical standards of a profession" (*OSMS,* 343 U.S. at 336). Justice Jackson's famous dictum, oft-repeated in subsequent cases, seemed difficult to reconcile with the Court's ruling, nine years earlier, in the Group Health case. What, if anything, had changed during the intervening years to explain the Court's position? Did Jackson, who failed to take part in the Group Health case, spurn prepaid group practice?

The context for the case, set against the Korean War and anticommunist fervor, likely influenced the Court's disposition. Investigations of communist sympathizers, led by Senator Joseph McCarthy, dominated the headlines, as did the espionage trial of Julius and Ethel Rosenberg. Antisocialist rhetoric clouded the debate over access to health care. In 1947, Marjorie Shearon, a former federal employee, accused certain individuals at the Federal Security Agency of conspiring to nationalize health insurance (Campion 1984:160). And in 1949, President Truman placed compulsory health insurance on the national agenda. Vehemently opposed to Truman's initiative, the AMA engaged Whitaker and Baker, a public relations firm, to stigmatize the president's plan. "The doctors of this country are in the front lines today of a basic struggle between socialism and private initiative," Whitaker and Baker declared (Campion 1984:159).

The opinion of the federal district judge in *OSMS* captured and highlighted the debate over socialized medicine. No "American court [should] hold that . . . organized medicine must remain a sitting duck while socialism overwhelms it," the judge asserted (*OSMS,* 95 F.Supp. at 113). "Constitutional Democracy is not a one-way road," he continued.

> Those who believe in things as they are, or who seek to retain them in modified form may oppose radical change, without becoming subject to the criminal laws. That certainly includes vitally interested parties whose way of living itself, is threatened. . . . Social forces, acting through the Government may impinge on me, but I can oppose them with all my might. That is one of the issues in this case. What is the purpose of the doctors in organizing the Oregon Physicians' Service? Was it to obtain a monopoly in the prepaid medical field, or was it to save themselves and their profession from threatened socialization? I hold it was the latter, and that nothing in the anti-trust laws deprives them of the right to fight to defend their independent professional status. (*OSMS,* 95 F.Supp. at 109)

Though attorneys at the Justice Department rightly claimed that judicial bias had affected the outcome of the case, the Supreme Court overlooked the trial judge's "soliloquies on socialized medicine" (*OSMS,* 343 U.S. at 332). When it came to the perquisites of professional sovereignty, neither the medical profession nor the federal courts sought to distinguish between governmental and commercial activities.

THE GOLDEN AGE OF MEDICINE

Some scholars have labeled the period from about 1945 to 1965 the golden age of medicine (see Burnham 1982; Freidson 1973). This was a period, sociologist Eliot Freidson professed, when medicine "was at a historically unprecedented peak of prestige, prosperity, and political and cultural influence—perhaps as autonomous as a profession could be" (1973:384). As this chapter has shown, medicine's rise from "virtual political impotence" to "monopolistic control of medical practice" hinged upon scientific advances, organizational changes, and educational reforms that unified the profession and undermined its competition (Burrow 1977:12; Rosen 1983:66). The ideas of progressive reformers—in particular, the notion that experts, as proxies of government, could regulate competition in the public interest—groomed medicine's path. By 1920, physicians had gained exclusive authority over the terms, conditions, and content of medical work. The first journal of a state medical society appeared in 1896; by 1917, twenty-seven state societies had their own journals (Burrow 1977:168). There were 166 medical schools in 1904; by 1922, there were only 81. Before 1900, "fierce conflicts raged" between allopathic physicians and sectarians; by the end of the Progressive Era, such conflicts "[had] been all but forgotten" (Burrow 1977:68).

During the 1930s, the philosophy that underlay professionalism—the pursuit of knowledge and a higher social calling—succumbed to the political and economic interests of physicians and their professional associations. The elevation to power of Morris Fishbein and other opponents of contract practice and government-sponsored health care transformed the AMA from an organization that promoted education and research to one that exploited professional authority. Though medical educators and some prominent specialists expressed disappointment and frustration with the profession's confrontational course, most private practitioners, who dominated the AMA, were unified in their goals and purposes.

Having achieved domination over health care delivery, the medical profession opposed any changes to the status quo. Despite the growing needs of a destitute and expanding population in the Great Depression, medicine rejected contract practice and any other proposal to expand health care delivery, whether government or market based. The only exceptions were indemnity insurance, which satisfied the AMA's ten principles, and Blue Shield plans, which doctors controlled. Commercial indemnity insurers upheld professional autonomy—insurers reimbursed patients, not physicians. In addition, indemnity insurers adhered to free choice of physician—patients could choose any doctor they wanted, generalist or specialist; the insurer was not involved. Although Blue Shield plans, which appeared in the 1940s, violated professional autonomy because such plans paid physicians directly for their work, the AMA granted an exception, albeit reluctantly, since "doctors ran the plan" (Starr 1982:306). Physicians, however, had to satisfy several conditions in order to receive payments from Blue Shield: they could not participate in competing plans; they could not engage in contract practice; and they had to adhere to fee schedules that Blue Shield and the professional societies agreed upon (U.S. Congress, Senate, 1974:1580 [Statement of John W. Riley]).

The antitrust laws, as interpreted and applied throughout the Progressive and New Deal eras, did little to discourage the anticompetitive practices of physicians and their professional associations. Progressive ideas bolstered medicine's claim that those who drafted the Sherman Act did not countenance the learned professions. New Deal reformers, moreover, advanced the notion that collaboration among independent producers, both large and small, was better for the economy than outright competition. Still, there were certain boundaries that medical societies, in the pursuit of power and hegemony, exceeded at their peril. When medical societies crossed these boundaries, as in the Group Health and *OSMS* cases, they had to pull back, but not very far.

The AMA's scant revisions to its Code of Medical Ethics in the years following the Group Health and *OSMS* cases indicated that the profession did not fear the antitrust authorities. Code revisions in 1949 moderated the restriction on contract practice (it "was no longer unethical per se"), yet reinstated past limitations on associating with unscientific practitioners. But these changes were superficial at best. A physician still "could not dispose of his professional attainments or services to any hospital, lay body, organization, group or individual, by whatever name called, or however organized, under terms or conditions which permit[ted] exploitation of the services of the physician for the financial profit of the agency concerned" (AMA Code of Medical Ethics 1949). To sociologist Jeffrey Berlant, the new language actually enhanced the ability of the AMA "to oppose organizational arrangements it did not favor, without making explicit its criteria for exploitation" (Berlant 1975:108).

In 1957, the AMA again revised the code. Though the revisions appeared to be extensive, the changes had negligible effect on the profession's anticompetitive activities. To a significant extent, the provisions of the 1949 code remained intact. Soon after its issuance, the Judicial Council even announced that "the 1957 edition . . . was not intended to and d[id] not abrogate any ethical principle expressed in [the 1949] edition" (AMA, *Opinions and Reports* 1969:v).

The failure of federal courts and agencies to stop anticompetitive practices of professional societies was not because the antitrust laws were deficient in their scope and purpose. Rather, the reticence of courts and agencies stemmed from a set of ideas that looked upon professional behavior as a model for others, including government and industry. In addition, the precapitalist configuration of health care delivery (independent practitioners and stand-alone hospitals) made it difficult to prove that a particular restraint of trade had a "substantial effect" on interstate commerce. Under the circumstances, medicine's dominance of the health care industry remained secure well into the 1960s.

2 Precursors of Change

The social climate of the post–World War II years reveals a steady erosion of support, not for the professional ideal, but for professional associations and their interest-group tactics. Critics emphasized excessive fees, indifference to the personal concerns of patients, attacks on chiropractors, osteopaths, and other providers, and the failure of medicine to police its own ranks (Burnham 1982; Wylie 1952). Supporters stressed professionalism, physicians' sense of mission and higher calling, patient trust, the dangers of commercialism, and the importance of competence and caring (Kass 1983; Mechanic 1998). The truth, of course, lay somewhere in between. According to historian Rosemary Stevens, "the professions were being socially reclassified, moving down a moral continuum away from the role of benevolent agents of the public and toward that of self-interested players in the economic marketplace, as if they could not be both at once" (Stevens 2001:334–335).

This chapter examines the political, social, and economic forces and events that presaged the replacement of the professional regime by the market regime in the 1970s. These forces and events were highly complex and intertwined. Much of the story concerns AMA efforts to maintain professional hegemony in the face of mounting pressures—pressures to increase the number of physicians, to allow prepaid group practice, to be more inclusive, to accept financial aid from federal and state governments, and to address rising health care expenditures. The profession's response to changing conditions would determine its role in a reconfigured health care industry.

THE MEDICAL PROFESSION AS A SPECIAL INTEREST

To many practitioners, the ten principles announced by the AMA in 1934 confirmed what they already believed. But on closer inspection, the ten principles reflected a change in outlook and disposition since the Progressive Era, when medical educators, such as Ray Lyman Wilbur, controlled the association. Wilbur, who had been president of the AMA in 1923, chaired the Committee on the Costs of Medical Care (CCMC) and served as secretary of the interior during the Hoover administration (Campion 1984:127). Not only did the CCMC, with Wilbur's approval, endorse group practice, but it also advocated government support for voluntary health insurance (Starr 1982:263–266).

The CCMC report signaled a growing trend among policy makers interested in expanding access to health care services. Supporters of government-subsidized health care sponsored legislation during the administrations of Presidents Franklin Roosevelt (the Wagner-Murray-Dingell Bill of 1943) and Harry Truman (the Truman plan of 1945). The AMA vociferously attacked both plans for many of the same reasons it resisted contract practice—interference with the terms of payment, with free choice of physician, and with clinical autonomy (see Stevens 1971:138–139). Again, the ten principles defined medicine's stance, and again, the course of events (World War II and fear of communism) advanced its position.

Dominated by an "active minority" primarily comprised of urban specialists, the AMA seemed unable or unwilling to adapt to changing circumstances (see Starr 1982:273; Garceau 1941:142). Efforts to restrict competition by eliminating poorly performing schools and by prosecuting so-called quacks and pretenders received support from progressives, who linked regulation in the early twentieth century to the public interest. But scientific progress and achievement in succeeding years changed the underlying calculus. Medical advances, such as chemotherapy, antibiotics, hormones, insulin, and vitamins, increased expectations, giving rise to a new set of issues "having to do with the availability, distribution, and financing of physicians and hospital services" (Campion 1984:129). "It was one thing to accept that a person could not afford to call in the average practitioner of 1915; it was quite another in 1935 to deny insulin to a diabetic," Rosemary Stevens noted (1971:180).

Morris Fishbein, the AMA's self-appointed spokesman, blocked consideration of any new and innovative initiatives. Over the protest of the California Medical Association, Fishbein rejected state aid to voluntary nonprofit health plans in California (Campion 1984:122). In a 1945 editorial in *JAMA,* Fishbein wrote: "The problem of establishing medical care for all under prepayment plans, whether voluntary or compulsory, is complex and susceptible to various detrimental influences. Much carefully controlled experimentation with voluntary plans . . . is needed before anything resembling a real answer to the problem of medical care for all the people will be forthcoming" (as quoted in Campion 1984:121). Convinced that Fishbein was acting beyond his authority, the California contingent and other members of the House of Delegates sought to curb Fishbein's "public relations" activities. Though initial efforts failed, opposition to Fishbein grew, and in 1949, the delegates engineered his ouster (Campion 1984:118–125).

Events surrounding Fishbein's departure conflated ongoing debate in the 1940s over the nature and extent of the AMA's political entanglements. Should the primary purpose of the association be scientific achievement and education, or should it be political advocacy on behalf of the economic interests of its members? Olin West, secretary–general manager of the AMA, advised the association to stick to science and education. "I maintain that the AMA has no excuse for existence except as a scientific and educational organization," he said (as quoted in Campion 1984:130). But in the end, following heated debate in several forums, members rejected West's admonitions. Rather than retreat from the political scene, the AMA opened an office in Washington, D.C., and "committed itself irrevocably to a new body, the Council on Medical Service and Public Relations, which had clear, non-scientific objectives" (Campion 1984:131).

Its direction more certain, the AMA committed an increasing share of staff time and attention to protecting the economic pursuits of private practitioners. Success in the political arena, however, required a steady source of income. Almost total reliance on revenues generated by *JAMA* exposed the organization to events beyond its control, in particular, dollars received from the advertising of pharmaceuticals, which were not guaranteed. To fund its opposition to the Truman plan, the AMA assessed each member $25 and resumed the collection of dues from physicians in 1950. Simultaneously, state medical societies in thirteen states, including New York, California, and Illinois, adopted a "unified membership" policy. Unified membership meant that doctors had to join the AMA as a precondition to affiliating with their state and local societies. Although a majority of state societies did not require physicians to join the AMA, the association relied on these societies for collection of dues, recruitment, and retention of members (Campion 1984:114, 174, 364–365).

Future success in the political arena also required that the AMA revamp its antiquated organizational structure. By the 1950s, policy making and workload was divided among almost seventy councils and committees (Campion 1984:195). Seeking to streamline its decision-making apparatus, the Board of Trustees hired an outside consultant to perform an operational study. Among the consultant's recommendations was the creation of a chief executive officer (an executive vice president). The House of Delegates implemented the consultant's recommendation and, in 1958, chose Francis Blasingame, a consummate insider, as the association's first executive vice president. Soon after his appointment, Blasingame reorganized staff and created five new operational divisions—legal affairs and legislation, business operations, communications, publications, and field work. The new executive vice president assumed control over the AMA's Chicago operations and over its lobbying activities based in Washington, D.C. (Campion 1984:197–203).

As the AMA entered the 1960s, it was, as Frank Campion claimed, "a far stronger organization than it was at the start of the decade" (1984:204). Yet despite internal restructuring that improved staffing and finances, the AMA's political operations had not reached their full potential. The "Washington operation was weak," and, because of federal law, the association could not engage directly in the electoral process (Campion 1984:209). Facing a renewed push in Congress for government-subsidized health care, this time targeted toward the elderly, in 1961 the AMA launched the American Medical Political Action Committee (AMPAC). Though technically separate from the AMA for legal purposes, the association appointed AMPAC's board and its executive director. Over the next several years, AMPAC would endorse and finance candidates for public office in an attempt to build "a bipartisan conservative coalition" (Campion 1984:226). With its formal entry into the political arena, the AMA brushed aside any pretense that its principal purpose concerned scientific and educational endeavors. Going into the 1960s, the AMA was, first and foremost, a trade association.

THE DOCTOR SHORTAGE AND PREPAID GROUP PRACTICE

Among the issues that occupied the attention of Blasingame and other medical leaders in the 1950s were a shortage of physicians and the festering problem of prepaid group practice. The first issue arose in conjunction with public demand for more and better services. New hospital construction under the 1946 Hill-Burton Act, coupled with the rapid spread of private health insurance after World War II, greatly expanded the number of paying patients. Physicians "had more than enough work" and a sufficient number of facilities in which to perform it (Rodwin 1993:32). Many hospitals offered to subsidize doctors' practices by providing office space and by charging low rents in return for patient referrals (Rodwin 1993:38). The only thing lacking was an adequate supply of physicians willing to fill the new buildings.

For years, the AMA had resisted efforts by the federal government to increase medical school enrollments (Ginzberg 1990:178–183). In 1933, the total number of applicants accepted to medical schools was 7,357. Almost twenty years later, in 1951, the total number of applicants accepted was 7,663 (Rayack 1967:79). A report prepared by Oscar Ewing, head of the Social Security Administration under President Truman, projected a shortfall of 42,000 physicians by 1960 (Ginzberg 1990:179). In response to the Ewing report, Senator Claude Pepper called for direct federal subsidies for medical education. Though the AMA balked at direct subsidies, asserting a "threat to academic freedom," it "reluctantly" approved federal grants to medical schools "for construction, equipment, and renovation" of school facilities (Campion 1984:178–180).

But the issue would not go away, though President Dwight Eisenhower, during his eight years in office, did not strongly pursue it (Ginzberg 1990:180). A study released in 1958 projected that there would be a shortfall of as many as 17,200 physicians by the mid-1970s (Ginzberg 1990:181). Under pressure from the administration of John Kennedy in the early 1960s and facing a renewed battle over national health insurance, the AMA finally relented. In 1963, Congress enacted legislation to provide direct federal support for medical education. Federal subsidies for medical education had immediate and long-lasting consequences. Between 1964 and 1987, the number of medical schools increased from 88 to 127. During that same period, the supply of new graduates more than doubled, from 7,409 to 15,872 (Ginzberg 1990:141).

The second major issue that the AMA confronted in the 1950s was the recurrent matter of prepaid group practice. Private practitioners who controlled the AMA and their state and local societies continued to resist prepaid health plans, such as those in California, New York, and Seattle, Washington. But their efforts were squarely in the face of industry trends. A large and growing segment of the physician population, as much as 15 percent by the late 1950s, were employees of private and public hospitals (Campion 1984:189). Courts, particularly those in Western states, increasingly supported such employment arrangements (see Campion 1984:188–191; Starr 1982:320–327). The influx of dollars from private insurers, moreover, encouraged physicians to engage in commercial practices previously forbidden. Eager to increase their incomes, doctors sought to "dispense medical products, own medical facilities, and enter into joint ventures with medical suppliers" (Rodwin 1993:35). Under the circumstances, ethical restrictions on certain commercial activities were more difficult to justify in the 1950s than in the 1920s and 1930s.

Responding to these trends, in 1959 the AMA formed a commission headed by trustee Leonard Larson. Following deliberations, the Larson commission interpreted "free choice" to mean patient selection of insurance plans as well as doctors (Starr 1982:327). Henceforth, the AMA would not "officially" oppose contract practice. But this was easier said than done. While independent practitioners welcomed the loosening of ethical restrictions concerning the dispensing of drugs and devices, the ownership of pharmacies, and affiliation with allied health providers, such as physical therapists (Rodwin 1993:36), many remained opposed to prepaid health plans. Reprisals against prepaid health plans, some subtle and some not so subtle, continued well into the 1970s (Weller 1984:1368–1369; *In the Matter of the American Medical Ass'n,* 94 F.T.C. 701, 899–907 [1979]).

EFFORTS TO RESTRICT COMPETING PROVIDERS

Just as the AMA constrained the number of doctors that graduated from medical school in the years following World War II, so it curtailed efforts of nonphysicians to provide health care services. Drawn to the field because of burgeoning demand and new sources of income, the number of providers in the older professions (pharmacists, dentists, and nurses) doubled between 1950 and 1967, while numbers in the newer professions (opticians, physical therapists, and dieticians, for example) tripled during the same period (Gross 1984:38). Nurse anesthetists, nurse midwives, chiropractors, podiatrists, and many other health care providers sought access to new technologies, hospitals, and private and public insurers. Fearing a threat to their monopoly over health care delivery, physicians intensified efforts to preserve their competitive position (see Kissam et al. 1982:654).

Battles between physicians and nonphysicians over money and turf had transpired in the United States for well over one hundred years. Indeed, the AMA was founded to help allopathic, or "regular," physicians oppose "unorthodox" practitioners (King 1982:1749). When scientific progress validated allopathic medicine in the late 1800s, public and political support accrued (Rosen 1983:16; King 1982:1750; Starr 1982:57–59). State licensing boards, which gained legislative approval in most states by the late 1800s, provided medicine with the legal means for sanctioning competitors. Licensing boards defined the practice of medicine broadly and prosecuted those who violated state laws governing the treatment and care of patients. From 1906 to 1936, boards brought more than fifteen thousand actions against chiropractors alone (Chiropractic: Its Cause and Cure 1942:42). But board actions were not the only means, nor even the most effective means, that medicine employed to restrict competition. Medical societies in several states, beginning with Wisconsin in 1925, persuaded legislatures to enact "basic science laws" in the belief that few sectarians, or unorthodox practitioners, could pass a test of basic science as a prerequisite to licensure (Pinkham 1921:1938).

As the number and type of competing providers increased in the twentieth century, orthodox medicine engaged private accrediting bodies to exclude sectarians from hospitals, government facilities, and insurance arrangements. Perhaps the most important was the Joint Commission on Accreditation of Hospitals, of which the AMA, along with the American College of Surgeons, the American College of Physicians, and the American Hospital Association, was a founding member. Formed in 1951, the Joint Commission inherited the duties of the American College of Surgeons, which had surveyed hospitals to assure compliance with minimum standards since 1919. Policy pronouncements of the Joint Commission in the postwar years closely tracked those of the association. In order to receive accreditation, for instance, hospitals had to have a fully functioning medical staff organization that subscribed to the Code of Medical Ethics (see Havighurst, Blumstein, and Brennan 1998:687–688; AMA House of Delegates, *Proceedings* [hereafter *Proceedings*], June 1991:103).

Medical staff of hospitals, comprised of allopathic physicians, possessed unfettered discretion before the 1960s to determine who could treat patients in health care facilities. Allopaths customarily embraced "quality" standards to justify decisions to exclude those who lacked degrees from "approved" medical schools (see Kissam et al. 1982:674–681). Suppression of competition, while apparent, was difficult to establish. The earliest court decisions, *Falcone v. Middlesex County Medical Society* (170 A.2d 324 [N.J. 1961]) and *Greisman v. Newcomb Hosp.* (192 A.2d 817 [N.J. 1963]), which helped osteopathic physicians gain hospital privileges, did not invoke the antitrust laws. Quality was not the central issue in *Falcone* and *Greisman;* rather, it was the AMA's Mundt Resolution, which linked hospital privileges to medical society affiliation. Holding in favor of the osteopathic physicians, the courts in *Falcone* and *Greisman* determined that the membership requirements at issue were arbitrary and against the public interest. Soon after the rulings in *Falcone* and *Greisman,* the Joint Commission abrogated the Mundt Resolution (AMA, *Legal Conference for Medical Society Representatives* [hereafter *Legal Conference*], 16–18 April 1964:314).

Some wished that the decisions in *Falcone* and *Greisman* had relied more closely on antitrust principles. The author of one influential treatise, for instance, noted that "the result of *Falcone* may prevent exclusion from medical societies as a tactic in combating competition, but unless antitrust remedies are expanded . . . society action short of exclusion may not be preventable" (U.S. Congress, Senate, 1974:1615 [Treatise by L. S. Helland, Re: Structure of Health Care Delivery]). AMA attorneys, nonetheless, recognized the close connection to antitrust principles. Addressing a group of AMA officials, attorney Karl Nygren said: "The other aspect of this case [*Falcone*], which I believe is the key to the decision, is the restraint on medical practice, resulting from exclusion from society membership of all osteopathic physicians who, like the members of the society, had an unlimited license to practice medicine. In this respect, the decision reads like an antitrust case or common law restraint of trade" (*Legal Conference,* 16–18 April 1964:381).

Allopathic physicians put aside their differences with osteopathic physicians in the 1960s, but not with chiropractors.* Indeed, the AMA's "war" against chiropractic intensified in the 1950s and 1960s (Wardwell 1988:174). In 1963, the AMA formed a Committee on Quackery to "contain and eliminate" chiropractic, and in 1966, the House of Delegates adopted a resolution that officially gave chiropractic "cult" status (Leffler 1983:186). The AMA based its opposition to chiropractic on scientific grounds. "To debate any merit of chiropractic before a knowledgeable audience," proclaimed the executive secretary of the Mississippi delegation to the AMA, "is to insult their intelligence. There is no shred of demonstrable evidence to support and validate the dogma of this cult" (*Legal Conference,* 16–18 April 1964:143).

The AMA's concern for poor quality notwithstanding, economic considerations figured prominently in its actions. When chiropractors sought privileges at hospitals, medicine's attorneys were quick to respond. "We have found two spots where chiropractors are trying to get hospital staff privileges," Robert Throckmorton, the association's general counsel, stated.

> Just as soon as we heard about it, we got on the telephone and at least indicated our concern and tried to make sure that things were well in hand because I'm sure we all feel that the first time a chiropractor gets on the staff of a hospital, this opens the door and causes problems for everybody. While it is a matter of local responsibility, at least to this

*Osteopathy, which began as an alternative to orthodox medicine in the late nineteenth century, took on many of the diagnostic and therapeutic tools and educational standards of allopathic medicine in the second half of the twentieth century (see Gevitz 1988:124).

> extent we are trying to be interested for the legal protection of the entire profession. There are anti-trust and other problems we would get into if we were too aggressive. (*Legal Conference,* 16–18 April 1964:211)

Throckmorton's emphasis on "opening the door" and "protecting the profession" suggested that more was at stake than quality considerations. His reference to "antitrust problems" if the AMA was "too aggressive" made it clear that the profession's economic interests were involved.

The increasing specialization of medical practice throughout the twentieth century had much to do with the hostile state of affairs by the 1960s (see Gross 1984:65). Obstetricians opposed nurse midwives; anesthesiologists fought nurse anesthetists; orthopedists countered podiatrists; psychiatrists confronted psychologists; and ophthalmologists battled optometrists. Taking advantage of their strategic position, medical specialists used a variety of tactics to marginalize providers who encroached on their turf. Medical staff of hospitals barred access to nurse midwives, nurse anesthetists, and podiatrists (see Gross 1984:67; U.S. Congress, House, 1999:162 [Statement of Jan Stewart]; *Proceedings* December 1977:78–79); psychologists and optometrists had trouble obtaining coverage from insurance plans, such as Blue Shield, that physicians controlled (U.S. Congress, House, 1982a:811 [Clarence Martin and Michael Pallak to Robert Kasten]; FTC Special Collections [Bureau of Competition, Staff Report and Proposed Trade Regulation Rule, April 1979:168–170]).

The purported basis for excluding nonphysicians from hospitals, technology, and insurers was the proper care and treatment of patients. A familiar refrain was that competitors lacked physicians' advanced training and expertise. Yet when nonphysicians sought to enhance their education, physicians criticized them for their efforts. A representative from the Wisconsin State Medical Society offered this advice at a 1964 forum: "Nurses, podiatrists, and optometrists spend too much time in training for what they should be doing and can properly do . . . they should cut out their four, five and six years of training because it is unwarranted and only leads to restlessness and ambitions beyond that training and beyond the possibilities of either technological specialties, limited professionalism or skilled craftsmanship" (*Legal Conference,* 16–18 April 1964:195–196).

Medicine's assertion that its competitors were incompetent most often was inaccurate. Its campaign against midwifery was a good example. Lay midwifery predated modern medicine, and, as late as 1910, midwives attended to over 40 percent of all births in the United States (Gross 1984:65). Studies showed that midwives significantly reduced infant mortality, leading some to believe that midwifery's success, not its failure, was the reason for its suppression (Gross 1984). "The assumption motivating activity suppressing midwives was that their very existence was an obstacle to the development of [obstetrics as a] specialty," psychologist Stanley Gross asserted (1984). In the mid-1940s, the National Organization of Public Health Nurses established a section for nurse-midwives, and in 1955, the American College of Nurse-Midwives formed and began to accredit nurse-midwifery programs (U.S. Congress, House, 1982a:649 [Testimony of the American College of Nurse-Midwives]). Despite the fact that nurse-midwives were licensed in forty-eight states by the late 1970s, insurers often failed to reimburse them and hospitals often refused to give them privileges for difficult deliveries (Gross 1984:67).

Nurse anesthetists also enjoyed a long and rich history. The first educational programs for nurse anesthetists predated World War I and, by the 1920s, operated in several academic health centers, including Johns Hopkins Hospital, the University of Michigan Hospital, Charity Hospital in New Orleans, Barnes Hospital in St. Louis, and Presbyterian Hospital in Chicago. Established in 1931, the American Association of Nurse Anesthetists instituted a certification program in 1945 and by 1955 accredited nurse anesthesia programs under the auspices of the U.S. Department of Education (www.aana.com). As in the case of nurse-midwives, physicians responded by constraining nurse anesthetists. Medical societies passed resolutions and adopted ethical principals that forbade physicians from participating in nurse anesthesia programs (U.S. Congress, House, 1999:162 [Statement of Jan Stewart]).

Not only did many nonphysicians furnish quality health care, they did it more cheaply than their physician counterparts. Before the advent of public programs of insurance (Medicare and Medicaid) in the United States, the poor and destitute chiefly relied on nurse-midwives and other alternative providers. Enhancements to technology and improved insurance coverage transformed the health care environment in the late 1960s. As nonphysicians clamored for inclusion in the burgeoning health care enterprise, the exclusionary tactics that medicine imposed came under closer scrutiny. But before the antitrust laws could come to the aid of nonphysicians, policymakers would have to change their approach to government regulation.

CHANGING VIEWS OF THE "PUBLIC INTEREST"

Discomfort with medicine's exclusionary tactics resonated in the 1960s, a decade that featured an unpopular war in Vietnam, confrontations over civil rights, and other social dislocations. The "high status necessary for professional authority," historian John Burnham concluded, "was being eroded" as the faults of physicians and the anticompetitive activities of medical societies became more transparent (Burnham 1982:1478). Burnham's observations were consistent with AMA surveys of the general population. These surveys, begun in the 1950s, indicated that public opinion was turning against the medical profession (*Proceedings* June 1983:142, 145).

Medicine's history of discriminating against women, blacks, and Jews for admission to medical schools came into sharper focus. Prejudice and elitism, common throughout society, permeated the medical profession. To economist Reuben Kessel, medicine operated much like a "social club" or clique composed primarily of individuals who shared similar views (Kessel 1958:46). Recruitment of like-minded individuals, Kessel suggested, made it easier to discourage activities, such as advertising or price-cutting. "Minority groups whose culture and values are different from those of the majority could rationally be discriminated against in admission to medical schools because they are more difficult to control by informal controls after they are out in medical practice than is characteristic of the population at large," Kessel wrote (1958:46).

The surge in criticism of the medical profession was not an anomaly. Those who rebelled against the "system" in the 1960s did not always differentiate among members of the "establishment." Public opinion showed "general disillusionment with many aspects of American life," not just physicians and their medical societies (Burnham 1982:1476). About 26 percent of the public in 1964 believed that a "few big interests" controlled public policy; by 1972, the number of individuals having similar impressions stood at 53 percent (see Zinn 2003:542). Like other institutions derided in the 1960s, the medical profession was undergoing a fundamental reassessment (see Smith-Cunnien 1990; Burnham 1982).

A large part of this reassessment concerned the consumer movement, which gained traction in the 1960s and 1970s. Consumerism reflected what historian Samuel Hays called "a third stage of consumption" (1987:24). This third stage of consumption "encompassed new material goods, new amenity elements of both necessity and convenience, and a host of new products reflecting the purchasing power that came to be called discretionary income" (Hays 1987:24). Consumers, Hays said, placed demands on government that producers often opposed.

Consumerism checked earlier conceptions of the "public interest." Under the public interest theory of regulation, government corrected market failures through "benevolent" regulation (see McCormick 1989:20). But benevolent regulation depended upon the goodwill of those who did the regulating. In health care, this meant that ethical codes designed to inhibit competition ostensibly were in the public interest. Scholars and journalists who favored the public interest theory of regulation sought to reconcile reality with democratic theory. The solution they proposed, "pluralism" or "interest-group liberalism," held that bargaining among special interests benefited most individuals. Though far from perfect, pluralism, they asserted, was "a more realistic and less dangerous mode of political organization than others which relied on mass mobilization" (see Holsworth 1980:17).

Revisionist democratic theory—"that rational participation by a majority in a large-scale society was improbable"—did not sit well with members of the counterculture (Holsworth 1980:16). Among the critics of pluralist theory was political scientist E. E. Schattschneider. In the words of Schattschneider: "The flaw in the pluralist heaven is that the heavenly chorus sings with a strong upper class accent" (1975:34). Bargaining among special interests did not benefit the underprivileged in society, Schattschneider asserted. The work of Schattschneider and others, such as Theodore Lowi, fueled the regulatory reforms of the early 1970s and the efforts of consumer activists, such as Ralph Nader.

Nader became the chief spokesperson for a consumer movement that opposed "corporate socialism," the "tyranny of the experts," and interest-group liberalism (Holsworth 1980:10, 13, 18). According to political scientist Robert Holsworth, Nader believed "that only a politicized society with consumers vigorously and constantly asserting their own interests can reduce the existing level of victimization" (1980:33). Consumerism, from Nader's point of view, was a defensive movement that comprised "representation in Washington, representation of the public good in private bureaucracies, and widespread participation by consumer-citizens on local levels" (Holsworth 1980:33). The public interest theory of regulation remained large in Nader's accounting, but the mix of groups and individuals engaged in the policy-making process was appreciably different. Nader injected the voice of consumers alongside those of business, labor, and the professions. If regulation was to be "benevolent," it required input from consumers.

During the 1970s, the consumer movement made great strides. Public interest groups gained access to Congress, the courts, and federal agencies. In the early 1970s, Congress created new entities to give consumers greater voice in the political process. While old regulatory agencies, such as the Interstate Commerce Commission and the Securities and Exchange Commission, catered to producers, new ones, such as the Environmental Protection Agency and the Consumer Product Safety Commission, focused on consumers (Hays 1987:24). Consumer advocates devised new labels to designate the altered state of affairs. In health care, physicians became "providers"; patients became "consumers."

MEDICARE AND MEDICAID

Further entering the mix in the 1960s was a renewed push for government-subsidized health care, which began with the introduction of the King-Anderson Bill. King-Anderson, unlike the Roosevelt- and Truman-backed initiatives, was not a comprehensive insurance scheme for the entire population. Rather, King-Anderson was more limited in scope, targeting those sixty-five years of age and over. The AMA aggressively countered the bill, spending $250,000 in the 1962 election campaign, an enormous sum at the time, on candidates who opposed the measure (Rayack 1967:12). In the words of Leonard Larson, the trustee who engineered the change in AMA policy concerning prepaid group practice, "We fight because the administration's medical care proposal, if enacted, would certainly represent the first major, irreversible step toward the complete socialization of medical care" (as quoted in Campion 1984:256).

But physicians "were not altogether of one mind" in resisting King-Anderson. Some favored it, others sought a countermeasure, and still others did not want any legislation whatsoever. Led by executive vice president Francis Blasingame and the Board of Trustees, this third group prevailed. Blasingame and the board succeeded in large part because Wilbur Mills, the powerful chair of the Ways and Means Committee of the House of Representatives, "refused to report the bill out of committee" (Campion 1984:267).

The AMA's lack of a countermeasure to King-Anderson marginalized its role when the political environment suddenly changed following the assassination of President Kennedy and the landslide victory of Lyndon Johnson over Barry Goldwater. Believing he could not forestall King-Anderson any further, Mills switched his position. Its gambit now foreclosed, the AMA belatedly developed and backed a proposal known as Eldercare, a scaled-down version of King-Anderson. Though it spent more than $950,000 in the first quarter of 1965 to advance its proposal, the association could not thwart the passage of more comprehensive legislation (see Rayack 1967:11). In the end, Congress amended the Social Security Act to provide hospital care (Medicare Part A) and medical services (Medicare Part B) to retirees and medical assistance to needy persons (Medicaid).

Opposition of physicians to the new legislation was so intense that several delegates at the annual convention of the AMA in 1965 called for a collective boycott. Only the fear of antitrust action stopped them. An AMA official who witnessed the debate stated:

> We had, prior to the meeting, at least thirty to forty resolutions that called for a total boycott by the divisions of the Medicare program. . . . Wes Hudson [legal counsel] addressed the House of Delegates to give them a primer on antitrust law and why adoption of the resolutions would result in direct action against the AMA by the Justice Department because it would constitute a boycott and there is no justification that would save it. In light of the resolutions, we had worked with the Judicial Council prior to the meeting to come up with an opinion, which, for all intents and purposes, said that each physician should decide for himself or herself whether or not to accept Medicare patients. . . . And so, even though the hearings lasted for hours and hours and hours, and we had numerous delegates who had tears streaming down their faces who would repeatedly come up to the microphone to talk about the disaster it was going to be, the result was that the House did not adopt any of the boycott resolutions and did, in fact, adopt the opinion of the Judicial Council. (Anderson 2003)

The focus now shifted to the development of regulations to implement Medicare and Medicaid. Seeking the cooperation of America's physicians, the undersecretary of health, education, and welfare, Wilbur Cohen, met with members of the association. During an initial "exploratory" meeting, Cohen agreed that the government would solicit the AMA's input at this crucial stage. Cohen's session with the AMA and others that followed marked the beginning of a "new relationship" (Campion 1984:280). "Instead of glowering at each other across a political battlefield, hurling slogans and accusations," Campion wrote, "the two sides now addressed each other in civilized tones around a conference table" (1984:280).

The final regulations that the federal government agreed to enforce embodied many of the AMA's recommendations. To a significant extent, the Medicare and Medicaid programs would satisfy the core beliefs of the medical profession—free choice, clinical autonomy, and self-regulation—as codified in the AMA's ten principles. There would be no limitation on free choice of physician, whether general or specialty practitioner. Physicians would have total freedom to diagnose, treat, and prescribe medications, the only constraints being that diagnosis and treatment had to be "reasonable and necessary" and charges had to be "usual and customary." The government's role, quite simply, would be that of a reimbursement agency. Physicians would deal with private insurance carriers, not with federal agencies; most insurance carriers would be Blue Shield plans, which doctors controlled through their medical societies (Stevens 1971:445–453).

RISING COSTS OF HEALTH CARE SERVICES AND INITIAL EFFORTS TO CONTAIN THEM

With the extension of private insurance to most employees and the addition of federal funds to cover the poor and elderly, demand for health care exploded. The result was a "medical arms race" in which physicians and hospitals offered more and better services (Robinson 1999:23). Now that government paid the bills for a new and growing segment of the population, it had its own interests to protect, and cost overruns were a potential problem. Since Medicare and Medicaid did not introduce any new mechanisms to control costs, other than utilization review committees in hospitals, much of the responsibility "rested on the integrity of the medical profession" (Stevens 1971:449).

Rising health costs were only one piece, albeit a big one, of a discouraging economic forecast. Before the decade of the 1970s ended, there would be two recessions (the first commencing in 1973 and the second in 1978) characterized by high unemployment and runaway inflation. The simultaneous occurrence of high unemployment and inflation, or "stagflation," as it came to be known, defied conventional wisdom. The causes of stagflation were numerous and complex. They included the costs associated with the Vietnam War and the Great Society programs, a downward trend in manufacturing that began in 1969, drought conditions in the agricultural sector, and significant production cuts in crude oil imported from the Middle East and other countries that comprised the Organization of Petroleum Exporting Countries, known as OPEC (Bernstein 2001:148–173).

Attempts by the federal government to address stagflation proved futile and, at times, exacerbated the situation. President Nixon imposed price controls in 1971 and 1973, including ceilings on physicians' fees and hospital charges. Although Nixon's first set of price controls temporarily slowed the rate of inflation, OPEC production cuts, announced in 1973, caused a new round of inflation. According to historian Michael Bernstein, "The OPEC price shock, while different in form and etiology, had many of the same consequences as the 1929 New York stock market debacle," including significant drops in real income, corporate investment, profit margins, and employment (2001:158).

Seeking to tame health care costs, Congress turned to government regulation. In 1972, Congress amended the Social Security Act to establish, among other things, Professional Standards Review Organizations (PSROs). PSROs engaged physicians to approve payment for medical services under Medicare and Medicaid. Two years later, Congress passed the National Health Planning and Resources Development Act. The 1974 act required all fifty states to enact certificate-of-need (CON) laws and created health systems agencies headed by boards with consumers in the majority. Congress hoped that CON legislation would discourage duplicative and unnecessary spending on buildings and equipment and that PSROs would curtail the costs of medical services. In addition, more than thirty states established rate-setting programs in the 1970s and 1980s to regulate hospital charges and payments (Patel and Rushefsky 1999:167–180; Kronenfeld 1997:80–92).

But if policy makers thought that government regulation would stem rising costs of health care, they were mistaken. In 1960, national spending on health care services totaled $26.9 billion, or 5.3 percent, of gross national product (GNP); by 1970, costs totaled $74.7 billion, or 7.5 percent, of GNP; and by 1980, national expenditures totaled $249 billion, or 9.5 percent, of GNP (Marmor and Klein 1994:108). Per capita spending in 1960 was $146; by 1970, it was $350; by 1980, it stood at $1049 (Kronenfeld 1991:20).

An important reason why government planning and regulation failed to stem costs concerned weak financial incentives. The retrospective method of payment that Congress adopted in 1965 gave physicians carte blanche to maximize fees and medical services. Physicians enhanced their incomes by doing more rather than less—by seeing more patients, by ordering more tests, and by performing more procedures. Consumers also had no incentive to curb their desire for health care services if they had insurance. Because others paid their bills for them, consumers spent more on health care than they actually required (see Feldstein 1999:50–51). Under the circumstances, the forces of supply and demand did not work as economic theory had predicted. Rather than lead to a decrease in demand, price increases fueled efforts toward more comprehensive insurance coverage (Robinson 1999:24). Absent a reversal of economic incentives, costs of health care would continue to climb in the near and distant future.

CONCLUSION

During the postwar years in the United States, the American public savored the fruits of technological success and rising economic prosperity. Americans who had experienced the Great Depression and the Second World War enjoyed, for the first time, a period of relative calm and stability. But a new generation, restless and unhappy with entrenched authority, rebelled against the old order. Rising social, political, and economic unrest spilled over to the health care industry.

As the 1970s began, professional associations, led by the AMA, faced challenges from several quarters—from the federal government, from alternative health care providers, and from physicians themselves, particularly those in academe who disagreed with the AMA's conservative agenda. Medicine had withstood efforts to change the system, often because principles of self-regulation, autonomy, and free choice enjoyed widespread support in business and government circles. But the cynicism that pervaded the 1960s exposed the profession to closer scrutiny. Economists, sociologists, and others argued that claims of altruism and quality masked policies that aided doctors and their economic interests.

In the years following World War II, the AMA had become a politically astute organization. Morris Fishbein's brash and confrontational style had given way to the polish and sophistication of those who specialized in public relations and political lobbying. Still, the association reflected the norms and beliefs of AMA leaders and those of its rank and file. These norms and beliefs increasingly were out-of-touch with powerful trends in American society. One powerful trend that challenged the medical profession was the consumer movement. Consumerism, as conceived by Ralph Nader and his followers, viewed politics as a defensive struggle. Nader asserted that consumers should organize to protect their interests from those of the business and professional lobbies.

Federal intervention in health care during the 1950s and 1960s circumscribed medicine's authority. As initially conceived, Medicare and Medicaid preserved the status quo—patients would have free choice of physician and there would be few, if any, limitations on doctors' autonomy. It was only a matter of time, however, before enhanced access to care and pressures to control costs made traditional forms of delivery and finance unworkable. Once that time came, and it would come soon, policy makers would begin their search for alternatives to the professional order. Countries such as Great Britain, Germany, and Canada already had chosen government-run or government-financed systems. But in the United States, another possibility loomed—America's free enterprise system.

3 The Triumph of Market Theory

The transition from regulatory policy to competition policy in the late 1970s, though seemingly abrupt, followed years of preparation and accumulated knowledge in academic and policy circles. As political scientist John Kingdon observed, "Agenda change appears quite discontinuous and nonincremental. But incrementalism might still characterize the generation of alternatives" (Kingdon 1995:82). Universities and think tanks, such as the American Enterprise Institute, were the sources of the theories and ideas that fueled deregulatory and antitrust policy (Derthick and Quirk 1985; Eisner 1991). The economic study of antitrust law, for instance, originated at Chicago, Harvard, and Yale in the 1950s, yet federal courts and agencies rarely employed economic analysis in their decision making until the 1970s and 1980s (Easterbrook 1984:9 n. 8).

This chapter provides the intellectual framework for the shift from the professional to the market regime. It traces the evolution of neoclassical market theory from its origins at the University of Chicago in the 1930s to its widespread acceptance by economists, legal scholars, and government decision makers in the 1970s. It relates the policy preferences that market theory put forth (deregulation and an efficiency-based antitrust policy), the movements that it inspired (law and economics), and the theoretical underpinnings for an economic theory of regulation (public choice and agency capture). Finally, this chapter explores the roles of prominent economists and legal scholars. If economists, such as Milton Friedman, provided the kindling for the health care revolution, then legal scholars Robert Bork, Richard Posner, and Clark Havighurst supplied the kerosene. Bork and Posner extended economic theory to the antitrust arena. Havighurst went a step further. He linked antitrust policy to market competition in the health care arena.

MILTON FRIEDMAN AND NEOCLASSICAL ECONOMIC THEORY

The economic theory of John Maynard Keynes and its most ardent supporter in the United States, Paul Samuelson, underlay public policy since the mid-1930s. Keynesian economics held that policy makers could "fine tune" the economy through the manipulation of taxes and spending (Bernstein 2001:118). Contrary to the classical economic theory of Adam Smith, Keynes believed that "there was nothing self-perfecting about a free market economy" and that government spending was necessary "to arrest the downward spiral of private expenditure" (Lowi and Ginsberg 1994:682). This demand-side approach to correcting downturns in the economy fostered many of the economic initiatives of the New Deal and of America's version of the welfare state.

Despite the doctrinal shift in economic theory that Keynes brought about, a "small beleaguered minority" remained steadfast supporters of Adam Smith (Friedman 1982:vi). This small minority was most closely associated with the Chicago School of Economics. Through a series of major faculty appointments and a rigorous training regimen for doctoral students "whose end result is an economist with the Chicago style of thought," the Chicago school assumed prominence in the 1930s and retained its influence in the years after World War II (Reder 1982:8–9). Though the faculty in the Department of Economics at the University of Chicago included several notable scholars, Milton Friedman was its most prominent member. According to Melvin Reder, a graduate student and "working economist" at the University of Chicago, "Friedman swiftly took over the intellectual leadership of one faction of the Department and energetically attacked the views and proposals of the others. His vigor in debate and the content of his arguments set the tone and public image of Chicago economics for at least a quarter century" (1982:10).

The Chicago School of Economics rested on several assumptions of classical market theory. Foremost, Chicagoans subscribed to the notion that individuals are self-interested maximizers, that is, they are rational decision makers who make choices based on their own personal preferences or objectives. In a free market, producers (seeking to maximize their profits) and consumers (seeking to maximize their well-being or utility) gravitate toward equilibrium, or a perfect balancing of their needs and desires. The optimal allocation of resources, known as Pareto optimality, refers to the situation in which "there is no alternative allocation such that any one decision maker could have his expected utility increased without a reduction occurring in the expected utility of at least one other decision maker" (Reder 1982:11).

Those critical of the Chicago school thought it "unrealistic, even fanciful" for "market actors [to] behave in conformity with a 'rational' assessment of all available information" (Bernstein 2001:160–161). Friedman's response to such criticism was that "businessmen generally behave *as if* they were engaged in maximization" (Bork 1978:120, emphasis in original). "Friedman's point," Robert Bork stressed, "is not that firms maximize perfectly any more than expert billiard players plan and execute every shot correctly. Perfection is the limiting condition to which the more successful come closer than their rivals." Success, in other words, "is measured against rivals rather than the ideal. . . . Profit maximization is the limiting point toward which success tends" (Bork 1978:121).

Friedman's ideas featured a strong normative component. Just as neoclassical economic theory viewed the state "as an inefficient instrument for achieving any given objective," so many Chicagoans believed that "it is wrong to entrust the control of resources to government officials no matter what social objectives they may be pursuing" (Reder 1982:31). "These two strains of anti-statist thought," Reder noted, "are not easily disentangled" (1982:31–32). Friedman himself freely professed the link between economic and political freedom. He wrote: "Historical evidence speaks with a single voice on the relation between political freedom and a free market. I know of no example in time or place of a society that has been marked by a large measure of political freedom, and that has not also used something comparable to a free market to organize the bulk of economic activity" (Friedman 1982:9). Friedman saw government's role as that of "an umpire to interpret and enforce the rules decided on," not as an active participant in the rule-making process (Friedman 1982:15).

Friedman was a member of the Mont Pelerin Society, a libertarian organization founded by Nobel laureate Friedrich von Hayek in 1947. The expressed objective of the society "was to facilitate an exchange of ideas between like-minded scholars in the hope of strengthening the principles and practice of a free society and to study the workings, virtues, and defects of market-oriented economic systems" (www.montpelerin.org). Members of Mont Pelerin viewed the modern welfare state as a threat to economic liberty and political freedom. They described themselves as "liberals" in the European or classical sense rather than the "current American sense," which favored government oversight and regulation. Several Chicagoans served as presidents of Mont Pelerin, including Friedman, George Stigler, James Buchanan, and Gary Becker. Other prominent Chicagoans who were members of the society included Richard Posner and Harold Demsetz. The society's influence was widespread throughout Europe and the United States. Eight members won Nobel Prizes in economics, including Friedman and Stigler; twenty-two members served as economic advisers on President Reagan's campaign staff (www.montpelerin.org).

Buchanan and Stigler extended neoclassical economic theory into the realm of politics. They spearheaded public choice theory, the notion that politicians pursue their own self-interests when making government policy. Public choice theory holds that efforts of politicians to gain reelection lead to the passage of laws that favor special interests. This is known as "rent-seeking" behavior. The line of reasoning is as follows: "If you were a vote-seeking politician what would you do? Clearly, little gain would be derived from supporting the interest of the largely uninformed and disinterested majority. Predictably, politicians will be led as if by an invisible hand to serve well-organized, concentrated interests. Support of such special interests will generate vocal supporters, campaign workers, and most importantly, campaign contributions" (Gwartney and Stroup 1990:469; see also McChesney and Shughart 1995).

Public choice theory had profound implications for government regulation. If government regulation was the product of rent-seeking behavior, then to what extent did it serve the public interest? Economists Martin Feldstein and Mancur Olson showed that much of the legislation in the health care field, from Medicare and Medicaid to tax subsidies for health insurance, benefited physicians and other special interests. Olson, for instance, laid much of the blame for rising health care costs on fee-for-service arrangements (Olson 1982:5). Medicare and Medicaid programs, Olson wrote, while built on notions of "egalitarian and humanistic feelings," were "designed and administered in such a way as to generate vastly increased incomes for physicians and some relatively well-to-do providers" (1982:4). Because prepaid group practices, HMOs, and other competitive approaches had the potential to undercut physicians' income, as well as their autonomy and authority, professional associations suppressed their operation.

Public choice theory, when tied to the notion of agency capture (the assertion that special interests "capture" and control the agencies that supervise them), countered the belief that government regulation was in the public interest. Both public choice theory and agency capture underlay a conservative political agenda. Several think tanks emerged in the 1970s for the purpose of advancing "competitive capitalism" (Blyth 2002:156). These think tanks included the Heritage Foundation (founded in 1973 by Antony Fisher, a member of the Mont Pelerin Society), the Hoover Institute, and the

American Enterprise Institute (AEI). Corporate donations in the 1970s swelled their coffers. Economists at the Chicago school found solace at all three, particularly AEI, where "a host of . . . conservative economists took up residency or conducted policy-focused research" (Blyth 2002:157). Within these various settings, the "disparate ideas of monetarists, supply-siders, rational expectations, and public choice theorists" congealed and formed the blueprint for combating inflation, regulation, corporate taxation, and rising expenditures for health care services (Blyth 2002:126).

DEREGULATION AND THE HMO ACT OF 1973

Deregulation was one of the policies spawned by neoclassical economic theory. Theorists claimed that deregulation, or the removal of government-imposed restrictions, would engender market competition. Between 1975 and 1980, the federal government deregulated the airlines, trucking, and telecommunications industries through legislation and administrative action. Removal of government impediments to competition was not, by any means, a partisan undertaking. Economists in the Carter administration, such as Alfred Kahn, supported deregulation of the private sector, as did consumer activists, such as Ralph Nader, and liberal senators, such as Edward Kennedy.

Political scientists Martha Derthick and Paul Quirk sought to explain why policy makers embraced deregulation in the late 1970s. How was it, they asked, that "a diffuse public interest articulated by a 'few lonely economists' got embodied in law, and why were the industry and union interests that had a stake in preserving regulation unable to protect themselves against change?" (Derthick and Quirk 1985:13). If conventional wisdom held that self-interest was the sole motivator of political behavior, then the results seemed inconsistent.

Derthick and Quirk discovered that ideas, and mass public sentiment in support of those ideas, overcame entrenched interests in airlines, trucking, and telecommunications. Their case studies revealed the following similarities: Most economists agreed that procompetitive deregulation constituted sound public policy. Powerful forums, such as the Brookings Institution and the American Enterprise Institute, disseminated economists' ideas to the broader intellectual community. Economists who touted deregulation gained employment in the upper echelons of the federal government and achieved prominence in policy circles. Congress and the executive branch were receptive to these ideas because they were easy to implement and because they responded to public concerns over inflation and big government. Finally, the affected industries were unable to mount a plausible argument to justify the continuation of protectionist policies (Derthick and Quirk 1985:246–252).

As in the cases of airlines, trucking, and telecommunications, restrictions on competition pervaded the health care industry. What was different, however, was the source of these restrictions. Rather than emanate from government, these restrictions emanated from the medical profession, with the government's backing. Thus, deregulation in health care meant the removal of impediments on price, entry, and delivery that the medical profession imposed through ethics, norms, and policies of professional associations and private accrediting bodies. Under the circumstances, Congress did not have to act to remove restrictions. Enforcement of the antitrust laws by government agencies, such as the Department of Justice and the Federal Trade Commission, was the purported solution to free-market competition.

But deregulation of health care was more problematic than in most other industries. First, it entailed the overthrow of the professional regime, and second, it called for the establishment of a competitive market. Application of the antitrust laws to the medical profession was not a simple undertaking. The Supreme Court, in the early 1970s, had yet to modify or eliminate certain barriers to legal action—the interstate commerce requirement, the "learned professions" exemption, and state-action immunity. In addition, there was the need to establish a competitive market if and when the antitrust laws applied. As Derthick and Quirk observed, "Deregulation called mainly for removing constraints on existing institutions and restoring markets in classic form. It stands in contrast . . . to the federal government's promotion of health maintenance organizations, a case in which an effort to strengthen markets encountered unforeseen difficulties in building a novel form of organization" (1985:246).

The initial attempt of the federal government to introduce prepayment for medical services was the HMO Act of 1973. HMOs were the brainchildren of Paul Ellwood, a physician and head of a Minneapolis-based think tank known as InterStudy. Ellwood's design called for the integration of finance and delivery. Organized groups of physicians, Ellwood envisioned, would provide comprehensive care to patients or subscribers who prepaid for their health care services. The proposal made use of market forces—HMOs would compete with each other and with indemnity-based plans on the basis of price and quality. Members of the Nixon administration embraced Ellwood's idea, in part because use of market forces to constrain costs entailed a limited role for government (see Kingdon 1995:6; Agrawal and Veit 2002:20–24).

Though the 1973 act preempted adverse state laws in the case of federally qualified HMOs, Congress nonetheless required that qualified plans provide comprehensive benefits and calculate their premiums on a communitywide basis, that is, without reference to claims experience or risk factors. Conditions such as these made it difficult for HMOs to compete with traditional insurers that used "experience rating" and offered lower-cost packages (see Agrawal and Veit 2002:31–32). To be sure, the AMA was behind many of the act's restrictive features. Community-based premiums and comprehensive benefits, among others, were grounded in the AMA's ten principles. Even after the legislation passed in a form that met certain of the AMA's tenets, professional associations sought to prevent HMOs from gaining a foothold in many areas. "The most familiar response," Lawrence Brown observed, was "an attempt by the medical society to deter or crush the nascent plan. If this fail[ed], the society . . . then move[d] to establish an independent practice association" (Brown 1983:43). Individual Practice Associations, or IPAs, were a type of HMO that comprised networks of independent, fee-for-service physicians.

THE MERGER OF LAW AND ECONOMICS

The Chicago school heralded the merger of law and economics. Interdisciplinary in nature, the movement sought to fuse economic methodology (statistics and price theory) with legal reasoning. Its founding father, though he published sparingly, was Aaron Director, a law professor who was a consummate teacher. In the words of Nobel laureate Ronald Coase, "Aaron was someone who by his personality as much as anything was able to make this great difference in the way that people looked at the law, even influencing people whose views were completely different from his own" (www-news.uchicago.edu/releases/04/040913.director.shtml). Milton Friedman, George Stigler, and Henry Simons were among Director's colleagues and contemporaries. Director introduced Friedman and Stigler to the Mont Pelerin Society, advanced the publication of *The Road to Serfdom* by Friedrich von Hayek, and taught courses in antitrust law alongside Edward Levi, President Gerald Ford's future attorney general.

A member of Chicago's law faculty as early as 1946, Director schooled Robert Bork and Richard Posner in his new way of thinking. Bork and Posner (as well as other legal scholars, such as Frank Easterbrook) would enhance and promote, through their writings and public service, the teachings of Aaron Director. Both would become law professors at prestigious universities: Bork at Yale Law School from 1962 to 1975 and from 1977 to

1981; Posner at the University of Chicago Law School from 1969 to 1981. Both would serve presidents or important government agencies: Bork as U.S. solicitor general from 1972 to 1977 and as acting attorney general of the United States from 1973 to 1974; Posner as law clerk to Justice William J. Brennan, Jr., as special assistant to FTC commissioner Philip Elman, and as a member of the staff of U.S. solicitor general Thurgood Marshall. And both would serve on the federal bench: Bork on the United States Court of Appeals for the District of Columbia Circuit from 1982 to 1988; Posner on the United States Court of Appeals for the Seventh Circuit from 1981 to the present.

The most significant contribution of Bork and Posner to the law and economics movement was their development in the mid- to late 1960s of an alternative approach to the so-called Harvard, or industrial organization, school of thinking (see Bork 1978; Posner 1976). Adherents of the industrial organization school, which prevailed from the 1940s to 1970s, examined the "structural" or "socioeconomic" characteristics of certain industries to discern the permissible degree of concentration. They believed that firms in concentrated industries could, through "a variety of collusive and exclusionary strategies," augment their positions and "realize monopoly profits" (Eisner 1991:100). To those immersed in this approach, the goals of antitrust policy were multifaceted and complex. For each industry, proponents advanced a "standard of fair conduct," "desirable economic performance," and "small" over "big" business (Kaysen and Turner 1991:188). Those in the industrial organization school believed that government regulation was in the public interest. Their analyses conflated values and concepts having political and social as well as economic dimensions. "Fair conduct," for instance, comprised notions of "equal treatment" and the elimination of "unfair tactics" (Kaysen and Turner 1991:186). Efforts to promote small business required policy makers to discern the "desirable distribution of social power" (Kaysen and Turner 1991:187).

In contrast to the Harvard school, Bork and Posner espoused one goal or value above all others—consumer welfare, which they equated with allocative efficiency. Efforts to further this goal, they said, required courts "to distinguish between agreements or activities that increase[d] wealth through efficiency and those that decrease[d] it through restriction of output" (Bork 1991:39). This "monolithic" approach, as law professor E. Thomas Sullivan called it, fused legal reasoning with economic analysis (Sullivan 1991:162). According to Sullivan:

> Marginal utility and price theory dominate the constructs. The geometry of the language speaks of demand and supply curves. Rational

> behavior in the market is defined in terms of profit motivation. The technical terms reference allocative efficiency as the central analysis. The style is characterized by reference to the sovereignty of the market; there is little concern for market failures and negative externalities. Perfect competition and the state of market equilibrium serve as the intellectual baselines. Competition, in turn, is defined as conduct that maximizes economic efficiency without regard to distributive consequences. The political economy of antitrust has not been important to the development of the modern period. The question asked, rather, is whether a certain allocation of resources is efficient. The distributional consequences of the allocation are irrelevant. (1991:162)

Bork and Posner excoriated proponents of the industrial organization school for their failure to develop a workable approach based on economic theory. Posner called the school's approach "particularistic and non-theoretical" (1991:197); Bork proclaimed that it could "never assist in the correct disposition of a case and may lead to error"(1991:42). Typical of his exegesis, Bork relied on legislative history to bolster his disposition. In the years immediately following passage of the Sherman Act, he said, "The dominant goal was the advancement of consumer welfare" (Bork 1978:17). It was not until later, he claimed, that conflicting goals, such as producer welfare, entered the calculus. The principal culprit was Justice Louis Brandeis. "Brandeis's approach," Bork wrote, "grew in importance in the later evolution of antitrust until, in the era of the Warren Court, it often became the dominant, though not the exclusive, goal" (1978:17).

Those opposed to the position advanced by Bork and Posner asserted that the framers of the Sherman Act did not view efficiency as the primary objective. They argued that political and social concerns predominated and that Congress's intention to protect small business was paramount. Historian Richard Hofstadter pointed to the events surrounding the act's passage, the so-called robber barons of the 1890s, Theodore Roosevelt's assault on the Northern Securities Company, and Woodrow Wilson's "case against the political power of monopoly" (Hofstadter 1991:30, 24–29). Law professor Herbert Hovenkamp declared that "the legislative histories of the various antitrust laws fail to exhibit anything resembling a dominant concern for economic efficiency" (Hovenkamp 1985:249). And law professor Robert Pitofsky, who years later would chair the FTC, wrote: "It is bad history, bad policy, and bad law to exclude certain political values in interpreting the antitrust laws" (Pitofsky 1979:1051).

Despite these contrary opinions, the views of Bork and Posner prevailed in the late 1970s. Their work, as well as that of the Chicago school economists, went far to undermine medicine's special status. The notion that physicians, as members of a "learned profession," should have immunity from the antitrust laws did not conform to the "monolithic" approach of Bork and Posner. When gauging anticompetitive behavior through the lens of economic efficiency, professional values, grounded in the need to correct market failures, lost their legal standing. Economic efficiency meant that courts should consider the welfare of consumers to the exclusion of all other values. The values of small producers, such as physicians, no longer entered the calculus. It did not matter who or what entity engaged in anticompetitive conduct or their motivations, even if altruistic. Boycotts and price-fixing, whether undertaken by the medical profession or any other group or occupation, violated neoclassical economic theory.

CLARK HAVIGHURST AND HEALTH CARE COMPETITION

Having started in the academy, the law and economics movement spread to the upper echelons of government and judicial circles. Its steady progress was due to entrepreneurial law professors who marketed their ideas to the wider policy community. Law professors gained access to the policy community through their identification with prestigious law schools; the widespread dissemination and acceptance of their research and expertise; and the students, colleagues, and networks they trained, fostered, and joined. Law professors who succeeded as policy entrepreneurs were often prolific writers for law reviews, law journals, scholarly magazines, and newspaper editorials. Their networks typically included other scholars with similar leanings; members of influential groups, think tanks, and government agencies; and important policy makers and politicians. Various legal organizations and think tanks provided a forum for their work and, in some instances, published their books. Prominent law professors often testified before congressional committees and subcommittees, served as consultants for presidents and government agencies, chaired important government commissions, and drafted legislation, rules, regulations, and government reports. Their students frequently served as law clerks to federal circuit judges and Supreme Court justices. References to their work appeared in judicial opinions. Many became federal judges themselves, agency heads, or leaders within the Department of Justice or other government agencies.

Despite broad acceptance of economic theory in academic and policy circles in the 1970s, few scholars stressed its application to the health care industry. Writing in the 1960s, before the advent of Medicare and Medicaid, economist Kenneth Arrow contended that the market for medical services lacked "one or more of the competitive preconditions" for success and that "nonmarket means," such as ethical proscriptions of the medical profession, sufficed to correct them (Arrow 1963:947). So too, Talcott Parsons, a sociologist, asserted that "the ideology of the profession lays great emphasis on the obligation of the physician to put the welfare of the patient above his personal interests, and regards commercialism as the most serious and insidious evil with which it has to contend" (Parsons 1964:43). The views of Arrow and Parsons remained in vogue for much of the 1970s as policy makers used regulatory approaches, including health planning and hospital rate controls, to stem rising costs of health care. Linking economic and legal theory to health policy required the persuasive abilities and intellectual standing of a skillful policy entrepreneur. Among the potential candidates, one in particular stood out: legal scholar Clark Havighurst.

Though he had "no specific scholarly agenda in mind" when he began teaching in 1964, Havighurst soon became intrigued by the complex problems that the health care industry faced (Havighurst 2004:107). Dissatisfied with the narrow "intersection of law and medicine" at the time, Havighurst went beyond the usual topics (medical malpractice and occupational licensure) to examine economic regulation. Using money from a small federal grant, Havighurst formed the Interdisciplinary Committee on Legal Issues in Health Care in 1969. Comprising prominent legal scholars, medical school faculty, and economists, such as Reuben Kessel, members of Havighurst's committee exchanged ideas, produced several memoranda, and otherwise stimulated thinking on a broad range of topics related to health care and economics (Havighurst 2003).

By 1970, Havighurst's research agenda had begun to take shape. Interested in antitrust theory and practice since law school, Havighurst was predisposed to market-based solutions that "gave people more choices" (Havighurst 2003). He opposed big government, big medicine, and a legal system "that tended to control people's lives" (Havighurst 2003). As editor of and a regular contributor to *Law and Contemporary Problems* (*L&CP*), a quarterly publication of the Duke University law school, Havighurst enjoyed a ready forum for his views and philosophy. Havighurst's work on HMOs and the health care market appeared in *L&CP* in 1970, as did some of his later work on deregulation and private accreditation. Dan Schwartz, an attorney at the Federal Trade Commission, consulted Havighurst before establishing the commission's health care program in 1975. According to Schwartz, the program "wasn't well developed. It wasn't very well focused, but it raised an issue related to an area of the economy that nobody had looked at—other than Clark Havighurst" (Schwartz 2003).

Havighurst's 1970 article on HMOs attracted the attention of Paul Ellwood. Inspired by the young professor's work, Ellwood helped to arrange Havighurst's sabbatical from 1972 to 1973 at the Institute of Medicine (IOM) of the National Academy of Sciences. Havighurst's experience at IOM was key to his early intellectual growth. Once there, he "tossed ideas around" with Carl Yordy, Ruth Hanft, and other staff at IOM and gained valuable insights "about how the industry worked" (Havighurst 2003). Havighurst's relationship with IOM would span several decades and would include his service on the institute's Board of Health Services.

In 1974, Havighurst testified before the U.S. Senate Subcommittee on Antitrust and Monopoly concerning an IOM report that he helped to write. The report was critical of the restrictions that Congress had placed on HMOs. Calling the HMO Act of 1973 a "white elephant" that would spawn "oversized and essentially clumsy" organizations, Havighurst proposed that Congress amend the act to remove certain obstacles to market competition (U.S. Congress, Senate, 1974:1041 [Statement of Clark C. Havighurst]). By far the biggest obstacle that Havighurst had in mind was the medical profession. Medicine, he testified, used several tactics, including Foundations for Medical Care, or FMCs (the forerunners to Independent Practice Associations), that "in their chief manifestation [comprised] prepayment plans sponsored by local medical societies." FMCs, Havighurst asserted, were "fighting ships" whose purpose was to sustain the medical monopoly. The approach, he said, was similar to that employed by the Oregon Physicians Service in the 1940s. Like the Oregon Physicians Service, once FMCs cornered the market on prepaid care, they would revert to traditional forms of finance and delivery (U.S. Congress, Senate, 1974:1041, 1083 [Statement of Clark C. Havighurst]).

Two important concepts guided Havighurst's analysis of the health care industry and of the medical monopoly in particular—public choice theory and the economic approach to antitrust policy. Havighurst gained familiarity with these concepts by reading the works of Mancur Olson and George Stigler and by attending the "summer camps" of Henry Manne, a prominent legal scholar who opened the field of corporate law to economic analysis. Olson and Stigler were the leading proponents of public choice theory, which underlay the economic theory of regulation; Manne founded the Law and Economics Center to spread the economists' creed to law professors and judges. A frequent lecturer at the Law and Economics Center, Harold Demsetz proclaimed: "Some who attended Manne's 'summer camp' got a good rest or a good tan, but most came away with more. Most found something in the economic analysis that changed the way they looked at a problem or a group of problems. And some found a new way of looking at things that fundamentally changed their approach to teaching and writing" (Demsetz 1999:256).

Havighurst first attended Manne's summer camp in 1972. The experience confirmed and strengthened his skepticism toward government regulation as a panacea for the health care industry. "I was very comfortable with a lot of the conclusions they reached and with the kinds of analysis they performed," Havighurst said (2003). The public choice theorists, he wrote in an article published in 1975, had shown that the "postulated public-interest objective" of regulation was a fallacy, that in the "political marketplace," a "pro-producer bias" held forth. But Havighurst's praise was not limited to proponents of public choice theory. He also noted that "such liberal heroes as Ralph Nader and his allies" had injected a strong dose of skepticism (Havighurst 1975:579–580).

Havighurst pointed to Professional Standards Review Organizations (PSROs), among other examples, as confirmation for his view that regulation could be counterproductive. Established by Congress in 1972, PSROs monitored the cost and quality of care under the Medicare and Medicaid programs. Close ties of PSROs to local medical societies, he asserted, made them a threat to the formation and development of HMOs. Havighurst predicted that PSROs would "behave like so many other regulatory and self-regulatory agencies," in that they would adopt "a regulatory program similar to that [of] an industry-wide cartel" (Havighurst 1974b:263). True to form, PSROs failed to take disciplinary action against poorly performing physicians by withholding payments in a systematic fashion (Dranove 2000:57–58). Congress replaced them in 1983 with Professional Review Organizations, which had fewer ties to professional associations.

The economic approach to antitrust policy, fostered by Bork and Posner, influenced the construct that Havighurst proposed. Though he did not believe that antitrust analysis "turn[ed] on efficiency and on weighing of consumer-welfare considerations in every case," Havighurst clearly favored the Chicagoans over the industrial organization school (Havighurst, Blumstein, and Brennan 1999:4). His foremost concern, as he put it, was "the protection of competition as a process" and not on "protecting competitors, efficiency, or consumer welfare as such" (Havighurst 2003). By ruling out values that had nothing to do with the competitive process, Havighurst aligned himself with the "monolithic," or single-valued, approach of Bork and Posner. Efforts of medical societies to justify anticompetitive conduct by claiming a "worthy purpose" or "quality enhancement" lacked standing in Havighurst's "competitive process" calculus (1978:349–353).

Policy analysts and academicians read his work, Havighurst suggested, because "there wasn't a whole lot out there to read" (2003). Antitrust was "a truly revolutionary idea" that had yet to resonate in policy circles. "To the extent you were trying to build friends in the medical community, as Ellwood was trying to do," he said, "you didn't want to be associated with someone like me who was declaring war on the community." While this may have been true in the early 1970s, it was not the case by the end of the decade when the political climate had changed. The case of *Goldfarb v. Virginia State Bar Association* would be the catalyst for Havighurst's auspicious agenda.

THE *GOLDFARB* CASE

Lewis and Ruth Goldfarb entered into a contract in 1971 to purchase a home in Fairfax County, Virginia, just outside Washington, D.C. A trial attorney at the Federal Trade Commission, Lewis Goldfarb would rise through the ranks to become an assistant director of the FTC's Bureau of Consumer Protection. Before they could close on their new home, the Goldfarbs' lender required title insurance and a title examination that, under Virginia law, only a member of the Virginia State Bar could perform. The Goldfarbs sent letters to thirty-six attorneys in Fairfax County, seeking the lowest possible rate. Of the nineteen attorneys who responded, none agreed to charge less than the minimum fee schedule, which the Fairfax County Bar Association had compiled for advisory purposes only—1 percent of the first $50,000 of the purchase price and .5 percent thereafter. This was in addition to the premium for the title insurance itself. Unable to obtain legal services below the minimum rate, the Goldfarbs sued the state bar and the county bar on behalf of similarly situated purchasers. They claimed that the minimum fee schedule constituted price-fixing in violation of section 1 of the Sherman Act.

Though the facts of the case were not in dispute, the Goldfarbs faced several legal hurdles. First, they had to prove that defendants had engaged in a conspiracy to fix prices. Second, they had to show that the defendant bar associations were involved in interstate commerce. Third, they had to overcome the defendants' contention that the practice of law did not involve "trade or commerce" within the meaning of the Sherman Act, the purported basis for the learned professions exemption. Fourth, they had to counter the defendants' assertions of state-action immunity.

Following a 1972 hearing, Judge Albert Bryan of the federal district court held that a price-fixing arrangement existed. He found the minimum fee schedule "hard to justify as having any relation to the labor involved" because of the separate charge for title insurance (*Goldfarb v. Virginia State Bar*, 355 F.Supp. 491, 494 [E.D. Va. 1973]). There also was sufficient evidence, he said, to satisfy the test for interstate commerce. A "significant portion of funds" for purchasing homes in Fairfax County came from outside Virginia, two of the principal loan guarantors resided in the District of Columbia, and those who purchased homes in Fairfax County often worked in other states or jurisdictions. As for the learned professions exemption, Bryan questioned "whether the adoption of a minimum fee schedule is itself 'professional'" (*Goldfarb*, 355 F.Supp. at 495). "There is a basic inconsistency between the lofty position that professional services, not commodities, are here involved and the position that a minimum fee schedule is proper," he wrote (*Goldfarb*, 355 F.Supp. at 495).

Having ruled for the Goldfarbs on the first three issues, Judge Bryan turned to the defense of state-action immunity. Bryan dismissed the assertion of the county bar—the decision to establish a fee schedule constituted "private," not state, action. But the state bar's claim was more complex and required closer scrutiny. Although the state bar had issued ethics opinions making it improper for attorneys "habitually to charge fees below those suggested in a minimum fee schedule," it had never disciplined any attorney for consistently charging less than the minimum amount. More important, the state bar had acted "within the scope of [its] statutory or rule-created authority" as an administrative agency of the Virginia Supreme Court. Based on these facts, Judge Bryan held that the activities of the state bar were immune from antitrust scrutiny (*Goldfarb*, 355 F.Supp. at 496).

Judge Bryan's rulings in favor of the Goldfarbs did not stand for long. In a 2–1 split decision, the United States Court of Appeals for the Fourth Circuit dismissed the Goldfarbs' claim. Though the circuit court agreed that "the fee schedule and the enforcement mechanism supporting it act[ed] as a substantial restraint upon competition," it determined that the learned professions exemption and the interstate commerce requirement barred the Sherman Act's application (*Goldfarb v. Virginia State Bar*, 497 F.2d 1, 13 [4th Cir. 1974]).

The Goldfarbs' only recourse, at this point, was a hearing before the U.S. Supreme Court, a difficult undertaking. At least four of the nine justices on the Court had to agree that the case was worthy of their full attention—that it had national significance. Stressing the importance of the case "for the medical profession and for the performance of the health services industry," Clark Havighurst filed an *amicus curiae* brief in support of the Goldfarbs' petition (Havighurst 1974a:ii, 2). Havighurst argued that the learned professions exemption remained in dispute and that the "antitrust laws

[were] potentially one of society's best defenses against elitism and monopoly in medicine." By cataloging numerous anticompetitive practices of the AMA and other medical societies, Havighurst expanded the Goldfarbs' claim to include issues common to all professions and to the health care industry in particular. The *OSMS* case, Havighurst asserted, had been wrongly decided. The Goldfarbs had given the Court an opportunity to clarify, if not rectify, a poor decision.

What effect Havighurst's "little brief," as he called it, had on the Court's decision to accept the case is, of course, a matter for speculation. Special interest groups often file briefs that take positions on issues of public policy, as occurred in *Goldfarb.* But Havighurst's brief undoubtedly stood out. Indeed, a law clerk of Justice Harry Blackmun mentioned the brief in a Court memorandum. He wrote: "There is an amicus brief from Clark C. Havighurst, a professor of law at Duke University School of Law, whose concern is with the issue of the 'learned profession' exception and its impact in the area of the provision of health care. He argues against the acceptance of a broad 'learned profession' exception" (Harry A. Blackmun Papers, Box 206, 74–70 [File Memorandum, 12]). Blackmun himself favored Havighurst's point of view. *Goldfarb* is "a good ripsnorter of a case," Blackmun wrote, one that would have a "rather profound effect in most aspects of the practice of law as well as that of the other so-called learned professions" (Harry A. Blackmun Papers, Box 206, 74–70 [File Memorandum, 3]).

On 16 June 1975, the Supreme Court announced its decision. By a unanimous vote, the justices rejected the ruling of the circuit court, breaking new ground on several important issues. First, the Court determined that the title examination was "an integral part of an interstate transaction," insofar as it included out-of-state lenders and federal agencies that acted as loan guarantors (*Goldfarb,* 421 U.S. at 783–784). Second, the Court swept aside the learned professions exemption. It held: "We cannot find support for the proposition that Congress intended any such sweeping exclusion. The nature of an occupation, standing alone, does not provide sanctuary from the Sherman Act" (*Goldfarb,* 421 U.S. at 787). Third, the Court dismissed the state-action claims of the state and county bars. "By providing that deviation from the County Bar minimum fees may lead to disciplinary action," the Court ruled, the State Bar "has voluntarily joined in what was essentially a private anticompetitive activity, and in that posture cannot claim it is beyond the reach of the Sherman Act" (*Goldfarb,* 421 U.S. at 791–792).

Without directly saying so, the Court effectively reversed its ruling in *OSMS.* The context, of course, had changed—the antisocialist rhetoric of the 1950s had diminished, and faith in the professions had reached its nadir;

this was the post-Vietnam, post-Watergate era. Contemporaneous court decisions in other areas, such as civil rights, paralleled the *Goldfarb* decision. The key premise in the civil rights cases was that federal laws could protect the public (and minorities) from entrenched private interests. State-action immunity, the interstate commerce requirement, and the learned professions exemption had to be restricted because they allowed private monopolies to engage in anticompetitive and discriminatory practices.

Perhaps the only sticking point among the justices was the learned professions exemption, the "hard issue," as Justice Blackmun called it in a Court memorandum. "There is some appeal to the thought of a learned profession's exemption," Blackmun wrote in the memorandum. The Court's decision to reject the exemption hinged, in part, on the fact that title examinations were, in Blackmun's words, "fairly standardized products" (Harry A. Blackmun Papers, Box 206, 74–70 [File Memorandum, 25 March 1975:6–7]). "Part of their problem [that of the state and county bars] is that they stopped acting like a profession and adopted a shoddy tradesmen's practice," Chief Justice Burger stated (Harry A. Blackmun Papers, Box 206, 74–70 [Burger Memorandum to Conference, 24 April 1975:3]). "I always abhorred these minimum fee schedules and felt somewhat convinced at least that they serve to help out the incompetent attorney who had a floor on which to rely for his fees," Blackmun added (Harry A. Blackmun Papers, Box 206, 74–70 [File Memorandum, 25 March 1975:3]). But this did not stop the Court from attempting to retain the spirit of the exemption in future cases. Footnote 17 of the Court's opinion, which held as follows, sought to accomplish this objective:

> The fact that a restraint operates upon a profession as distinguished from a business is, of course, relevant in determining whether that particular restraint violates the Sherman Act. It would be unrealistic to view the practice of professions as interchangeable with other business activities, and automatically to apply to the professions antitrust concepts which originated in other areas. The public service aspect, and other features of the professions may require that a particular practice, which could be viewed as a violation of the Sherman Act in another context, be treated differently. We intimate no view on any other situation than the one with which we are confronted today. (*Goldfarb*, 421 U.S. at 788–789 n. 17)

Though *Goldfarb* went far to resolve important issues, questions still remained concerning the precise boundaries and limits of professional power. Would the Court, for instance, subscribe to the position of Bork and Posner that consumer welfare was the only criterion for judging anticompetitive practices? Or would the Court embrace values closely related to the notion of professionalism, as footnote 17 suggested?

CONCLUSION

Neoclassical economic theory, as cultivated in the Chicago school, underpinned government policy in the late 1970s. In industries such as airlines, trucking, telecommunications, and health care, deregulation was the chosen remedy for constraints on competition. But in health care, unlike most other industries, the medical profession, not government, stood in the way of a free and unfettered market. Medical societies had deterred, indeed had prohibited, the formation of alternative forms of finance and delivery. Consequently, the federal government in the 1970s had to establish a framework in which health maintenance organizations and other innovative forms of finance and delivery could develop and prosper.

Antitrust law as applied by courts and agencies was the antidote to the medical monopoly. But the application of antitrust laws to the medical profession was not a simple undertaking. Adherents of the Harvard, or industrial organization, school hindered the overthrow of the medical monopoly. Professional values, as articulated by economist Kenneth Arrow, sociologist Talcott Parsons, and others buttressed a "multivalued" approach to antitrust theory. Even if anticompetitive, Arrow asserted, ethical constraints were needed to overcome market failures related to "uncertainty in the incidence of disease" and disparities in expertise, including the acquisition of knowledge and information. The *OSMS* case, decided at the height of the Harvard school of antitrust enforcement, reflected the predominant ideology. "Forms of competition usual in the business world," the Supreme Court asserted, "may be demoralizing to the ethical standards of a profession" (*OSMS*, 343 U.S. at 336).

The law and economics movement, augured by the writings of Bork and Posner, attacked the notion that regulation prevented or mitigated market failure. One value, not several, formed the basis of their antitrust analysis. This was the principle of consumer welfare that they equated with allocative efficiency. Stripped of contrary values, considerations, and interpretations that bolstered ethical proscriptions, the "monolithic" approach of the legal economists threatened medical hegemony. Clark Havighurst, who viewed the medical monopoly as the central impediment to market competition in the health care industry, sought to apply antitrust concepts wholesale to the anticompetitive practices of physicians and their professional associations. "Aside from the dictum in the [*OSMS*] case, there seems to be no authority" for the position that physicians should be treated differently than other groups, Havighurst contended (1978:352).

Legal principles, such as the learned professions exemption, the interstate commerce requirement, and state-action immunity, hindered enforcement efforts. The *Goldfarb* decision, decided by the Supreme Court in 1975, altered the predominant legal calculus. The Court threw out the learned professions exemption, loosened standards for interstate commerce, and narrowed state-action immunity. After *Goldfarb,* the Department of Justice and the FTC could pursue the learned professions in most jurisdictions.

For several reasons, *Goldfarb* was a product of the shift in thinking during the 1970s. First, the antitrust principles that the Court applied in *Goldfarb* were part of a broader effort to stimulate the economy and control costs through market competition. Second, public choice theory as formulated by Chicago school economists furnished the justification for ending the learned professions exemption. Third, the law and economics movement opposed consideration of noneconomic values, many of which were embodied in ethical codes of professional associations, ostensibly for purposes of consumer protection. Though footnote 17 mitigated the Court's ruling in *Goldfarb,* the concerns expressed in footnote 17 fell short of those in *OSMS.*

The decision in *Goldfarb* exposed medicine to antitrust scrutiny, but it did not alter medicine's domination of the health care industry. It was one thing to articulate a theory; it was another to dismantle the laws and ethics that comprised the medical monopoly. Whether Havighurst and other reformers eventually succeeded would depend upon their ability to mobilize the support of the federal antitrust agencies. Medicine still possessed sufficient clout to fend off a legislative assault. Those opposed to the professional monopoly needed a powerful champion. That champion would be the Federal Trade Commission.

4 The Federal Trade Commission Takes the Lead

The lead agency in the fight against the anticompetitive practices of the medical profession was the Federal Trade Commission. This chapter sets the stage for the agency's initial confrontation with the AMA, addressed in the next chapter, and the series of investigations, probes, and administrative actions that struck at the heart of the medical monopoly. It explains why the FTC took the lead in these matters and how the agency organized for action. Finally, it examines the state of affairs at the AMA in the 1970s.

The timing of these initiatives was no fluke—they reflected the intellectual consensus that had formed among economists and the subsequent effect of economic theory on legal doctrine and federal antitrust policy. Still, this did not fully explain why the FTC, not the Department of Justice, became the lead proponent of market competition in the health care arena. Much of the answer lay in Congress's political and financial support for the commission for most of the 1970s, the working relationship that developed between FTC lawyers and economists on health care issues, and the agency's ability to control its agenda through the administrative process.

REORGANIZATION AT THE FTC

Established in 1914 to administer the antitrust and trade regulation laws, the FTC lacked political clout for much of its existence (Wells 2002:111). The consumer movement woke the FTC from its bureaucratic slumber. Two 1969 reports, one from Ralph Nader's Study Group and the other from the American Bar Association (ABA), criticized the commission for its poor performance and recommended systemic change. The Nader report stressed political cronyism, while the ABA report emphasized managerial deficiencies (Green, Moore, and Wasserstein 1972:328). Both reports led to signifi-

TABLE 1. *Succession of Federal Trade Commission Chairs, 1961–2007*

Chair (Party Affiliation)	*Term of Service*
Dixon (D)	March 1961–December 1969
Weinberger (R)	January–August 1970
Macintyre* (D)	August–September 1970
Kirkpatrick (R)	September 1970–February 1973
Engman (R)	February 1973–December 1975
Dixon* (D)	January–March 1976
Collier (R)	March 1976–April 1977
Pertschuk (D)	April 1977–March 1981
Clanton* (R)	March–September 1981
Miller (R)	September 1981–October 1985
Calvani* (R)	October 1985–April 1986
Oliver (R)	April 1986–August 1989
Steiger (R)	August 1989–April 1994
Pitofsky (D)	April 1995–June 2001
Muris (R)	June 2001–August 2004
Majoras (R)	August 2004–present

*Acting

cant changes in organization and personnel. Congress was very supportive. In 1971, the FTC's annual budget was about $21 million; by 1979, it was over $65 million (Clarkson and Muris 1981:20–21). It was not uncommon for Congress during this time to appropriate more money than the agency actually requested.

Most of the changes in organization and personnel occurred in the early 1970s under the leadership of Caspar Weinberger, Miles Kirkpatrick, and Lewis Engman. President Nixon appointed Weinberger in January 1970. When Weinberger left several months later to become deputy director of the Office of Management and Budget, Miles Kirkpatrick, the principal author of the ABA report, took his place. Engman succeeded Kirkpatrick in 1973 when Kirkpatrick returned to the private practice of law in his native Philadelphia. Table 1 shows the succession and party affiliation of FTC chairs from Paul Rand Dixon to Deborah Platt Majoras.

Although Weinberger stayed for only six months, he initiated changes that altered the commission's internal culture. Weinberger replaced existing bureaus with the Bureau of Competition and the Bureau of Consumer

Protection, thereby restructuring the commission along functional lines (antitrust and consumer protection). He also inaugurated a series of personnel changes that Miles Kirkpatrick continued. By 1973, nearly one-third of the agency's employees had been replaced, often with young, energetic, and aggressive attorneys (Clarkson and Muris 1981:5). Daniel Schwartz, an assistant to the director of the Bureau of Competition, came to the commission in 1973 because of the changes in personnel and performance. "The FTC was becoming a very exciting place," he noted (Schwartz 2003).

Most everyone agreed that the commission needed to improve strategic planning. Lack of planning prompted a "mailbag" approach to case selection that mired the agency in "trivia" and encouraged "persistent complainers" (Green, Moore, and Wasserstein 1972:387; Clarkson and Muris 1981:1). Seeking to remedy the situation, Kirkpatrick oversaw the formation of the Evaluation Committee at the Bureau of Competition in 1972. The committee's purpose was to develop "broad enforcement plans" for entire industries (Katzmann 1980:32). Included on the Evaluation Committee were members of the Bureau of Economics, another FTC unit (Schwartz 2003). This changed the overall tone of case selection. "Prior to the 1970s, there is little evidence that economic criteria played a significant role in agency affairs," political scientist Mark Eisner wrote (Eisner 1991:171–172). "The Bureau of Economics was isolated and relatively unintegrated into agency activities. The same could not be said by the end of the 1970s. Economists were regular participants . . . and were directly involved in the definition of the caseload."

Robert Katzmann, also a political scientist, summarized the various reform initiatives of the early 1970s and their effect on FTC policy and operations. According to Katzmann:

> In its efforts to change the character of the case load (and devote more attention to structural and industrywide investigations and less to simple conduct matters), the commission leadership of the 1970s proceeded in three major stages. First, decision makers redesigned the agency's structure to increase the leadership's control of the operating bureaus and eliminate organizational barriers that reinforced parochial attitudes held by many attorneys. Second, they removed incompetent attorneys and replaced them with persons of proven ability or promise. Third, Bureau of Competition officials developed an evaluative process to facilitate the fashioning of a coherent antitrust policy, closed many cases unworthy of agency resources, and took away the staff attorneys' authority to open cases. (1980:127–128)

Congressional support in the form of increased funding for agency operations had certain strings attached, of course. During committee hearings in the early 1970s, members of Congress prompted the agency to take on entire industries, to act boldly, and even to experiment (Kovacic 1982:632). Among those members who pushed the hardest were Warren Magnuson (chair of the Senate Commerce Committee) and Gale McGee (chair of the subcommittee of the Senate Appropriations Committee). Magnuson urged Weinberger to "maintain the right kind of morale by recruiting strongly and expanding the existing Trade Commission programs" (as quoted in Kovacic 1982:632); McGee told Kirkpatrick, "We would rather you make a mistake innovating, trying something new, rather than playing so cautiously that you never make a mistake" (as quoted in Kovacic 1982:633). Members of Congress targeted specific sectors for investigation. These included the food, energy, and health care industries (Kovacic 1982:637–640). In the case of health care, Representative Jamie Whitten of the House Appropriations Committee urged the FTC to look into the problem of "increased medical costs" (as quoted in Kovacic 1982:640 n. 255). Acting on the instructions of Congress, the agency pursued litigation against manufacturers of breakfast cereals, the eight largest petroleum companies in the United States, and organized medicine in 1972, 1973, and 1975, respectively (Kovacic 1982:646).

The FTC was in a good position in the 1970s to do Congress's bidding. An independent regulatory commission with broad administrative powers, it could proceed by rule making or adjudication to police an entire industry. The choice between rule making and adjudication was strategic and depended on the scope, timing, and novelty of the initiative as well as the industry's political clout. For several reasons, litigation was the FTC's primary weapon: first, the commission controlled the forum (agency lawyers tried their cases before an administrative law judge who was a member of agency staff, not in a courtroom before a federal judge); second, opposing parties seldom could appeal or otherwise sidestep the process until the commission rendered its final decision; third, the commission had enormous discretion to fashion a remedy; and fourth, the scope of judicial review was relatively narrow, making an agency ruling difficult to overturn on appeal (Asimow, Bonfield, and Levin 1998). Because administrative agencies held "all the cards" in adjudication, they were often immune to interest group pressure (see Meier 2000).

New leadership and new personnel stimulated the agency's inchoate authority. Section 5 of the Federal Trade Commission Act, as amended in 1938, prohibited "unfair methods of competition in commerce and unfair or deceptive acts or practices in commerce." Violations of this provision left much to the discretion of commissioners and legal staff. Consequently, changes in public policy or legal doctrine augured new approaches and new legal actions. The only other requirement for issuance of a complaint was whether the action was in the "public interest." Again, this criterion was rather broad and vague. Perhaps the only significant legal constraint on case selection was the Sherman Act and interpretive court rulings. Although section 5 was more expansive than the Sherman Act, the commission rarely exceeded Sherman's scope for prudential reasons (Havighurst 2003).

THE BATTLE BETWEEN THE NADERITES AND THE CHICAGOANS

Political scientist Kenneth Meier has observed that "the incorporation of professionals into bureaus also incorporates their professional values" (Meier 2000:60). This was certainly true of the Federal Trade Commission. Many of the economists and attorneys at the FTC in the early 1970s favored the "old antitrust," that is, the approach of the Harvard or industrial organization school. The addition of new personnel and the replacement of old ones transformed the agency's perspective. Many of the new economists and attorneys either adhered to the antitrust doctrine of law professors Robert Bork, Richard Posner, and Clark Havighurst or were at least receptive to it.

The commission's determination to proceed, beginning in 1972, against the food, petroleum, and transportation industries was bold (Kovacic 1982:646). It reflected changes in outlook and strategy that had their roots in consumerism as embodied in the Nader report. Congress had delegated broad authority to the FTC to "combat virtually all" unfair methods of competition. Yet, followers of Nader complained, the commission had "*never* lodged a monopolization charge against a major American industry" (Green, Moore, and Wasserstein 1972:392, emphasis in original). The report's introduction, written by Nader himself, conflated the consumer movement with antitrust enforcement:

> It may not be too sanguine to say that from the present on, antitrust and its brace of phrases will start to become household words; that the prices that people pay for their bread, gasoline, auto parts, prescription drugs, and houses will be more and more related to antitrust violations and the costs of concentration; that the air they breathe and the consumer hazards they suffer will be increasingly connected to industrial collusion and controlled markets; that those aggrieved by antitrust violations will more and more directly reach toward the companies and their executives for suitable redress and other sanctions through the courts. Contrary to Richard Hofstadter's comment on the antitrust

> movement as "one of the faded passions of American reform," antitrust enforcement—private and public—will make a comeback to show the modern relevance of this traditional wisdom first formulated into law by a conservative Republican Congress in 1890. (Green, Moore, and Wasserstein 1972:xi)

Nader's reference to "the costs of concentration" foretold the forthcoming struggle between those who favored the industrial organization school and those who promoted neoclassical economic theory. Contrary to the Chicagoans, the Naderites believed that industrial concentration through mergers, joint ventures, and the like decreased competition, raised prices, encouraged inflation and unemployment, and threatened democracy. There was "a political and social price to pay for corporate bigness," they asserted (Green, Moore, and Wasserstein 1972:21).

Louis Engman, who chaired the commission from 1973 to 1975, represented an early departure from the erstwhile perspective of the followers of Ralph Nader. Though he had a "strong proconsumer bent," Engman's consumerism proceeded from that of Adam Smith, not that of Ralph Nader (Critser 2005). Engman was among the first to present a coherent case for government deregulation to advance competition. In a 1974 speech to financial analysts, he said: "Much of today's regulatory machinery does little more than shelter producers from the normal competitive consequences of lassitude and inefficiency" (as quoted in Critser 2005:12). "Engman's speech," Timothy Muris proclaimed, "may be considered one of the first contemporary examples of successful competition advocacy," an approach that advanced economic theory and its applications through speeches, testimony, and written submissions to regulatory agencies and committees of Congress (Muris 2002).

Under Engman, the Office of Policy Planning and Evaluation (OPPE) became a key player in case selection. Engman's choice of Wesley James "Jim" Liebeler to direct OPPE in 1974 led to greater emphasis on economic analysis and program development. A graduate of the University of Chicago School of Law, Liebeler had served on the staff of the Warren Commission, which had investigated the assassination of President Kennedy. Though Liebeler's service was brief, about two years, he left an indelible mark on policy planning. Arthur Amolsch, the publisher of *FTC:Watch*, an independent newsletter that reported the agency's affairs, described Liebeler's reign in colorful terms:

> In its most recent incarnation, under the direction of [Liebeler], OPPE was an Olympian observer loosing bursts of thunderbolts on the most obnoxious mortals down below. At least once a year, at budget time,

> Olympus would erupt, raining rhetorical destruction left and right (but mostly left). Led by its stormy genius, Liebeler's OPPE once suggested that the Bureau of Consumer Protection could best serve consumers by abandoning its cigarette program and transferring the extra money into its funerals program. Liebeler's OPPE, we also note, invented the Prescription Drug Advertising Rule, launching the FTC on a deregulatory track which is still bearing fruit. (*FTC:Watch* 1 July 1977:1)

Liebeler was a few years ahead of his time. When he arrived at the FTC, Chicago school theory and practice had yet to take hold. "Chicago school economic analysis was very new and there was bureaucratic resistance," Dan Schwartz observed (2003). Liebeler and his "bright, aggressive, confrontational, and young" staff at OPPE (which included a recent graduate of the law school at UCLA, Timothy Muris) established a bridgehead against the "old antitrust" (Schwartz 2003). The industrywide cases had "nothing to do with economic analysis" and could "be understood only in political terms," Liebeler and Muris professed (Clarkson and Muris 1981:96–97). While ensconced at OPPE, Liebeler and his small staff critically examined past and ongoing commission activities. Though they failed to stop investigations of concentrated industries, they launched several new initiatives intended to curtail state and federal regulation, such as the occupational licensure program. Calvin Collier, who succeeded Lewis Engman as commission chair, supported Liebeler's efforts, but Collier remained for only one year, giving way to a regime that opposed Chicago school theory (Clarkson and Muris 1981:295).

Collier's replacement, Michael Pertschuk, a Democrat and Carter appointee, was cut from the Ralph Nader mold. Described as "an innovator with clearly defined goals but with no desire for confrontations" (*FTC:Watch* 25 February 1977:4), Pertschuk soon belied at least part of the characterization. He relentlessly attacked big business, earning for himself the title "Tyrannosaurus Rex of regulation" (*FTC:Watch* 15 December 1978:20). Having served as chief counsel to the Senate Commerce Committee at a time of Democratic control, Pertschuk embraced the views of the committee's liberal senators, Warren Magnuson, Frank Moss, and Philip Hart (Kovacic 1982:632). At his confirmation hearing, Pertschuk attacked "corporate bigness." He declared:

> I am not convinced by those economists who argue that an organization of an industry that has persisted for a long period of time in the absence of legal restrictions on entry is optimal because it fundamentally reflects underlying cost conditions. . . . [E]ven if economies are present in a given case, that does not end the inquiry. There are political reasons,

> in the best sense of the word, which justify a governmental policy aimed at reducing concentration—for example, the deeply held American belief that power should be fragmented and that decision centers should be multiple. Huge corporations can be more compelling in their influence on individual lives and community welfare than sovereign states. (*FTC:Watch* 8 April 1977:14)

Upon taking office, Pertschuk inherited some problematic and protracted cases, such as those against the petroleum industry and cereal manufacturers. Eager to advance his agenda, Pertschuk turned to rule making, which he believed would move things more quickly. Passage of the Magnuson-Moss Warranty Act in 1975 had clarified and expanded the commission's rulemaking powers. Claiming he had a mandate to make rules for entire industries, Pertschuk set out to meet the professed goals of Congress as expressed in committee and subcommittee hearings. By the end of 1978, "nineteen major rule or rule amendment proceedings were underway." These included proposed rules for mobile homes, food advertising, funerals, used cars, prescription drugs, protein supplements, and children's advertising (U.S. Congress, House, 1984:151–152 [Report of Michael Pertschuk]).

Pertschuk's liberal views and colorful rhetoric made him a perfect foil for Timothy Muris and other members of the opposition. During Pertschuk's tenure, from 1977 to 1981, Chicagoans successfully advanced their ideas in academic and policy circles, from Muris at the University of Miami to Liebeler at UCLA, from Milton Friedman at the University of Chicago to James Buchanan at Virginia Tech, and from Mancur Olson at the University of Maryland to Robert Bork at Yale. Henry Manne's Law and Economics Center made its home in these years at the University of Miami School of Law. It was at Miami that Muris "helped form his own government in-exile" (*FTC:Watch* 25 September 1981:22).

Keenly aware that Chicagoans would attempt to undermine his agenda, Pertschuk sought to ensure that those in charge of the FTC's various bureaus and divisions shared his perspective. This required some housecleaning at the Office of Policy Planning and Evaluation. Pertschuk's selection for director of OPPE was Robert Reich, who was later secretary of labor in the Clinton administration. Reich's style was quite different from Liebeler's—in Amolsch's words, "tête-à-tête, not toe to toe." "Whereas OPPE was once assigned the role of Devil's Advocate in the budget process," Amolsch observed, "under Reich this function will cease" (*FTC:Watch* 1 July 1977:2).

Pertschuk also scrutinized the leadership at the Bureau of Economics, which, in the late 1970s, became "prominent" in the selection of cases for FTC prosecution (Clarkson and Muris 1981:294). Most economists at the

FTC were advocates of the industrial organization school in the early 1970s, but "free-market thinking" was in vogue when Pertschuk arrived in the second half of the decade (*FTC:Watch* 13 January 1978:19). The intellectual shift among economists at the Bureau of Economics mirrored changes occurring in the broader academic community. According to one of Amolsch's sources, "It sometimes seems that as fast as the antitrust lawyers identify a suspicious industry, the economists give the industry a clean bill of health" (*FTC:Watch* 13 January 1978:19). This placed a premium on the person who headed the bureau.

The economist in charge of the Bureau of Economics when Pertschuk arrived was Darius Gaskins, hardly a Chicagoan. Yet his views came under close scrutiny. The following news item from *FTC:Watch* demonstrates the intensity of the vetting process:

> FTC:WATCH learned that James Adams, an economist at the University of Michigan, is under consideration for appointment as Director of the Bureau of Economics. Although informed sources indicated that Chairman Pertschuk is not necessarily determined to replace the present director, Darius Gaskins, the record so far indicates that Pertschuk is moving to put his own people in all senior positions. This, naturally, is the key to a chairman's ability to control the agency far beyond the power he exercises through his one vote as a Commissioner. Adams is described by one knowledgeable source as *"more anti-Chicago than Darius."* (22 April 1977:7, emphasis added)

Pertschuk's tenure at the FTC proved inauspicious from the start. Several senators who had supported Pertschuk either retired or lost in the 1976 general election, including Philip Hart, Vance Hartke, Mike Mansfield, Gale McGee, Frank Moss, John Pastore, and John Tunney (Kovacic 1982:653). Frank Moss, the chair of the consumer subcommittee of the Senate Commerce Committee, was, according to *Business Week*, "one of the Hill's most prolific sources of interventionist consumer protection legislation" (Congress Waits for Carter's Signal 1977:94). Moss's replacement, Senator Wendall Ford of Kentucky, though also a Democrat, instructed subcommittee staff "not to go searching for new worlds to regulate" (Congress Waits for Carter's Signal 1977:94).

Had Pertschuk not expanded the FTC's agenda at a time of intense congressional oversight and industry unrest, his reign as chair might have been less controversial. Rule making, more so than litigation, riled big business. Several industries successfully pressured Congress to terminate the agency's activities. Congressional review, budgetary retrenchment, and adverse court rulings crippled Pertschuk's agenda. According to William Kovacic: "Divisions within both chambers over the extent of restrictions to be imposed were so severe that the Commission's funding lapsed on two occasions, forcing the agency to close its doors for the first time ever. The Commission had gone without an authorization bill for fiscal years 1978, 1979, and 1980—a portent of the discontent that surfaced graphically in congressional consideration of the Federal Trade Commission Improvements Act of 1980" (1982:665). The 1980 act, though it restored funding to the commission, curbed several programs as well as the agency's statutory authority.

The 1980 presidential election of Ronald Reagan signaled the Chicagoans' forthcoming control of the Federal Trade Commission. Reagan's transition team included Timothy Muris, who assumed the lead role in preparing the team's report. Senior advisors included law professors Havighurst and Liebeler, former chairs Engman and Collier, and future U.S. Supreme Court justice Antonin Scalia. The transition team recommended substantial budget cuts—6.5 percent in fiscal year 1981 and a whopping 24.9 percent in fiscal year 1982 (*FTC:Watch* 23 January 1981:1). David Stockman, director of the Office of Management and Budget (OMB) in Reagan's first term, proposed even deeper cuts and called for an end to antitrust enforcement. But Stockman appeared to be bluffing, and the OMB withdrew its proposal in the face of congressional and special-interest opposition (*FTC:Watch* 6 March 1981:2).

Though the Reagan administration reduced the commission's staff from over 1,700 employees in 1981 to fewer than 1,300 employees by 1984 (substantial cuts occurred in the regional offices and at the Bureau of Competition), the number of economists remained about the same (U.S. Congress, House, 1984:18 [Report of Michael Pertschuk]). The new chair, economist James Miller, had been a resident scholar at the American Enterprise Institute before assuming the helm and had taught industrial organization and microeconomics at Georgia State University and Texas A&M. Miller recognized that a healthy FTC could further the agenda of the new administration. He picked Muris to head the Bureau of Consumer Protection. The Bureau of Consumer Protection was the source of Pertschuk's rule-making initiatives, many of which Muris subsequently stalled, killed, or curtailed (U.S. Congress, House, 1984:149–150 [Report of Michael Pertschuk]).

As was his prerogative, Pertschuk remained on the commission in a watchdog role where he launched his assault on the new administration. He ended his tenure in 1984 with a rhetorical flourish. "The current leadership" he declared, "has been consumed with a single-minded determination to undo the past—not just the immediate past—but the very foundations of antitrust and consumer protection law laid down by Congress in 1914, in 1938, in 1950, and in 1975, laws forcefully implemented by bipartisan Commissions" (U.S. Congress, House, 1984:1 [Report of Michael Pertschuk]).

CONGRESS HELPS TO FRAME THE COMMISSION'S HEALTH CARE AGENDA

Despite important differences in philosophy and approach, Naderites and Chicagoans could agree on one program in particular—the health care initiative that targeted the medical monopoly. "Of course, James Miller and the Reagan majority on the FTC have done some things right," Pertschuk conceded, "most significantly, their continued spirited defense of the Commission's authority to challenge anticompetitive professional self-regulation" (U.S. Congress, House, 1984:6 [Report of Michael Pertschuk]). Timothy Muris felt the same way about Pertschuk. The "only possible exception" to Pertschuk's "deficient" agenda worth noting, Muris and his colleague Kenneth Clarkson wrote, was the FTC's "recent moves against guildism in the 'learned' professions" (Clarkson and Muris 1981:96). Naderites and Chicagoans achieved consensus not because they shared similar philosophies, but because they disdained the monopolistic practices of the medical profession. As Pertschuk observed: "It is not exactly surprising that economic conservatives and liberal consumer advocates should have found common ground in the FTC's professions program: the conservatives, nurtured in the Chicago School of Economics, abhor all forms of market regulation, including self-regulation, because such regulations impair the free market. Liberal consumer advocates abhor such rip-offs as price fixing and monopolization. The learned professions managed to breach both thresholds of obnoxiousness simultaneously" (1986:91).

Liberals and conservatives, Democrats and Republicans, agreed that organized medicine was an appropriate target of law enforcement (Muris 2003; Havighurst 2003). During hearings before the Senate Subcommittee on Antitrust and Monopoly in May 1974, Senator Edward Kennedy asserted:

> One of the major characteristics of the health care industry is the dominance of interlocking relationships between providers of health care services. Over the years physicians, medical societies, hospital boards, and health insurance entities have developed close and sometimes excessive relationships. . . . Evidence seems to be accumulating that providers of health care services, through their extraordinary dominance of the mar-

ketplace, make the possibility of meeting consumer involvement remote or nonexistent. Through these hearings the subcommittee will attempt to determine whether antitrust action by the Federal Government against various organizations representing providers of health care services is justified. (U.S. Congress, Senate, 1974:1561)

Six days of hearings before the Senate subcommittee in 1974 produced extensive documentation concerning efforts of organized medicine to discourage competition. Mickey Leland, a state representative from Texas, testified: "A small group of very powerful men . . . control both the cost and the availability of medical services in Texas" (U.S. Congress, Senate, 1974:95). John Nelson, the executive director of a New York HMO, stated: "The pattern of opposition from the organized medical community in Rochester . . . was not . . . much different from the historic opposition of several generations of physicians to closed panel prepaid medical group plans" (U.S. Congress, Senate, 1974:1478). And Robert Biblo, the president of the Harvard Community Health Plan, asserted: "Developing HMOs have to contend with what could be described as a 'physician monopoly'. . . . One of their major reasons they are not operational is their inability to recruit physicians. Medical societies sometimes find it difficult to remain neutral when faced on the local level with the realistic possibility of a competing system to fee for service" (U.S. Congress, Senate, 1974:1439).

Experts who testified before the subcommittee proposed that the antitrust agencies take action. "[An] antitrust victory against the medical profession would be one of the most fortunate developments that could occur in trying to get the health services marketplace in order," Clark Havighurst asserted (U.S. Congress, Senate, 1974:1046). Getting physicians to move from fee-for-service to group practice "simply isn't going to happen until we do something to remove those restraints that first prohibit the physician," John Riley, president of the University of Washington Law School, contended (U.S. Congress, Senate, 1974:1576).

Though congressional opposition to the medical monopoly signaled support for market competition, how far did this carry? The HMO Act of 1973 was riddled with restrictions that hampered the development of prepaid group practice. Those who testified before the subcommittee decried certain features of the act. "The National HMO Act has produced such monstrous demands upon HMOs that it threatens to destroy the very concept that it seeks to encourage," physicians who managed a group health plan in St. Paul, Minnesota, stated (U.S. Congress, Senate, 1974:1469). "The HMO Act contains a number of important provisions bearing on the regulation of HMOs, many of which extend beyond proposed requirements for the rest of the health care system," the Institute of Medicine reported (U.S. Congress, Senate, 1974:81).

Notwithstanding efforts of special interests to restrict the development of HMOs in the 1970s, Congress moved inexorably toward market competition in the health care arena. Even those who promoted universal health care, such as Senator Kennedy, favored new forms of delivery. Kennedy's 1978 proposal for universal coverage "was a striking departure from earlier liberal programs," Paul Starr observed. "Instead of a public system," Starr indicated, "it called for private health plans (HMOs, independent practice associations, Blue Cross, commercial insurance) to compete for subscribers, who would receive a health insurance card entitling them to hospital and physicians' care and a variety of other basic health services" (1982:413).

Despite the ascendancy of Jimmy Carter to the presidency in 1976, Democratic control of the executive and legislative branches of the federal government would be short-lived. Economic conditions improved by the mid-1970s but turned sour again during the Carter administration. Legislative initiatives in Carter's first year in office tracked the regulatory tradition—a minimum wage bill and significant public works programs. These efforts stoked the fires of inflation. According to historian Bruce Schulman: "The cost of living leaped up at double-digit rates: interest rates reached 20 percent; the value of savings eroded; the prices of meat, milk, and heating rose out of sight" (Schulman 2001:131). The administration's initial response—voluntary wage and price controls—did not slow inflation, and in October 1978, Carter announced a fiscal austerity program that included substantial budget cuts. As the economy continued to decline, Carter sought fresh perspectives. He hired Alfred Kahn, who as chair of the Civil Aeronautics Board had deregulated the airlines industry, to advise him on inflation, and Paul Volker to head the Federal Reserve Board. Volker slowed inflation by choking the money supply, which, in Schulman's view, "produced a recession that complicated the administration's woes" (2001:134).

The tax revolt of 1978 signaled a shift in public attitudes and beliefs—smaller government, faith in markets, and individual self-reliance. Tax reform began in California where protestors, upset with soaring property taxes, approved Proposition 13. Following California's lead, several states passed similar measures to cap government spending. Some states took preemptive action, "hoping to avoid the fiscal straitjacket that California voters had wrapped around their government" (Schulman 2001:212). Congress joined the fracas. It cut the tax rate on capital gains from 48 to 28 percent (Edsall 1984:65). The effect was that of a "modern Boston Tea Party," the *New York Times* reported (Lindsey 1978). According to historians Michael

Schaller and George Rising: "The tax revolt spread throughout the nation after 1978, producing momentous consequences. It helped create a coalition against the liberal welfare state, gave the conservative movement a unifying issue, shaped an antigovernment ethic, and generated disaffection with the Democratic Party. It also strengthened the links between ideological conservatives, business leaders, and the Republican Party" (2002:76).

A prime example of Congress's swing to the Right was President Carter's failed initiative to lower the costs of health care spending. First introduced in April 1977, the president's proposal sought to cap spending on hospital care at 9 percent in 1978 and at lower rates over the next three-year period. The proposal targeted hospitals because they were responsible for 40 percent of total health care spending and their inflation rate of 15 percent in 1976 exceeded all other industry segments (Pave 1977:36). Opposed by the hospital and physicians' lobbies, the president's bill floundered; in 1979, the House of Representatives struck it down by a substantial margin, 234 to 166. Ninety-nine Democrats joined 134 Republicans in voting against the initiative (Congress: The Big Battalions 1979:46). Expounding on the reasons for the bill's demise, *The Economist* stated: "Lobbying was not the only factor in this defeat. Regulation has become a dirty word; the consumer movement has fallen out of favour" (1979:46; see also Weissert and Weissert 1996:278–282). To Clark Havighurst, "The health revolution got its start in 1979, after the defeat of President Carter's proposal to cap spending" (2003).

THE COMMISSION GOES TO WORK

The Senate hearings in 1974 provided a jumping-off point for the FTC. For many years there had been complaints about the anticompetitive practices of the AMA, but the commission had not taken action, choosing instead to let the Antitrust Division at the Department of Justice address complaints ad hoc, as in the Group Health and *OSMS* cases. At Jim Liebeler's urging, the commission in 1975 created a task force on occupational licensure and housed it at the Bureau of Consumer Protection (Muris 2003; Schwartz 2003). Almost immediately, the task force commenced an investigation into attempts by state licensing boards to suppress competition. Although the investigation bore fruit, the state-action doctrine prevented legal action. Undeterred, members of the task force took their case to the antitrust divisions of several states. The strategy worked. By the early 1980s, many states either had revised or rescinded anticompetitive provisions contained in board rules and regulations (Zeitlin 1985:10–11).

Unlike the initiative concerning occupational licensure, efforts to investigate the anticompetitive practices of the medical profession met internal resistance. This was not because commission attorneys feared the AMA. Rather, it was because managers at the Bureau of Competition, where such an initiative likely would commence, worried that a large undertaking would divert limited funds from their own programmatic initiatives (Schwarz 2003). In addition, staff attorneys within the Bureau of Competition did not like cases that took years to develop. For many such attorneys, the FTC was a stepping-stone toward more lucrative employment in the private sector. Assignment to a case that required extensive investigation before trial might hinder career advancement. Most lawyers preferred smaller cases that promised early trial experience (Katzmann 1980:83).

But Dan Schwartz, who was an assistant to the director of the Bureau of Competition in 1975, saw things differently. To Schwartz, Liebeler's "fresh ideas" provided an opportunity. Sometime in early 1975, Schwartz approached Robert Liedquist, the acting director of the Bureau of Competition, about Liebeler's suggestions. Liedquist told Schwartz to "take about three months to look at the issue" and, if promising, recommend it to the Evaluation Committee (Schwartz 2003). The Evaluation Committee, composed of the principals of the Bureau of Competition and the Bureau of Economics, screened all nonmerger cases before committing resources to a formal investigation (Katzmann 1980:22–25). In the vernacular of the FTC, Liedquist authorized Schwartz to commence a preliminary investigation of the anticompetitive practices of physicians and their professional associations (see Katzmann 1980:60–65).

Schwartz admittedly knew little about the health care industry when he began. He enlisted the support of staff attorneys at the Bureau of Competition, among them Jonathan Gaines, David Wilson, George Wright, Maynard Thomson, and Lawrence Gray. For the next couple months, Schwartz and his team gathered information, spoke to experts in the field, and performed legal research. Among the experts that Schwartz consulted was Clark Havighurst. Schwartz met with Havighurst in Durham, North Carolina, for about half a day. According to both accounts, the meeting was highly productive. As Schwartz related, "There were just a ton of issues to which no one paid any attention except Clark Havighurst. In those days, the idea of applying the antitrust concept to the health care industry was foreign. Clark Havighurst had that idea, and he was about the only person who did" (Schwartz 2003). Maynard Thomson, assigned by Schwartz to peruse the AMA Code of Medical Ethics for antitrust violations, met with Havighurst at a later date. The exchange between Havighurst and Thomson would lay the groundwork for the FTC's eventual case against the AMA

(FTC Special Collections [Thomson Memorandum to Evaluation Committee, 2 June 1975:25]).

On 6 June 1975, only ten days before the Supreme Court announced its decision in *Goldfarb,* Schwartz presented his findings to the Evaluation Committee. He recommended that the Bureau of Competition open "seven new preliminary investigations in the health care area" (FTC Special Collections [Schwartz Memorandum to Evaluation Committee, 6 June 1975:3]). These included (1) professional domination of Blue Cross/Blue Shield, (2) restrictions on the development of HMOs, (3) the suppression of physician advertising and other forms of competition through ethical standards, and (4) the use of relative value scales to fix prices. Schwartz's memorandum also examined but did not recommend "at this time" an investigation into the shortage of doctors in the United States and its connection to AMA "control . . . over the education, testing and certification of physicians" (FTC Special Collections [Schwartz Memorandum to Evaluation Committee, 6 June 1975: 21–22]).

The Evaluation Committee met on 12 June 1975 to discuss the recommendations of Schwartz and his team (FTC Special Collections [Bureau of Competition, Agenda for Evaluation Committee, 12 June 1975]). According to Schwartz, the meeting was "long and contentious" (2003). Lack of agency experience with the health care industry, Schwartz surmised, engendered much caution. In the end, the committee approved most of the recommendations that Schwartz had made, including those on medical ethics (2003).

Before proceeding further, the Bureau of Competition, in accordance with standard operating procedures, obtained clearance from the Antitrust Division of the Department of Justice. Had the department been more involved with the health care industry, it might have denied clearance to the FTC. But that was not the case here. According to Schwartz: "Up to now, the health care industry, as such, has been largely ignored by the antitrust enforcement agencies. The Department of Justice has a large number of investigations allegedly underway, but the Department has made very little effort to deal with the health care industry as a special area with special problems. In response to this general neglect, some of the low-cost investigations recommended herein are designed to, among other things, bring an antitrust presence to this industry" (FTC Special Collections [Schwartz Memorandum to the Evaluation Committee, 6 June 1975: 9]).

Schwartz's proposal triggered the budget review process within the commission. Following the introduction of program-based budgeting in 1975, FTC commissioners and the Office of Policy Planning and Evaluation had to carefully scrutinize new programmatic initiatives. Schwartz's proposal, grounded in Jim Liebeler's earlier work on occupational licensure, received widespread support (Muris 2003). The commissioners added "physician services" to "the health care program," which, when launched in 1974, comprised prescription drugs, medical laboratories, and hospital supplies (FTC Annual Reports, 1974 and 1975). Over the next several years, the agency devoted substantial resources to the "physician services" side of the ledger. Anticompetitive practices of physicians and their professional associations (in particular, the AMA) came under intense scrutiny.

THE HEALTH CARE SHOP

Assistant directors for litigation are among the most influential and powerful individuals within the Bureau of Competition. Because bureau directors "cannot personally supervise every detail of each case," they must rely on their assistant directors "to oversee most of the investigations" (Katzmann 1980:16). Assistant directors typically control the flow of information within their unit, or "shop," select the attorneys who will handle specific cases or investigations, and otherwise manage staff development and strategic direction. Perhaps the most important of these is information control. According to political scientist Robert Katzmann:

> The ability of the assistant director to affect the course of an investigation stems in part from his access to and control of information that flows through his *shop* of twenty to thirty lawyers. . . . He is the first to read the mailbag complaints that the Evaluation Office forwards to his shop for analysis; he has the right to review all incoming correspondence directed to the staff attorneys; he can examine all documents that the staff lawyers have gathered; he can review letters of inquiry from his staff to firms involved in an investigation; he can edit communications that the staff might direct to the bureau director and the commissioners; and he serves as the intermediary between the bureau hierarchy (principally the bureau director) and the staff, conveying the views and desires of one party to the other. (Katzmann 1980:16, emphasis in original)

Alan Palmer, a former law clerk to Supreme Court justice Potter Stewart, became the first assistant director of the health care shop in April 1976. The shop, during Palmer's tenure, comprised about twenty attorneys, including Arthur Lerner, a recent graduate of Harvard Law School (Palmer 2003). In 1978, the commission divided the shop into two components—the Professional Health Service Program (formerly physician services) and the Hospital, Drug, and Medical Supplies Program—and increased its resources (*FTC:Watch* 16 December 1977:5). Most staff members were assigned to the

TABLE 2. *Heads of the Professional Program of the Health Care Shop of the Federal Trade Commission, 1976–1985*

Health Care Shop Heads	*Years of Service*
Alan Palmer	1976–1977
Jonathan Gaines	1978
Walter T. "Terry" Winslow	1979–1982
Arthur J. Lerner	1982–1985

"professional" program and its new assistant director for litigation, Jonathan Gaines (Lerner 2003). Near the end of 1978, Walter T. "Terry" Winslow succeeded Gaines and remained as assistant director until he became deputy director of litigation of the Bureau of Competition in 1982. Lerner followed Winslow as assistant director of the health care shop from 1982 to 1985. Table 2 depicts the succession of assistant directors of litigation who oversaw the professional program of the health care shop from 1976 to 1985.

Resources were plentiful; workload and staffing needs meshed (Palmer 2003). According to Robert Reich, "health services matters" claimed thirty-four "economist and attorney work years," or about 5 percent of the total economist and attorney work years in fiscal year 1978 (FTC Special Collections [Office of Policy Planning and Evaluation, Briefing Book, 5 June 1979: 32]). Even after Congress began to cut funding to the commission in 1978, support for the shop remained strong. Indeed, the report of the transition team for the Reagan administration contained the following endorsement: "The FTC has pursued several worthwhile initiatives against explicit collusion, including its recent efforts to expose guildism in the professions. We believe that the agency's work in this area is in the public interest and should be expanded" (*FTC:Watch* 3 April 1981:2).

Graduates of the country's top law schools applied to the FTC, some for the exciting and cutting-edge cases that the health care shop pursued (Schwartz 2003). In Alan Palmer's words: "We had a mix of people—some aggressive litigators, some who were merely doing a job, and others who thought what we were doing was really neat, that it was right, and were true believers" (2003). Among the "true believers" were Terry Winslow and Arthur Lerner. According to Timothy Muris, Winslow and Lerner "grew up in the health care shop, and became very interested, very ingrained, and very committed to the program" (2003). But this did not make them card-carrying Chicagoans or advocates of any particular point of view. Lerner, in fact, served as an advisor to Pertschuk from 1979 to 1981 before returning to the shop as Winslow's deputy. There was genuine agreement among the attorneys in the health care shop that the basic principles of antitrust law, learned in law school, should apply to the learned professions (Palmer 2003; Lerner 2003; Schwartz 2003).

FINANCIAL PROBLEMS AT THE AMA

While the power and prestige of the FTC grew during the 1970s, that of the AMA declined. Much of the AMA's freefall was due to rising costs of health care, accompanied by social unrest and political discontent, some of it directed toward the anticompetitive practices of professional associations. But not all of the association's problems lay with forces outside its control. The AMA also faced financial and leadership deficits of its own creation. These deficits would lessen the capacity of the association to respond to outside legal pressures.

Financial difficulties began when advertising revenues in *JAMA* and other AMA publications plunged by $2.7 million between 1967 and 1969 (Campion 1984:364). The decline in revenues, though related to reversals in the pharmaceutical industry, highlighted the association's overreliance on *JAMA* as a source of income, a throwback to the Morris Fishbein era. Indeed, advertising revenues from AMA publications in 1967 represented 43 percent of total income, an exceedingly large share. Membership dues, on the other hand, comprised only 37 percent. In addition, the AMA still relied on state and local medical societies to collect annual dues and to recruit new members (Campion 1984:364).

Lost revenues from drug advertising in the late 1960s led to a string of financial shortages in the early 1970s. The AMA had no choice but to raise dues for new and existing members. Few alternative sources of income existed, and the association could not continue to draw from its liquid reserves. In 1970, the association increased dues by $40 (from $70 to $110) and, in 1975, by $140 (from $110 to $250) (Campion 1984:363–391). The first dues increase provided only temporary relief, but the second one, when combined with budget cuts and improved financial management, turned things around (*Proceedings* December 1976:175).

AMA efforts to improve its financial situation through higher dues engendered substantial risk. Several states with large numbers of practitioners, including New York and California, had adopted "unified membership" around 1950 in an attempt to bolster the AMA's fight against the health care plan of President Truman. Unified membership meant physicians had to join the AMA if they wanted to become members of their state and local medical societies. But an increase in dues disproportionately affected physicians living in states with unified membership, and they rebelled accordingly. The percentage of doctors who were members of the AMA declined from 64.5 percent in 1970 to 46.9 percent in 1979 (AMA Special Collections [Historical AMA Membership]). Almost 8,000 physicians left the AMA when New York discontinued "unified membership" in 1970; another 5,500 physicians left when California terminated the policy in 1977 (Campion 1984:368, 391).

Frustrated with political and financial setbacks in the late 1960s and early 1970s, members questioned the effectiveness of AMA leadership (Campion 1984:285–301). The first casualty was Francis Blasingame, who in 1968 resigned his position as executive vice president. Described as a "strong-willed administrator," Blasingame faced opposition from the Board of Trustees, which "thought he failed to consult with them sufficiently, especially on financial matters" (Campion 1984:284). Once Blasingame left, "the initiative and dynamism within organized medicine seemed to shift from the AMA to AMPAC" (Campion 1984:289). For most of the 1960s, rancor had existed between the two operations, the former based in Washington, D.C., and the latter based in Chicago. "Dr. Blasingame always maintained that it was AMPAC that dumped him," a member of the Board of Trustees said (as quoted in Campion 1984:295). The animosity that existed between leaders of the respective offices likely stemmed from profound differences in philosophy. While those in Washington favored "socioeconomic and political" pursuits, many in Chicago, including Blasingame, still thought the organization should stick to "medical and scientific" matters (Campion 1984:295–296).

Blasingame's successor, Ernest B. Howard, faced the brunt of the social, political, and economic turmoil that the late 1960s and early 1970s had to offer. Determined to retire in 1975, Howard engendered a political contest between factions in Washington and those in Chicago. The eventual winner, James Sammons, represented the Washington contingent. After entering practice in Baytown, Texas, Sammons became president of the Houston Academy of Medicine, director and chair of AMPAC, president of the Texas Medical Association, and chair of the AMA Board of Trustees. Though "displeasure" lingered among AMA delegates over the choice of Sammons, the new executive vice president quickly demonstrated his leadership abilities. Under Sammons's direction, the association restored its fiscal integrity, restructured its councils and committees, and reorganized its staff. The new regime imposed a tighter, more centralized framework and a budgeting system that stressed program management (Campion 1984:370–421).

The AMA emerged from internal discord to confront a new enemy in the FTC. Sammons accepted the challenge on behalf of the association. Only the AMA, he later reported, "had the resources to battle the FTC . . . to preserve medicine's role in self-regulation" (*Proceedings* June 1981:19). Sammons's frustration with the commission seemed evident from the start. Refusing to bow to the agency's new pronouncements, Sammons offered this view of "governmental bureaucracy" in a 1977 report to the House of Delegates: "It is a cancerous, relentless, mindless blob of a force that oozes through the cracks and seeps under the doors, and as soon as you can stop it in one direction, it creeps in on you from another" (*Proceedings* June 1977:31). In years past, the association had occasioned such rhetoric for "socialized medicine." But the problem for Sammons and the AMA was that this new adversary donned capitalist, not socialist, garb.

CONCLUSION

By overturning the learned professions exemption, the U.S. Supreme Court in *Goldfarb* altered the rules of engagement. Everything was in place in the second half of the 1970s for a classic confrontation. After remaining in the shadows for much of its existence, the Federal Trade Commission readied for battle. Vibrant leadership, a young and dedicated staff, and an expanded budget gave the agency new swagger. But more than the individuals and organizations involved, it was contrasting ideas, worldviews, and philosophies that made this confrontation so consequential. At one end of the spectrum, the AMA and its membership stood for professionalism—for self-regulation, for clinical autonomy, and for free choice of physician. At the other end of the spectrum, antitrust reformers and the FTC stood for market competition—for bureaucratic oversight, for the integration of finance and delivery, and for the ability of hospitals and insurers to choose their own providers.

Congressional support for the FTC's agenda as articulated by Dan Schwartz and others seemed secure in the mid-1970s. The 1974 hearings before the Senate Subcommittee on Antitrust and Monopoly set the tone for a series of investigations, probes, and legal actions. There were few malcontents—the Naderites and the Chicagoans, often for different reasons, opposed the anticompetitive practices of the medical profession. The case against the AMA, discussed in the next chapter, got its start when Louis Engman chaired the commission. Michael Pertschuk strongly supported the measure; so did James Miller, Pertschuk's successor. Although the Reagan administration curtailed several programs in the early 1980s, it continued to back the FTC's health care agenda.

A larger question remained, however. This involved the depth of political support for market competition. It was one thing to overthrow an existing regime; it was quite another to replace it with a viable alternative. At the end of the 1970s, the market creed seemed intact. Much of this was due to an ideological shift from the public interest theory of regulation to the economic theory of regulation as expressed in general elections. The 1979 defeat of President Carter's measure to cap hospital spending signaled the shift in thinking. "Regulation" was out of favor, the *Economist* duly noted. Ronald Reagan's success in the presidential election of 1980 confirmed the transformation. "Republicans and Democrats," political scientist Vincent Navarro claimed, "interpreted the 1980 elections in precisely the same way: a popular mandate to reduce government intervention, including social expenditures" (Navarro 1994:8).

By combining their forces, Naderites and Chicagoans could withstand the political clout of organized medicine. But the reason for the attraction, a medical monopoly that harmed consumers and suppressed competition, was unlikely to last once a market regime was established. Michael Pertschuk's torrid attacks against the policies of James Miller and other Reagan appointees demonstrated the depth of the division. In time, fundamental differences between advocates of the "old" and the "new" antitrust would carry over to health care, severing the link that existed. For now, however, Naderites and Chicagoans maintained their alliance. This would be particularly important as congressional discontent with the FTC coalesced in the late 1970s and early 1980s, giving the AMA a good opportunity to seek an exemption from the agency's jurisdiction.

5 The *AMA* Case

The crowning achievement of the FTC's early campaign for a more competitive environment in the health care industry was its case against the AMA (*In the Matter of the American Medical Ass'n,* 94 F.T.C. 701 [1979]). Begun in 1975, the *AMA* case targeted ethical restrictions on physician advertising, solicitation, and contract practice. Advertising and solicitation lay at the heart of the distinction between professional and commercial behavior. Medical societies strenuously objected to such practices, asserting that they undermined professional integrity. Contract practice, on the other hand, had little if anything to do with personal appearance and character. On the advice of the Larson commission, the AMA had ended its outright ban on contract practice. Nonetheless, the profession still regulated salaried arrangements. Indeed, certain activities of state and local medical societies indicated that efforts to enforce the ban persisted.

The *AMA* case conflated several important issues, many of them highly controversial. These included the FTC's jurisdiction over professional associations, the contours of professional ethics in the business arena, and the boundaries of professional self-regulation. How and to what extent should the antitrust laws apply to the medical profession? Was there a distinction between profession and trade for purposes of government regulation and antitrust enforcement? What did the Supreme Court mean in the *Goldfarb* case when it said, "It would be unrealistic to view the practice of professions as interchangeable with other business activities, and automatically to apply to the professions antitrust concepts which originated in other areas" (*Goldfarb,* 421 U.S. at 788–789 n. 17)?

THE FTC GIRDS FOR ACTION

Goldfarb was the trigger for the FTC's decision to proceed against the American Medical Association and its component professional societies. The

Court's pronouncements in *Goldfarb* on interstate commerce, the "learned professions" exemption, and state-action immunity removed important barriers to legal action. Maynard Thomson, who months earlier had supported Dan Schwartz's proposal to the Evaluation Committee, set forth the case against the association (FTC Special Collections [Thomson Memorandum to Commission, 12 December 1975]).

As in *Goldfarb*, the *AMA* case involved a series of ethical prohibitions adopted and enforced by a chain of professional societies. Physicians who violated bans on advertising, solicitation, and contract practice faced loss of license in states where medical boards embraced ethics standards as grounds for disciplinary action. But state-sanctioned disciplinary action, as the Court had stated in *Goldfarb*, did not preclude enforcement of the antitrust laws, where such action "was essentially a private anticompetitive activity" (*Goldfarb*, 421 U.S. at 791–792). Just as attorneys adhered to the minimum fee schedule in *Goldfarb* out of a desire to comply with professional norms, so many physicians disdained advertising and contract practice because they considered such activities to be unethical.

Jim Liebeler's work on drug advertising and Clark Havighurst's study of HMOs underlay Thomson's evaluation (see Havighurst 1970). "'Ethical' proscriptions," Thomson wrote, "against advertising and other forms of 'soliciting' patients, as promulgated and enforced by the AMA and the state and county associations, deprive consumers of valuable information." "The absence of competition," he concluded, "has blocked or distorted the emergence of new methods for delivery of medical services, methods which have the potential of slowing the rise of health costs" (FTC Special Collections [Thomson Memorandum to Commission, 12 December 1975: 3–4]).

Havighurst's 1974 testimony before the Senate Subcommittee on Antitrust and Monopoly, based on the Institute of Medicine Report that he helped to write, had stressed the conflict between medical ethics and marketplace innovation. The IOM Report, Havighurst testified, "rather dramatically illuminates the possibility that HMOs will spring up spontaneously in a market where obstacles to their creation have been removed" (U.S. Congress, Senate, 1974:1040 [Statement of Clark C. Havighurst]). "A substantial antitrust victory against the medical profession," he claimed, "would be one of the most fortunate developments that could occur in trying to get the health services marketplace in order" (U.S. Congress, Senate, 1974:1046 [Statement of Clark C. Havighurst]).

Dan Schwartz and Maynard Thomson were familiar with Havighurst's views favoring market competition. As Schwartz had done before him, Thomson met with Havighurst in March 1975, a few months in advance of the *Goldfarb* decision. When making his recommendations to the Evaluation Committee, Thomson paid homage to the eminent professor. "One authority in the area feels that an action against doctors' ethical codes would have great 'symbolic value,'" Thomson wrote. "By this Professor Havighurst meant that doctors, for perhaps the first time, would be forced to examine their practices with a view towards conforming them to societal values beyond those deriving from traditional medical ethics." The strategy that Thomson proposed embraced Havighurst's position:

> An antitrust attack on ethical codes would state forcefully that the day when the professions could be laws unto themselves was on the wane. By moving against all the anti-competitive provisions, this end would be accomplished far more thoroughly than by moving against only minimum fee schedules and, to a certain extent, bans on bidding. The restriction on advertising, for instance is at the very core of the nice conceit that the "professional" is somehow above the vulgar fray of trade, and thereby above the risks and costs and rules of trade. . . . From the foregoing, it is obvious that a "domino theory" is contemplated, whereby an attack on doctors' advertising bans simply heralds the demise of *all* such bans. (FTC Special Collections [Thomson Memorandum to Evaluation Committee, 2 June 1975: 25, emphasis in original])

Thomson's approach targeted certain state and local medical societies as well as the AMA. "Without the AMA," Thomson argued, "the local societies would have no unifying thread ensuring continued adherence to the ban on advertising." But "without the local societies . . . the agreements not to advertise would be even shorter-lived" (FTC Special Collections [Thomson Memorandum to Evaluation Committee, 12 December 1975: 41]). In an attempt to undercut a potential claim of state-action immunity, Thomson singled out the Connecticut State Medical Society and the New Haven County Medical Association for inclusion in the legal proceedings. Connecticut law, Thomson discovered, prohibited advertising and solicitation only to the extent that it was "untrue, fraudulent, misleading or deceptive" (FTC Special Collections [Thomson Memorandum to Evaluation Committee, 12 December 1975: 9]). Unconditional bans on advertising of the type at issue exceeded Connecticut's grant of authority.

Lloyd Oliver and James Folsom of the Bureau of Economics concurred with Thomson's reasoning. Folsom believed that the lawsuit would have more than "symbolic" effect. "I think the effect will be substantially greater than a placebo," he wrote (FTC Special Collections [Thomson Memorandum to Evaluation Committee, 12 December 1975: 49]). Though the commission approved issuance of the complaint on 16 December 1975, its chair, Louis Engman, expressed certain reservations. "Agreements not to advertise may be *per se* violations for most businessmen, but some narrow advertising restrictions among doctors conceivably could be reasonable," he cautioned. "In particular," Engman stressed, "the public health defenses which the AMA will raise may be more difficult than staff suggests" (FTC Special Collections [Engman Memorandum to Commission, 16 December 1975]). Footnote 17 of *Goldfarb* loomed large in Engman's opinion.

PEREMPTORY STRIKE

On 19 December 1975, the FTC brought action against the AMA, the Connecticut State Medical Society, and the New Haven County Medical Association for breach of the antitrust laws, specifically section 5(a) of the FTC Act pertaining to unfair and deceptive trade practices. The commission claimed that the medical societies had conspired to prevent or hinder physicians from "soliciting business, by advertising or otherwise; engaging in price competition; and otherwise engaging in competitive practices" (*AMA*, 94 F.T.C. at 702–703). The conspiracy arose from the collective promulgation and enforcement of anticompetitive ethics standards.

None of the attorneys in the health care shop attempted to contact the AMA before taking legal action; nor did they conduct a formal precomplaint investigation as protocol seemed to require (Anderson 2003; Katzmann 1980:60–72). Much of the fact finding, or "discovery," occurred after the FTC brought the case (*AMA*, 94 F.T.C. at 706). This was extraordinary. Ernest Barnes, the administrative law judge assigned to the *AMA* case, was perplexed by the agency's actions:

> When we had the first pre-hearing conference in this case, the complaint counsel told me that they had done no discovery. That kind of shocked me. They would have to conduct their entire discovery after the complaint issued. That's a little unusual; in fact, it's very unusual and kind of upsetting because that meant the case would be . . . delayed while they investigated. I had to issue subpoenas to a number of medical societies and they all contested the subpoenas, and so we had quite a battle while the complaint counsel were completing their discovery. . . . The Commission always had discovery after a complaint, but not discovery from scratch, like here. (Barnes 2003)

The apparent breach of protocol by commission attorneys reflected, to some extent, the unusual posture of the *AMA* case. *AMA* was part of a comprehensive strategy by the FTC to finally terminate the anticompetitive practices of the medical profession. Several FTC bureaus and divisions (the Bureau of Economics, the Bureau of Competition, and the Office of Policy Planning and Evaluation) had a role in bringing the action. *AMA* was not a simple "conduct" matter that began at the Bureau of Competition. Rather, it originated with Liebeler at the Office of Policy Planning and Evaluation (Muris 2003). "I'm positive," Muris recalled, "that [*AMA*] came out of the occupational licensure task force and Liebeler's efforts with regard to advertising" (2003). Because of the unique origins of *AMA*, there were no standard operating procedures.

Still, FTC attorneys could have approached the association to discuss code revisions before filing the complaint. There was a strong likelihood, moreover, that AMA attorneys would have been receptive (Bierig 2003). Indeed, the Judicial Council of the AMA met in November 1975 before FTC attorneys filed suit to revise the Code of Medical Ethics (*AMA*, 94 F.T.C. at 912; Appeal Brief of Respondent AMA, 1979:48). But FTC attorneys did not want to settle and, for several reasons, chose to litigate instead.

Most important, there was the unresolved question of the agency's jurisdiction. Section 4 of the FTC Act stated that the commission could regulate corporations "organized to carry on business for [their] own profit or that of [their] members." Because the AMA was a nonprofit organization, commission attorneys would have to prove that the profit motives of association members were apparent. FTC attorneys desired to prove their case at the earliest possible date before an administrative law judge of the FTC, where they had "home court" advantage (Costilo 2003).

The stakes were high. The entire initiative against the anticompetitive practices of the medical profession (and other health care professions, such as dentistry) hung in the balance. Jurisdiction would give the commission the authority to monitor the activities of the AMA and its component medical societies over the next several years. Jurisdiction would allow the agency to pursue investigations into medical society control of Blue Shield plans, prosecutions of specialty societies for boycotts and price-fixing, and rules to curtail anticompetitive practices. Finally, jurisdiction over the AMA would serve as precedent for actions against other professional organizations. The American Dental Association, for example, signed a consent order with the FTC in 1979 that tracked the result in *AMA*. If the FTC lost "on the merits or for lack of jurisdiction," its case against the American Dental Association also would fail (*AMA*, 94 F.T.C. at 1033).

There was little reason to believe, based on past history, that settlement discussions would serve any useful purpose other than to give the AMA the time it needed to mount a political offensive or to revise its Code of Medical

Ethics. Code revisions, even those that were incomplete, could render the case moot before it even started. "If you tell them we're investigating and they change the rules," Havighurst said, "then you lose the chance to make the point you want to make. For years, the medical profession restrained trade in serious ways. That's a pretty good reason for not putting them on notice" (2003). Settlements typically involve compromise and are often subject to differing interpretations. A court pronouncement, on the other hand, that government, not the AMA, had the authority to regulate the health care industry would have greater force and effect (see Havighurst 1978:375). The FTC required a favorable and decisive judicial ruling to further its long-range objectives.

FTC attorneys moved expeditiously, albeit somewhat hastily, to file their complaint. "We do not believe the pre-complaint work in this matter needs to be extensive," Dan Schwartz advised the Evaluation Committee. "We would hope to be able to move very quickly after the *Goldfarb* decision is handed down by the Supreme Court," he said (FTC Special Collections [Schwarz Memorandum to the Evaluation Committee, 6 June 1975: 19]). But in "moving very quickly," FTC attorneys failed to include an important allegation—the complaint made no specific reference to contract practice. Once he took over the case, Barry Costilo, a veteran trial attorney, discovered and corrected the omission (Palmer 2003; Costilo 2003). Months later, Commissioner Elizabeth Hanford Dole exclaimed: "I was somewhat surprised to learn . . . that complaint counsel are now challenging such alleged practices as restrictions on physicians' contracting with third parties, including 'medical care plans.' As I recall, this case was presented to the Commission as simply challenging restrictions on advertising and solicitation of patients" (FTC Special Collections [Dole Memorandum to Commission, 12 April 1977]).

The FTC's failure to put the association on notice before filing the complaint or to discuss a possible settlement frayed relations between the attorneys. Jack Bierig, the AMA's lead counsel at trial, recalled: "I remember we had a couple meetings in Washington that were very upsetting, where we thought we had offered what we regarded as very reasonable terms. Our position all along was we should be allies with the [FTC] . . . but it was very confrontational and exactly why the FTC was so extreme, it's hard to know" (2003). Notwithstanding Bierig's protest, his client seemed no more receptive to settlement than did the commission. Immediately after the filing of the complaint, AMA president Max Parrott and board chair Raymond Holden expressed their uncompromising support for restrictions on advertising and solicitation. They declared:

> We are somewhat hampered in responding to the FTC complaint since we received a copy of it—unofficially—only after it had been made public through the media. The complaint is directed at the AMA's code of ethics, more than 100 years old. It is ironic that the FTC should attack a code devised and operated as a standard of conduct in the best interests of the patient. Advertising by a professional is the very antithesis of professionalism. Physicians should not solicit patients. A patient should go to a doctor on the basis of need, not on the basis of advertising. Do patients want to be treated in accordance with the best professional's judgment concerning their health and safety? Or do they want medical services that are sold and promoted? We think there is enough hucksterism in this country without hucksterism in medicine. And we're going to fight it. (AMA Vows to Fight FTC Attempt to End Ban on Ads by Physicians 1976)

ADVERTISING AND SOLICITATION

For much of the twentieth century, bans on advertising and solicitation were central features of the Code of Medical Ethics. Principle 5 of the code (1957) stated that a physician "should not solicit patients." Based on this brief but critical phrase, the Judicial Council prohibited efforts of physicians to provide the public with most any kind of useful information. About the only type of information that doctors ethically could convey was their name, type of practice, office location, and hours of service (*Opinions and Reports*, Section 5 [1971]). According to the Judicial Council: "The doctor may ethically furnish this information through the accepted local media of communication, which are open to all physicians on like conditions. Telephone listings, office signs, professional cards, dignified announcements, all are acceptable media of making factual information available to the public." In addition, the council prescribed the conditions for holding an open house, follow-up announcements, the opening of a new practice, listings in commercially sponsored advertising directories, and signage.

By requiring all physicians, no matter their affiliation, to adhere to the same ethical standards for advertising and solicitation, the ban adversely affected efforts of medical clinics and group practices to market their products. "As is well-known," the Judicial Council related, "there is a tendency for physicians to organize themselves into so-called groups under various designations, such as group clinics, diagnostic clinics, group medicine, medical institutes, the (blank) medical academy, and similar names. Some of these groups are advertising in a manner that would be considered most reprehensible if done by an individual physician. The Council is unable to see any difference in principle between a group of physicians advertising themselves under whatsoever title they may assume and an individual physician advertising himself" (*Opinions and Reports,* Section 5 [1971]).

The AMA attempted to justify its restrictions on advertising and solicitation by appealing to the sentiments expressed by the Supreme Court in *Goldfarb* and other cases. A ban on advertising "served socially beneficial purposes unrelated to price," lawyers for the AMA asserted (Trial Brief of Respondent AMA, 1977: 45). These "socially beneficial purposes" included efforts to avoid consumer deception, maintain the public's confidence or trust, and ensure the quality of medical services. AMA attorneys adduced the following noneconomic justifications for advertising restrictions: "Possibilities for deception are particularly serious in the area of medicine because most consumers lack the training to evaluate medical claims and because many are vulnerable to superficially appealing promises or suggestions of cures. And the consequences of deception can be more horrible than in perhaps any other area. As the Supreme Court noted in the context of legal advertising, 'misstatements that might be overlooked or deemed unimportant in other advertising may be found quite inappropriate in legal advertising.' If anything, such misstatements are all the more important where people's health is at stake" (Trial Brief of Respondent AMA, 1977: 54).

A 1977 decision of the U.S. Supreme Court, *Bates v. Arizona State Bar Association* (433 U.S. 350, 383 [1977]), appeared to buttress the AMA's position. In *Bates,* a disciplinary rule of Arizona's highest court barred attorneys from advertising in newspapers or other media. Two lawyers violated the rule when they advertised certain "routine" legal services—uncontested divorces, uncontested adoptions, simple personal bankruptcies, and changes of name—"at very reasonable fees" (*Bates,* 433 U.S. at 354). Because state-action immunity restricted the application of the antitrust laws (a disciplinary rule of the Arizona court was at issue), the Court decided the case on First Amendment grounds.

In a 5–4 decision, Justice Blackmun, writing for the majority, held that Arizona's blanket prohibition on lawyers' advertisements violated free speech. Five justices (Blackmun, Brennan, White, Marshall, and Stevens) rejected the argument of the Arizona State Bar (*Bates,* 433 U.S. at 368); four justices (Powell, Burger, Stewart, and Rehnquist) dissented. In a blistering attack on the majority decision, Justice Powell declared: "The area into which the Court now ventures has, until today, largely been left to self-regulation by the profession. . . . The problem of bringing clients and lawyers together on a mutually fair basis, consistent with the public interest, is as old as the profession itself. . . . The Court's imposition of hard and fast constitutional rules as to price advertising is neither required by precedent nor likely to serve the public interest" (*Bates,* 433 U.S. at 402–403).

Having opened the door to advertising by the legal profession, the Court struggled to maintain some semblance of order. Professional associations would retain a role in self-regulation, the Court indicated, but it provided little guidance for future cases: "Advertising that is false, deceptive, or misleading of course is subject to restraint," Blackmun proclaimed (*Bates,* 433 U.S. at 402–403). "We recognize," he continued, "that many of the problems in defining the boundary between deceptive and nondeceptive advertising remain to be resolved, and we expect that the bar will have a special role to play in assuring that advertising by attorneys flows both freely and cleanly" (*Bates,* 433 U.S. at 384). By way of example, Blackmun favorably cited a revised statement of the AMA issued in 1976. The revised statement allowed doctors to furnish " 'biographical and other relevant data for listing in a reputable directory . . . [including] fee information.' " "Even the medical profession," Blackmun related, "now views the alleged effect of advertising in a somewhat different light from the [Arizona State Bar]" (*Bates,* 433 U.S. at 371 n. 20).

Blackmun's reference to the revised statement signaled support for the AMA's position. But, as the commission's investigation had disclosed, there was evidence that state and local medical societies maintained certain restrictions on advertising and solicitation, notwithstanding the revised statement (Proposed Findings of Fact, 1978: 276–281). Moreover, the Judicial Council did not issue the revised statement until after the *AMA* case had begun. "The basic issue in this case," Barry Costilo contended, "is not the AMA's *current* position on advertising and solicitation, but rather whether respondents have, over the years leading up to the complaint, engaged in concerted practices which have unreasonably restrained physician advertising and solicitation" (Reply Brief, 1978: 10, emphasis in original).

CONTRACT PRACTICE

Although the AMA did not view contract practice as unethical per se when the FTC filed its complaint in 1975 (sixteen years earlier, the AMA's Larson Commission had ended the association's blanket opposition to prepaid group practice), certain restrictions remained. Principle 6 of the Code of Medical Ethics was the source of those restrictions. According to Principle 6, "A physician should not dispose of his services under terms or conditions which tend to interfere with or impair the free and complete exercise of his medical judgment and skill or tend to cause a deterioration of the quality of medical care" (1957). As recently as 1971, the Judicial Council interpreted Principle 6 to prohibit certain contractual arrangements. These included:

1. When the compensation received is inadequate based on the usual fees paid for the same kind of services and class of people in the same community.
2. When the compensation is so low as to make it impossible for competent service to be rendered.
3. When there is underbidding by physicians in order to secure the contract.
4. When a reasonable degree of free choice of physicians is denied those cared for in a community where other competent physicians are readily available.
5. When there is solicitation of patients directly or indirectly. (*Opinions and Reports,* Section 6 [1971])

The council also barred certain relationships between physicians and hospitals, the practice of medicine by lay corporations, and certain arrangements between physicians and nonphysicians (*Opinions and Reports,* Section 6 [1971]).

While the *AMA* case was pending, the U.S. Supreme Court resolved all questions about the efficacy of professional restrictions on contract practice in the case of *National Society of Professional Engineers v. United States.* In 1972, the Department of Justice sued the National Society of Professional Engineers under the Sherman Act, claiming that a ban on competitive bidding suppressed competition. By way of response, the engineering society raised public safety concerns. It argued that the ban protected the public because "the lowest possible price would adversely affect the quality of engineering" (*Professional Engineers,* 435 U.S. at 685). A federal district court refused to consider the society's justification for the ban, holding it illegal (*Professional Engineers,* 389 F.Supp. 1193 [D.C. 1974]), and the United States Court of Appeals for the District of Columbia affirmed (*Professional Engineers,* 555 F.2d 978 [D.C. Cir. 1977]). In a unanimous decision, authored by Justice John Paul Stevens, the Supreme Court agreed with the rulings of the lower federal courts. Paying scant attention to the sentiments expressed in footnote 17, Stevens viewed noneconomic justifications for restraining competition, so-called worthy purpose defenses and the like, as irrelevant. Rule of reason analysis, Stevens declared, "does not open the field of antitrust inquiry to any argument in favor of a challenged restraint that may fall within the realm of reason. Instead, it focuses directly on the challenged restraint's impact on competitive conditions" (*Professional Engineers,* 435 U.S. at 648).

Though they agreed with the ultimate disposition of the case, several justices (Blackmun, Burger, and Rehnquist) claimed that the majority opinion had gone too far. "Certainly, this case," Blackmun wrote, "does not require us to decide whether the 'Rule of Reason' as applied to the professions ever could take account of benefits other than increased competition" (*Professional Engineers,* 435 U.S. at 699). "My skepticism," Blackmun continued, "arises from the fact that there may be ethical rules which have a more than *de minimus* anticompetitive effect and yet are important in a profession's proper ordering" (*Professional Engineers,* 435 U.S. at 700). Blackmun, in other words, still valued the views expressed in footnote 17. He undoubtedly believed that business and professional pursuits, for purposes of the antitrust laws, were not entirely "interchangeable."

Professional Engineers sealed the fate of the AMA's earlier pronouncements on contract practice. The assertions that inadequate fees undercut "competent service" and that certain corporate arrangements inhibited "free choice of physician" failed the Court's test in *Professional Engineers.* Conceding that "some language" in "earlier editions" of the Code of Medical Ethics was "obsolete," AMA attorneys argued that the association had "abandoned" any restrictions on contract practice. "In recent years," they claimed, "neither the AMA nor any state or local society has placed any unreasonably anticompetitive restriction on the development of non-fee-for-service modes of health care delivery" (Trial Brief, 1977: 86–87). Medical ethics, they said, no longer barred physicians from employment in medical schools, group practices, clinics, or HMOs, so long as such arrangements did not mislead patients or expose them to inferior health care (Trial Brief, 1977: 86). But the AMA's claims did not hold up under careful scrutiny. As the evidence produced in the case showed, many medical societies still constrained certain forms of contract practice.

THE PROBLEM OF INSTITUTIONAL BIAS

Administrative agencies combine executive, legislative, and judicial functions without the checks and balances inherent in the constitutional structure of American government. Although this enhances efficiency and effectiveness, it creates the appearance of bias. The appearance of bias becomes most acute when an administrative law judge with ties to an agency conducts the hearing and determines the respondent's fate. Those who face an administrative complaint rightly believe "that the agency acts as a legislator, investigator, prosecutor, judge and jury" (Asimow, Bonfield, and Levin 1998:117). So it was with the AMA. "This procedure, to which we have strenuous objections," the association's chief executive declared, "bears only an Orwellian resemblance to the judicial process, for the prosecutor, the judge (who also acts as the jury) and the appeals panel are all employees or officials of the adversary, the FTC. The process is a legislatively authorized exercise in which a federal agency enjoys the amiable practice of grading its own examination papers" (*Proceedings* June 1982:14). Newton Minow (who, along with Jack Bierig, was the AMA's outside counsel) also objected: "We feared we would not get a fair, unbiased proceeding because the Commission had already displayed its hostility to organized medicine. Furthermore, the administrative law judge assigned to the case had been for many years a prosecutor for the Commission. Finally, we knew that, incredible as it might seem to a non-lawyer, we would have to appeal the initial decision of the administrative law judge to the full Federal Trade Commission—the very people who directed the complaint in the first instance" (*Proceedings* December 1978:14).

Despite these protestations, there was nothing untoward about the relationship between the administrative law judge, Ernest Barnes, and the FTC. Agency know-how and expertise are desirable traits in an administrative law judge. Judge Barnes started his career with the FTC in 1955 as an attorney investigator, was assistant director of the Bureau of Competition from 1969 to 1972, and was an administrative law judge from 1972 until his retirement in 1987 (Barnes 2003). Although AMA attorneys expressed concern about Barnes's ties to the agency, there was no evidence that Barnes had a personal or financial stake in the outcome of the case or had prejudged the situation, the principal criteria for disqualification. The Federal Administrative Procedures Act provides that formal adjudications, such as *AMA*, "shall be conducted in an impartial manner." But this does not mean that an administrative law judge has to avoid the "appearance of bias," a standard often applied to federal or state judges (Asimow, Bonfield, and Levin 1998:130). In administrative proceedings, the law requires "actual bias," a more stringent standard (Asimow, Bonfield, and Levin 1998:130). Newton Minow, a former chair of the Federal Communications Commission, undoubtedly grasped the situation. He wanted to make sure that his client did as well.

Of greater concern was the potential bias of FTC chair Michael Pertschuk. Pertschuk voiced his opposition to professional self-regulation on at least three separate occasions during the proceedings in *AMA*. On one such occasion, he equated medical societies with "medieval guilds" (Motion for Recusal, 1979: 4). Pertschuk wrote:

> Many of the problems of an antitrust nature which I perceive in the health care field stem from the striking degree of physician self-regulation which exists and from a relative lack of participation by representative groups with at least potentially different interests—most notably consumers. It would not be far-fetched, in fact, to suggest that the medical profession is our closest contemporary equivalent to the guild system of medieval times, in which neither government regulation nor competition was permitted to impede the efforts of the tradesman or artisan to achieve professional success and economic prosperity. It seems appropriate, therefore, to consider whether there exists in the health care field today a proper mix of government regulation, competition, and self-regulation. I believe there does not. (Motion for Recusal, 1979: 5–6)

AMA attorneys moved to disqualify Pertschuk on the grounds that he had "prejudged key issues in the case" (Motion for Recusal, 1979: 1), but Pertschuk refused to step down. In his defense, Pertschuk declared: "The speeches and congressional statements cited by respondents can only be read as reflecting an underlying philosophy concerning the broad policy issues such as the role of professionals and professional licensing in our society, competition in the health care sector of the economy, and the problem of rising health care costs" (Memorandum in Response to Motion for Recusal, 1979:3).

There often is a fine line between prejudgment of "individualized facts" and prejudgment "about law, policy, or legislative facts" (Asimow, Bonfield, and Levin 1998:130). Individuals in Pertschuk's position are expected to provide direction on policy issues. Still, they have to be careful not to prejudge the facts of a particular case. Courts are lenient but, on occasion, take action.

Perhaps the leading case on the issue of prejudgment in administrative proceedings concerned Paul Rand Dixon, who, ironically, was one of the four commissioners to decide the *AMA* case. Dixon, like Pertschuk, was outspoken during his tenure as chair of the Federal Trade Commission. In a 1968 speech, Dixon admonished certain newspapers for displaying advertisements that were deceptive in nature. He gave as examples "ads that offer college educations in five weeks . . . or [the opportunity to become] an airline's hostess by attending charm school" (*Cinderella Career and Finishing Schools, Inc., v. FTC,* 425 F.2d 583, 589–590 [D.C. Cir. 1970]). Dixon's remarks dovetailed with a case before the commission that involved deceptive advertising—indeed, by a charm school. A federal circuit court held that Dixon had prejudged the matter. The court stated: "There is a marked difference between the issuance of a press release which states that the Commission has filed a complaint because it has 'reason to believe' that there have been violations, and statements by a Commissioner after an appeal has been filed which give the appearance that he has already prejudged the case and that the ultimate determination of the merits will move in predestined grooves" (*Cinderella Career and Finishing Schools,* 425 F.2d at 590).

Though Pertschuk's statements suggested that the case would "move in predestined grooves," the United States Court of Appeals for the Second Circuit (which would hear the association's appeal in *AMA*) affirmed Pertschuk's nonrecusal. "At most," the court said, "the public statements brought to our attention by the petitioners indicate that the chairman was informing the Congress and the public as to FTC's activities and policies in general . . . including those in the medical field" (*American Medical Ass'n v. F.T.C.,* 638 F.2d 443, 449 [1980]). Judge Walter Mansfield, who dissented from the opinion of the circuit court in other respects, agreed. "[Chair Pertschuk's] statements have the earmarks of prejudgment," Mansfield wrote, "[but] I am willing in this instance to give the speaker the benefit of the doubt" (*AMA,* 638 F.2d at 455).

TRIAL AND ORDER

Administrative hearings can be long and grueling affairs. Complex proceedings, such as *AMA,* require several days of trial to accommodate large numbers of witnesses and documents. There are few incentives to keep such proceedings short. The stakes are often high and the rules of evidence are more relaxed than in typical judicial trials. Attorneys expect that an administrative law judge will place few limits on witness testimony and the documents they seek to introduce. Such judges may even entertain hearsay evidence in instances where courts might not. Judge Barnes, for instance, admitted several documents that contained hearsay communications between professional associations and individual physicians (*AMA,* 94 F.T.C. at 964).

The first day of the hearing was 7 September 1977; the last day was 5 May 1978. Judge Barnes partitioned the matter into several discrete phases. The FTC's case-in-chief took place in Washington, D.C. (twenty days and twenty-five witnesses); the AMA's defense transpired in Chicago, Los Angeles, and Washington, D.C. (twenty-seven days and fifty-two witnesses); the state and local medical societies from Connecticut put on their defense in New Haven (four days and eight witnesses); the FTC's case in rebuttal returned to Washington, D.C. (three days and three witnesses); finally, the AMA's surrebuttal occurred in Chicago (three days and seven witnesses) (*AMA*, 94 F.T.C. at 707). All told, there were almost three thousand exhibits and ten thousand pages of transcript (*AMA*, 94 F.T.C. at 708). The cost to the AMA in outside legal fees for the trial alone was about $750,000 (Anderson 2003).

Because of the logistics involved in lengthy trials, such as document production and witness preparation, both sides often have several lawyers and legal assistants. Barry Costilo's trial team included five attorneys. The AMA engaged the Chicago law firm of Sidley and Austin to represent its interests. Jack Bierig, a young associate, assumed the role of lead counsel at the hearing. He received support from Newton Minow and Robert Youle. Minow appeared at key stages of the trial, argued the case on appeal, and lobbied Congress to rein in the FTC. The AMA's in-house lawyers, Bernard Hirsh and B. J. Anderson, also were present. In addition, the Connecticut respondents had their own attorneys.

Administrative hearings like *AMA* place much pressure on the lawyers, particularly lead counsel. This was among the reasons why the FTC entrusted the case to Costilo, a seasoned trial attorney. Bierig, on the other hand, was a relative newcomer. A 1972 graduate of Harvard Law School, Bierig heard about the case while enjoying his first vacation since joining Sidley and Austin three years earlier (Bierig 2003). Although no one reasonably expected Bierig to win before the commission, he shouldered the responsibility for putting on a vigorous defense and for establishing a detailed record should his client appeal. Bierig fought hard in a losing cause. Indeed, the trial was a tense affair that featured much acrimony between the attorneys and their respective clients. According to *FTC:Watch:* "The recently completed trial of charges that the American Medical Association has illegally restrained competition in the health care field . . . was conducted in an atmosphere so emotional that at one point opposing counsel spent 50 pages of the transcript attacking each other for alleged noncooperation in the cross-examination of witnesses. Administrative Law Judge Ernest G. Barnes was so offended by the language and nature of the allegations that he excised all 50 pages from [the] trial record" (15 December 1978:8).

The pivotal issue in *AMA* was the FTC's jurisdiction over nonprofit organizations. For guidance, Judge Barnes turned to the test set forth by the United States Court of Appeals for the Seventh Circuit in *F.T.C. v. National Commission on Egg Nutrition* (88 F.T.C. 89, 177 [1976], *aff'd*, 570 F.2d 157

[7th Cir. 1977]). Based on *Egg Nutrition,* Barnes ruled that the commission could assert jurisdiction over "nonprofit organizations whose activities engender a pecuniary benefit to its members if that activity is a substantial part of the total activities of the organization, rather than merely incidental to some noncommercial activity" (*AMA,* 94 F.T.C. at 923). To satisfy the test, Costilo had to show that a "substantial part" of the AMA's activities provided a "direct economic benefit" to its members. Bierig, on the other hand, could defeat Costilo's claim by demonstrating that any economic activities were "incidental or subordinate" to the scientific, educational, and public health pursuits of the association. As often happens when important factual distinctions are involved, a battle of the experts ensued.

Costilo's evidence consisted primarily of the lobbying activities of the AMA before Congress and certain federal agencies—opposition to federal price controls on physicians' fees, reimbursement practices under Medicare, national health insurance, federal funding of HMOs, relicensure of physicians, continuing medical education, and hospital cost containment. In addition, Costilo showed that the AMA had devoted substantial resources toward passage of the Keogh Act (which created tax benefits for physicians and other self-employed individuals), medical malpractice reform, use of relative value scales, restrictions on allied health professionals, and Professional Standards Review Organizations. Additional activities of a pecuniary nature included the AMA's involvement with Blue Shield and other insurers, its promotion of foundations for medical care, and its sponsorship of the American Medical Political Action Committee (AMPAC) (*AMA,* 94 F.T.C. at 739). AMPAC reported campaign fund transfers of more than $1 million in 1976, making it (at the time) the second-largest political action committee in the United States (*AMA,* 94 F.T.C. at 740).

Bierig countered with expert testimony from Frederick Sturdivant, a professor of business at Ohio State University. Based on a detailed analysis of the AMA's budget, Sturdivant concluded that "92.3 percent . . . went toward noncommercial activities" (*AMA,* 94 F.T.C. at 768–769). He then compared the AMA's budget to that of "major trade associations." "On the basis of an objective comparison to other associations," Sturdivant asserted, "the AMA was fundamentally different from commercial trade associations in that its purpose [was] not to seek the profit of its members" (Memorandum of AMA in Reply to Post-trial Brief, 25 August 1978:17).

Paul Feldstein, an economist from the University of Michigan, challenged the underlying assumptions of Sturdivant's findings. Feldstein testified that Sturdivant mischaracterized "all of AMA's legislative and so-called 'government interface' expenditures as not providing any direct or indirect economic benefits to AMA members" (*AMA*, 94 F.T.C. at 769). "Political activities are the most significant aspect of AMA's benefits to its members," Feldstein asserted (*AMA*, 94 F.T.C. at 769). Feldstein further criticized Sturdivant for failing to include dollars spent on economic research, physician placement services, and reinsurance for medical liability companies "to promote legislative and political goals" (*AMA*, 94 F.T.C. at 770).

Judge Barnes agreed with Feldstein. He found that the approach that Sturdivant used was "unreliable" (*AMA*, 94 F.T.C. at 768). "Dr. Sturdivant's comparative [findings]" Barnes determined, "[are] premised largely on an unsupported assumption—that associations of individuals in the education field are not oriented toward promoting the economic interests of their members" (*AMA*, 94 F.T.C. at 771). Based on the record before him, Judge Barnes concluded that the AMA and the Connecticut societies operated primarily for the "economic well being of their members" (*AMA*, 94 F.T.C. at 924).

Having resolved the jurisdictional issue in favor of the commission, Barnes rejected the contention that the AMA had "abandoned" certain ethical pronouncements. He noted that in 1974, only one year before the case commenced, the Judicial Council had issued the *Report on Physician-Hospital Relations*, which prohibited physicians from signing contracts "whereby any hospital, corporation or lay body . . . may offer for sale or sell for a fee [their] professional services" (*AMA*, 94 F.T.C. at 897). "[For] many years," the *Report* stated, "it has clearly been AMA's position that no lay organization should profit from fees received for physicians' services" (*AMA*, 94 F.T.C. at 897). The association, it seemed, had yet to drop the prohibition. Moreover, certain state and local medical societies, the evidence showed, still enforced the ban on contract practice. Indeed, in 1977 the Judicial Council of the Florida Medical Association declared that employment contracts between physicians and a Daytona Beach HMO were unethical. Armed with these facts, Barnes reasonably could conclude that "discontinuance or abandonment was never intended" (*AMA*, 94 F.T.C. at 969).

The only matter left for Barnes to decide was the appropriate remedy (or penalty) for respondents' transgressions. "It is necessary," he said, "to devise a remedy that will open the channels of communication and prevent obstruction to physicians and . . . HMOs" (*AMA*, 94 F.T.C. at 969). Notwithstanding Justice Blackmun's pronouncement in *Bates* concerning the importance of professional self-regulation, Barnes did not allow medical societies to police physician advertising. "It cannot be concluded in this proceeding or, indeed, in any proceeding," Barnes declared, "that government regulation of false and deceptive advertising, though at times perhaps imperfect, must give way to private regulation to protect the public" (*AMA*, 94 F.T.C. at 971–972). Barnes ordered the AMA to revise its ethics standards on advertising and solicitation but disallowed their reissuance for two years, and then only after obtaining approval from the commission (*AMA*, 94 F.T.C. at 976). In addition, he required the association to end its affiliation with any component organizations that engaged in prohibited activities.

Barnes's proposed order, along with his ruling on agency jurisdiction, comprised the most controversial features of his three-hundred-page decision. Even Costilo acknowledged that the relief Barnes prescribed exceeded his expectations (Costilo 2003). AMA leaders were apoplectic. Robert Hunter, who chaired the Board of Trustees, exclaimed: "We don't feel that lawyers, dentists, engineers, and other professionals, labor unions, business entities, charitable organizations, state and local government entities, should have to ask the federal government if they can issue ethical guidelines to their members and what those guidelines should say" (AMA Will Challenge FTC Decision on Ads 1978). Newton Minow grumbled: "After reading [the decision of the administrative law judge], I submit that George Orwell's 1984 has arrived six years early. The world of Big Brother, seeking to take over the independent, professional practice of medicine, has arrived in 1978" (*Proceedings* December 1978:14). James Sammons joined the chorus of protestors. The FTC, he said, "wants the practice of medicine to descend to the lowest level of the marketplace. As far as the AMA is concerned, 'Let the buyer beware' is an ethic which has no place where human life and health are at stake. Patients should choose their physician on the basis of who is the best doctor, not who is the best advertiser" (Patients Will Be the Real Losers 1978:13).

CONCLUSION

The FTC had won the first battle. This was to be expected, since the initial confrontation occurred in an administrative forum. Moreover, many of the substantive issues in the *AMA* case—the learned professions exemption and the viability of ethical pronouncements on advertising and contract practice—had been resolved by the Supreme Court in favor of the commission either before or during the proceedings. Based on the Court's decision in *Bates*, Judge Barnes could safely conclude that restraints on advertising and solicitation harmed consumers. Based on the Court's holding in *Professional Engineers*, he could find that restrictions on contract practice discouraged the entry of new providers, such as HMOs, that competed with the fee-for-service sector.

The crux of the case, as reflected in the voluminous testimony of expert economists, was the commission's jurisdiction over professional associations and, to a lesser extent, the AMA's claim of abandonment. Jurisdiction over professional associations had not been fully addressed in the past, and an adverse court ruling would have crippled the agency's efforts. Though AMA attorneys strenuously objected to the assertion of commission authority, past events had weakened their position. Since at least the 1930s, the medical hierarchy had pursued the economic interests of AMA members, thus failing to heed the advice of Ray Lyman Wilbur, the head of the Committee on the Costs of Medical Care, and Olin West, the association's former secretary and general manager. Both individuals favored the AMA's pursuit of scientific and educational endeavors. Under the circumstances, the FTC had good reason to assert jurisdiction. The Supreme Court and Congress would now weigh in.

6 A Question of Jurisdiction

Because a ruling of an administrative law judge is subject to internal review, it does not represent the final decision of an administrative agency. Though Michael Pertschuk and his fellow commissioners could reverse Judge Barnes's proposed order, they were not likely to do so, despite threatened action in Congress. In the end, the commissioners modified the order to allow medical societies greater leeway to regulate physicians (a possible response to political pressures) but upheld the ruling on the merits, as well as the assertion of jurisdictional authority.

The ink was barely dry on the FTC's decision when the AMA announced it would appeal to a federal circuit court (AMA Plans Appeal of FTC's Ruling on Physician Advertising 1979). No one should have been surprised. Speaking before the House of Delegates almost a year before the commission had issued its final order, Newton Minow proclaimed: "While we are not optimistic about the results before the FTC, we are hopeful that we shall find justice when we have our day in the federal courts. We will not rest until this misguided decision [of the administrative law judge]—so contrary to the public interest and so alien to our basic American traditions of freedom—is overturned" (*Proceedings* December 1978:15).

THE CIRCUIT COURT REVIEW

As was their prerogative, AMA attorneys sought judicial review in the United States Court of Appeals for the Second Circuit, which was home to the Connecticut and New Haven County medical societies. Although Newton Minow and Jack Bierig could have filed their appeal in the Seventh Circuit, which heard cases in Chicago (the AMA's "home turf"), they selected the Second Circuit because, in Bierig's words, "the Second Circuit had come up with some fairly anti-FTC rulings" (2003). Minow and Bierig, moreover, sought to avoid the Seventh Circuit because it had decided *F.T.C. v. National Commission on Egg Nutrition,* the case that Judge Barnes had used to impose agency oversight. Instead, they relied on the decision of the Eighth Circuit in *Community Blood Bank of Kansas City Area, Inc. v. F.T.C.* (405 F.2d 1011 [8th Cir. 1969]), which had held that the commission lacked jurisdiction over a nonprofit blood bank and several nonprofit hospitals.

Though Minow and Bierig were optimistic about their chances in the Second Circuit, a three-judge panel voted to affirm the decision of the FTC. Judges William Timbers and Dudley Bonsal ruled for the commission, while Judge Walter Mansfield dissented in support of the association. In a short, eleven-page decision, Judge Bonsal held that the commission's findings were "supported by substantial evidence" (*AMA,* 638 F.2d at 449). Bonsal dismissed the AMA's jurisdictional claim, stating, "The business aspects of the activities of the petitioners fall within the scope of the [FTC Act] even if they are considered secondary to the charitable and social aspects of their work" (*AMA,* 638 F.2d at 448). This formulation exceeded the test of *Egg Nutrition.*

According to an item appearing in the *AMA News,* the association's trade journal, "a major portion of the oral arguments" concerned the issue of "mootness," that is, whether the AMA had abandoned its anticompetitive practices (FTC's Action Improper, AMA Tells U.S. Court 1980). In order to avoid dismissal for mootness, a "case or controversy" must exist at all stages of a court proceeding and not simply at the time that a party files a complaint against another party (Gunther 1991:1628). The AMA sought to show that no "case or controversy" existed at the time of the hearing before the circuit court, that belated revisions to the Code of Medical Ethics in 1977 and 1980 had rendered the case moot. But a majority of the panel disagreed. While it is "not clear that the 1977 revisions rescinded prior ethical standards," Judge Bonsal wrote, the revisions nonetheless failed to satisfy the requirements of the antitrust laws (*AMA,* 638 F.2d at 451). "The ban on 'solicitation' . . . was left unchanged," he said, "and the [new] definition of that term incorporates many of the catchwords of earlier restraints" (*AMA,* 638 F.2d at 451 n. 6). The 1980 *Principles* enacted by the AMA only months before the circuit court's decision also failed the test. Not only was "the language of the 1980 *Principles* . . . general and imprecise," Bonsal determined, but "the various written interpretations of the 1957 *Principles* . . . remain in effect" (*AMA,* 638 F.2d at 451).

Judge Mansfield, however, took issue with his colleagues' interpretation:

> I respectfully dissent, for the reason that the steps promptly taken by the [AMA] to modify and up-date its ethical standards after the Supreme

> Court's decision in *Goldfarb* [citation omitted]—revisions that were commenced prior to the FTC's initiation of the present proceeding—satisfy me that the Commission proceeding has been unjustified, unnecessary, and a waste of administrative and judicial resources. In essence the Commission's order, as somewhat watered down by the majority opinion here, is based on outdated facts that long since have ceased to exist. . . . Notwithstanding the mootness of the issues . . . the Commission insisted on pressing for its pound of flesh. In my view the FTC is engaged in the futile business of beating a dead horse. (*AMA*, 638 F.2d at 457)

Fueled by Mansfield's dissent, the AMA promised to fight on. "We shall continue through whatever channels are appropriate," James Sammons insisted, "to work to overturn this decision so that the medical profession can continue to serve the public by establishing ethical standards for its members." "Professionalism itself is at stake," he declared (AMA to Continue FTC Battle 1980). Next in line to review the case was the U.S. Supreme Court.

THE JUSTICES SPLIT

On 23 March 1982, an equally divided Supreme Court (four justices voted to affirm, four voted to reverse) issued a one-line *per curiam* (unsigned) decision that upheld the ruling of the circuit court. Justice Blackmun took "no part in the consideration or decision of [the] case" (*American Medical Ass'n v. F.T.C.*, 455 U.S. 676 [1982]). To Jack Bierig, the outcome was "the greatest anticlimax you could imagine." He and his colleagues had "worked very hard to get the Supreme Court to take the case." "We were elated when the writ of certiorari was granted," Bierig said, "and we worked really hard to write exceptionally good briefs" (2003). At the very least, Bierig anticipated a "thoughtful" dissent that might clarify the issues for members of Congress and for other policy makers. But the Court's split decision denied Bierig and the AMA their consolation prize as well. It was as if the Court had refused to consider the case in the first place.

The *per curiam* decision created much uncertainty and speculation. "Summarily decided cases," Court scholar David O'Brien has observed, "enable the Court to cut down on its workload. But they also engender confusion among the lower courts. . . . Like denials of certiorari petitions, they invite confusion over how the Court views the merits of a case and the lower court ruling" (O'Brien 1990:243). Who were the justices who voted for and against the AMA and the FTC? What were their reasons for doing so? Was jurisdiction the principal stumbling block, or was it the issue of abandonment? Why did Justice Blackmun recuse himself? How would he have voted, and what effect would he have had on the outcome had he participated in the Court's deliberations?

Bierig viewed Blackmun's failure to participate as "a very ominous thing" (2003). "We didn't think we were going to get the liberal wing on the Court," he said, "but we figured we'd probably get the conservative wing." Absent Blackmun's involvement, Bierig contemplated a 4–4 tie. "We thought Blackmun would be very sympathetic to us," Bierig said, because of his former ties to the medical profession. (Blackmun had been counsel to the Mayo Clinic.) Blackmun, moreover, was a swing vote, a moderate who believed that the learned professions should be given special consideration under the antitrust laws.

Aside from Blackmun's prior opinion for the Court in *Bates v. State Bar of Arizona* and his concurring opinion in *National Society of Professional Engineers v. United States,* there was evidence that Blackmun sympathized with the AMA's position. One of Blackmun's law clerks highlighted the assertion of jurisdictional authority by the commission in a legal memorandum. "The issue of extension of FTC [jurisdiction] to the petitioners and similar groups may merit review," the clerk wrote. "The Court has given clear signals [in *Bates*] that responsible professional self-regulation is permissible. . . . Arguably, the disapproval of the 1976 guidelines that is inherent in [*AMA*] undercuts the ability of professional organizations to provide meaningful guidance to their professions" (Harry A. Blackmun Papers, Box 351, 80–1690 [File Memorandum, 8]).

Although law clerks do not speak for the justices they serve, they often mirror their views on crucial issues by virtue of time spent together, similar intellectual proclivities, and knowledge of past decisions. In this instance, Blackmun's law clerk captured the justice's temperate approach toward professional self-regulation. Indeed, Blackmun's opinion for the Court in *Bates* envisioned a greater role for professional associations in fashioning ethical standards than did the opinions of Judge Barnes and that of the full commission. Whether Blackmun would have voted to reverse on grounds of mootness or for lack of jurisdiction ultimately calls for speculation.

The positions of the eight justices who participated in *AMA* are more certain. The meticulously prepared conference notes of Justice Blackmun contain the comments of his colleagues during their deliberations. According to Blackmun's conference notes, Chief Justice Burger and Justices Powell, Rehnquist, and O'Connor voted to reverse, while Justices Brennan, White, Marshall, and Stevens voted to affirm (Harry A. Blackmun Papers,

Box 351, 80–1690 [File Notes]). This simple breakdown, which resembled the existing liberal and conservative blocs on the Court, belied important but subtle differences. Powell and O'Connor, for instance, believed that the FTC did not have jurisdiction over the learned professions. "A learned profession was not a 'business' in 1914 [the date Congress passed the FTC Act]," Powell declared; Congress did not intend to cover the "learned professions," O'Connor claimed. But Rehnquist did not agree—"[The] FTC Act can change," he stated, "just as the antitrust laws did." Rather, like Judge Mansfield, Rehnquist subscribed to the abandonment position. Chief Justice Burger professed a third point of view—one based on the merits. Burger asserted that the commission had not proven that the AMA and its component societies had engaged in price-fixing. The "FTC has gone wild here," Blackmun reported Burger as saying (Harry A. Blackmun Papers, Box 351, 80–1690 [File Notes]).

Ironically, the Court's mostly conservative bloc opposed the Reagan administration and its Chicago school disciples. Though he did not argue the case before the Court, William Baxter, a Stanford law professor whom President Reagan had appointed to head the Antitrust Division of the Department of Justice, appeared on the brief with Howard Shapiro, an FTC attorney, and Barry Costilo. Baxter, in Clark Havighurst's words, represented the "high water mark" of Chicago school thinking at the Department of Justice (2003). To Chicagoans, "the only relevant question in evaluating a restraint of trade is whether the restraint promotes or suppresses competition" (Gerhart 1982:321). Noneconomic considerations, which Blackmun, Rehnquist, and Burger had refused to ignore in earlier cases, were irrelevant under Chicago school principles.

Justices Stevens and White were the principal advocates of an antitrust analysis that treated business and professions alike. They countered Chief Justice Burger's spirited defense of the Code of Medical Ethics. A graduate of the University of Chicago and Northwestern Law School, Stevens practiced antitrust law in Chicago until appointed to the federal bench in 1971. While teaching antitrust part-time at Chicago and Northwestern Law Schools in the 1950s, Stevens undoubtedly crossed paths with Milton Friedman. Stevens was a friend of Edward Levi, who, as dean of Chicago Law School, became attorney general in the administration of President Gerald Ford (Canon 1991:343). Though both Stevens and White would later break with the Chicagoans over other matters, they adhered, as did Clark Havighurst, to the view that competition and the factors affecting it were the only relevant considerations.

Justices Brennan and Marshall, according to Blackmun's conference notes, did not offer any substantive comments during deliberations. Predisposed to the liberal camp, Brennan and Marshall lacked ties to those who supported the professions or the economic theory of regulation. As champions of civil liberties and equal protection, they undoubtedly disdained medicine's checkered past, particularly its discriminatory and exclusionary practices. "Whether the issue was political, racial, gender, or economic equality," Brennan and Marshall "forcefully articulated the egalitarian ethic" (Grunes 2003:226).

The beliefs of liberal consumer advocates, such as Brennan and Marshall, intersected with those of Chicago school economists in the FTC's assault on the anticompetitive practices of organized medicine. By a narrow margin, an untidy majority of the U.S. Supreme Court kept the agency's agenda intact. While some legal scholars proclaimed the demise of footnote 17 following *Professional Engineers* (Greaney 1989:616–618), the distinction between business and profession that Justices Stewart and Burger had articulated still resonated in *AMA*. Because the restraint on competitive bidding in *Professional Engineers* was, in Blackmun's words, "grossly overbroad," the case did not display the full range of individual opinions. Nor did any of the other antitrust cases involving the learned professions that the Court decided in the late 1970s and early 1980s. Yet a "deep split in the Court" existed (Muris 2000:286), as the *AMA* case clearly attested. The split would surface again in several First Amendment cases, many of them decided in the 1980s and 1990s, in which certain justices announced their opposition to *Bates* (Muris 2000:280–288).

THE BATTLE IN CONGRESS TO STRIP THE FTC OF JURISDICTION OVER STATE-REGULATED PROFESSIONS

Chief Justice John Marshall established the power of the Supreme Court "to say what the law is" more than two hundred years ago (*Marbury v. Madison* [1803]). But individuals and organizations who were dissatisfied with a Court decision could still lobby Congress to change or clarify existing law. On 24 March 1982, one day after the Supreme Court issued its *per curiam* decision in *AMA*, the association reaffirmed its support for congressional legislation to exempt state-regulated professions from FTC oversight (AMA Special Collections [Statement of James Sammons, 24 March 1982]). Spokespersons for the association implied that the reason for the 4–4 split was that the justices were divided over the scope of agency jurisdiction. "Four Justices of the Supreme Court apparently have concluded that the FTC does in fact lack jurisdiction over the professions," Newton Minow said. "Yet not only did the Commission deny our efforts to raise the jurisdictional issue, but the Administrative Law Judge, a career employee of the FTC, imposed serious sanctions against the AMA for even raising the issue" (U.S. Congress, House, 1982a:410 [Statement of Newton Minow]).

There was precedent for congressional relief from the antitrust laws—public utilities, securities and commodities exchanges, the insurance industry, labor unions, agricultural cooperatives, and others had received special exemptions of one sort or another. But the AMA's initiative was more circumscribed. Its problem was not so much with the antitrust laws as with the commission itself. "Only the forum would be changed," James Sammons testified before Congress. "The U.S. Department of Justice can enforce the federal antitrust laws, state attorneys general have enforcement powers, and civil antitrust actions [would be] available," he said (AMA Special Collections [Statement of James Sammons, 24 March 1982:4–5]). Clearly, the FTC had struck a nerve.

Efforts of the AMA to restrain the FTC commenced in 1977, when the association successfully opposed the agency's attempt to have Congress clarify its authority over nonprofit organizations (*Proceedings* December 1977:21). In 1979, 1980, and 1981, the AMA backed various proposals to curtail the commission's asserted authority. Debate centered on two pieces of legislation—a Senate bill, known as McClure-Melcher (S. 1984), and a House bill, known as Luken-Lee (H.R. 3722). McClure-Melcher offered total exemption from investigations, rule makings, and adjudications, while Luken-Lee sought to place a moratorium on commission actions concerning state-regulated professions.

Sponsors of McClure-Melcher and Luken-Lee reintroduced their initiatives in the 1982 session of Congress, soon after the Supreme Court decision in *AMA*. The timing seemed auspicious. Members of Congress and the Reagan administration were unhappy with commission efforts to regulate certain industries during the 1970s. "Now, with a Reagan administration and a sympathetic Congress intent upon dismantling all forms of regulatory restraint," Pertschuk proclaimed, "the AMA and its allies seemed poised on the brink of triumph" (1986:83). At a hearing before a House subcommittee on 1 April 1982, Representative Gary Lee stated: "As we begin these hearings on the reauthorization of the [FTC], I have to admit that I do not approach this particular issue with the same sense of optimism just expressed by some of my colleagues on the subcommittee. While it is correct that legislative jurisdiction over the [FTC] was only recently vested with the subcommittee, my experiences with the FTC as a member of the subcommittee have been anything but encouraging. I might add that if these experiences are at all indicative of the future, the outlook is bleak" (U.S. Congress, House, 1982a:4 [Statement of Gary A. Lee]).

But AMA leaders were wrong to assume that that the White House would back their efforts. As proponents of the Chicago school, the administration's appointees opposed trade restraints, whether government or private. James Miller, who replaced Pertschuk as the new head of the FTC, was an outspoken critic of a special exemption. In an opinion piece for a Washington news service, Miller wrote: "The main argument advanced by professional groups in support of an exemption is that we interfere with legitimate forms of self-regulation and state control. If that were true—if FTC oversight were simply another layer of needless, bureaucratic regulation—I'd be the first to say so and to recommend change. But it is just not true" (Miller 1982:11). David Stockman, in a letter to Congressman James Florio, backed Miller's position. "The Administration would not support proposals, such as those contained in S. 1984 and H.R. 3722, to grant blanket immunity to the professions from Commission's antitrust and consumer protection jurisdiction," Stockman declared (AMA Special Collections [Stockman to Florio, 31 March 1982]).

Stockman's letter piqued James Sammons and others at the AMA. "We must protest strongly the recent letter from David Stockman . . . and the fact that no professions were consulted by the Administration [before it announced its] position," Sammons stated in telegrams to Michael Deaver, James Baker, and Edwin Meese. "I cannot emphasize too much how important this issue is to AMA and other professions who have supported this Administration on its key goals," Sammons continued. "You may recall that we have discussed this in every meeting with the President and in meetings with you and your staff" (AMA Special Collections [Sammons Telegrams, 2 April 1982]).

In addition to key members of the Reagan administration, various consumer groups and allied health practitioners also opposed McClure-Melcher and Luken-Lee. The Consumer Federation called McClure-Melcher the "Professions Income Maximization Act of 1982" (U.S. Congress, House, 1982a:334 [Statement of David I. Greenberg]); the American Association of Retired Persons argued that "consumers will suffer direct and tangible injury" (517 [Statement of the National Retired Teachers Association and the American Association of Retired Persons]); Public Citizen's Congress Watch judged the proposal "offensive" (468 [Statement of Jay Angoff]). Nurses complained about barriers to competition (544–545 [Statement of Patricia A. Jones]); chiropractors noted the "long history" of "price fixing, bans on advertising, boycotts and other anticompetitive practices" (572–

573 [Statement of Bruce Nordstrom]); psychologists declared that "the most abusive profession in regard to psychology is the medical profession" (810 [Clarence Martin and Michael Pallak to Robert Kasten, Jr.]). U.S. newspapers echoed these positions. According to Michael Pertschuk, the tally was 0 in favor of the exemption, 154 against (1986:93). The *Wall Street Journal*, normally a foe of government regulation, stated: "On this one, we are on the side of the Feds" (as quoted in Pertschuk 1986:92).

Though the forces aligned against it were formidable, the AMA had extensive resources and allies of its own. Joining the AMA were several specialty societies, including the American Society of Anesthesiologists, the American Society of Internal Medicine, the American Academy of Ophthalmology, the College of American Pathologists, and the American Academy of Orthopaedic Surgeons. Also on the side of the AMA were engineers, dentists, veterinarians, and several state bar associations. Engineers professed, "The historic standards of professional practice must not be reduced to the marketplace standard of buyer and seller" (U.S. Congress, House, 1982a:431 [Statement of Milton F. Lunch]). Veterinarians asserted, "The orientation and mandate of the [FTC] are focused solely on economic and commercial questions. This entails the further assumption that professional services are essentially fungible, which common sense tells us is not true" (655 [Statement of the American Veterinary Medical Association]).

Despite the exemption's appeal to several professions, the battle to remove the FTC's jurisdiction was primarily about the AMA. According to Jay Angoff, who led the campaign against the exemption for Congress Watch: "When I was at the FTC in 1979 and 1980 and when the AMA issue started, it was always referred to as the 'professions exemption.' Who cares about the 'professions exemption?' We just all the time called it the 'AMA exemption.' We didn't talk about lawyers, dentists, architects; this was the AMA" (as quoted in Pertschuk 1986:97–98). The association, moreover, bankrolled the effort. On 10 June 1982, the *Washington Post* reported: "192 of the 196 members of the House of Representatives who cosponsored the legislation received a total of $1.14 million from the [AMA]" (Mayer 1982).

On 11 May 1982, the Senate Commerce Committee voted ten to five in favor of the exemption, while a majority of House members, flush with AMA dollars, agreed to cosponsor Luken-Lee. Sensing an imminent victory for the association, opponents changed tactics. With the backing of the Reagan administration, Congressman James T. Broyhill proposed a compromise to Luken-Lee that would "preclude the Commission from second guessing State judgments on licensing, education and quality of care issues" yet would leave intact the agency's authority over commercial and consumer protection matters (U.S. Congress, House, 1982b [Statement of James T. Broyhill]). But AMA leaders were in no mood to compromise. Joseph Boyle, chair of the Board of Trustees, wrote members of Congress: "While it has been said that [Broyhill's substitute] addresses only the 'business' side of professional practices, a reading of this substitute amendment shows that this characterization is wrong. Moreover, business aspects cannot be so neatly separated from professional practice" (AMA Special Collections [Boyle to House members, 20 September 1982]).

A battle ensued in the House between those who favored Broyhill's compromise legislation and those who favored Luken-Lee. Five members of Congress—Richard Cheney, Delbert Latta, Bill Frenzel, James Quillen, and Trent Lott—circulated a letter opposing the Broyhill substitute. They wrote:

> The Broyhill substitute can hardly be considered a compromise when it would give the FTC everything it wants and the other side nothing. Because of its breadth, it would not have prevented one single act of harassment by the Commission toward the professions over the last seven years. No amendment is perfect, but given the 4–4 Supreme Court split and all the controversy, differences of opinion and doubt surrounding this issue, the moratorium approach of the Luken-Lee amendment would certainly seem to make more sense. We urge you to give the benefit of the doubt in this case to someone other than the regulatory bureaucracy for a change—and to oppose the Broyhill substitute to the Luken-Lee amendment when it comes up on the floor. (AMA Special Collections [Cheney et al. to House members, 23 September 1982])

Notwithstanding the opposition of key House Republicans, the Reagan administration remained firm. On 27 September, Vice President George Bush wrote to Broyhill to extend his support (AMA Special Collections [as stated in Rial to Schweiker, 4 November 1982]). Furious over continuing efforts of administration officials to defeat Luken-Lee, AMA president William Rial admonished Vice President Bush:

> We are very disappointed that we were not consulted by your office prior to the sending of your letter [of 27 September]. . . . Many believe that the FTC under former Chairman Mike Pertschuk epitomized everything that was wrong with federal regulation. . . . The election of President Reagan . . . gave many of us hope that unnecessary or duplicate federal regulation would be eliminated. In many areas, this has happened. Yet the FTC continues to assert authority over professionals and continues to try to expand its powers. We would expect the Administration to oppose these efforts as inconsistent with its program of deregulation. Yet, to our concern you are actively supporting them. FTC Chairman Miller,

> a self-proclaimed deregulator, is also supporting these efforts. It is regrettable that on this issue Mr. Miller and Mr. Pertschuk are in agreement. (AMA Special Collections [Rial to Bush, 20 October 1982])

Rial also wrote to President Reagan on 25 October. His letter reminded the president of the AMA's support in the recent election and demanded his aid in return:

> As you may recall from several visits by AMA leaders with you—first as Presidential nominee, later as President-Elect and recently as President—our position in these areas has been consistently one of support for your ideals. . . . We believe, however, that actions the [FTC] has taken against the professions are the antithesis of your views. . . . To overcome these actions of the FTC, legislation is now pending to make clear that Congress has not given the FTC authority over professionals or their nonprofit associations. . . . The AMA was shocked when OMB Director David Stockman wrote earlier this year opposing the legislation. . . . We find it hard to understand how an Administration spokesman can publicly espouse views on this issue which seem to us so divergent from your own. . . . We certainly hope that you will make it clear to your associates that support of the FTC on this issue is contradictory to the fundamental goals of your administration to reduce federal regulation and to enhance state and individual responsibility. (AMA Special Collections [Rial and Boyle to Reagan, 25 October 1982])

In their responses to Rial, prominent members of the Reagan administration affirmed that Broyhill's proposal satisfied the president's goals. "Representative Broyhill's substitute . . . is, in our view, an appropriate compromise between the Commission's present unrestricted authority over the professions and Representative Luken's proposal to exempt the professions totally from FTC law enforcement," the vice president said (AMA Special Collections [Bush to Rial, 8 November 1982]). "The President has not wavered from his goals of eliminating unnecessary regulation and encouraging increased state responsibility," Reagan's counsel, Fred Fielding, stated. "It is his firm belief, however, that exempting professional groups from the FTC is not consistent with these goals. . . . The letter written by OMB Director Stockman that you mentioned, as well as the letters written by Vice President Bush and HHS Secretary Schweiker in support of Representative Broyhill's proposal, were written only after the President's position was clear" (AMA Special Collections [Fielding to Rial, 12 January 1983; Fielding to Boyce, 12 January 1983]).

The showdown over the Broyhill compromise and Luken-Lee occurred in the House on 1 December 1982, a week earlier than expected. "Finding itself with a murderous calendar and a free hour," Arthur Amolsch reported, "the leadership called up the FTC's pending authorization bill and with it the emotional controversy over language proposed by Congressman Donald Luken to exempt the 'professions' from FTC enforcement jurisdiction." Taken by surprise, House Representatives who backed the commission failed to muster the votes needed to pass Broyhill's proposal and defeat Luken-Lee. The Broyhill substitute lost by 13 votes (208–195, with 31 abstentions), while Luken-Lee won by a comfortable margin (245–155), thus "indicating that the compromise had been worth 44 votes to FTC backers" (*FTC:Watch,* 3 December 1982:6).

Attention now shifted to the Senate. During an all-night session on 17 December, senators debated the merits of McClure-Melcher, which now appeared as an amendment to a year-end appropriations bill (Pertschuk 1986:82). Supporters argued that the "amendment is fully consistent with the original purposes of the [FTC]." "The Clayton Act," they said, "specifically did not direct the FTC to investigate nonprofit professional associations for antitrust violations. [Moreover,] the Sherman Act specifically delegated to the Justice Department—not the FTC—responsibility for investigating these nonprofit associations for alleged antitrust violations" (U.S. Congress, Senate, 1982 *[Senate Record Vote Analysis]*).

Unlike House members, senators who opposed the exemption were prepared. Their champion, Warren Rudman, "had, in the previous 48 hours, personally lobbied every member of the Senate" (Pertschuk 1986:84). Immediately before a vote to table the amendment, Rudman spoke:

> For the first time in 20 years doctors are making housecalls. Physicians are swarming around the Dirksen and Russell Senate Office Buildings. Some doctors are so concerned about the health of the Members of this Chamber that they have filled the reception room to capacity. We are not fooled. It is time to give the American people a break. The McClure-Melcher amendment would strip the FTC of any power to enforce this Nation's antitrust laws with respect to State-regulated "professionals," and would exempt such professionals from Federal laws against consumer fraud and deception . . . this amendment is a clever attempt by some very high-priced lobbyists to get a large Christmas present for their clients. The amendment is anticonsumer and anticompetitive. The overwhelming public response is that this broad exemption is wrong: It is bad economics, bad politics, and, most importantly, it is simply unfair. (U.S. Congress, Senate, 1982 *[Senate Record Vote Analysis]*)

The succeeding vote tally was fifty-nine senators for tabling the amendment, thirty-seven against. Party affiliation was not a factor. Sixty percent of Republican senators and 64 percent of Democratic senators voted to table the amendment. Four senators did not vote, two from each party (U.S. Congress, Senate, 1982 [*Senate Record Vote Analysis*]). Though the issue would resurface in succeeding years, victory would continue to elude the association.

The results of the final vote in the Senate captured the political alliance that existed between consumer advocates and free-market proponents. Consumer advocates, such as Michael Pertschuk and Jay Angoff of Congress Watch, pressed liberal members of the House and Senate, while market proponents, such as James Miller, David Stockman, and other high-ranking officials in the Reagan administration, solicited neoconservatives. Medicine's support for Ronald Reagan in the presidential election of 1980 was not enough to overcome the administration's opposition to a special exemption. A special exemption ran in the face of the market-based principles that President Reagan and his advisors frequently and consistently espoused. Superior funding and organization did not always guarantee victory. Ideology trumped self-interest in this particular matter.

THE REACH OF *AMA*

More than a decade after the Supreme Court ruled in *AMA*, the parties still clung to their trial-hardened positions. Angry over a 1993 speech in which the commission claimed credit for "the development of managed care plans," James Todd, executive vice president of the AMA, wrote FTC chair Janet Steiger to express his displeasure. "The FTC's 1979 Order against the AMA was not 'necessary to the creation of managed care plans,'" Todd asserted. "Any AMA-imposed restrictions on the ability of physicians to contract with such plans had ended before 1950, and all vestiges of such restrictions had been voluntarily eliminated well in advance of the Commission's 1979 Order," he declared (FTC Special Collections [Todd to Steiger, 23 March 1993]). Steiger responded: "It may well be that the degree of AMA's opposition to contract practice had lessened by the time of issuance of the FTC complaint, but the Commission found, after a full trial on the merits, that the ethical rules continued to have anticompetitive effects." "In sum," Steiger said, "there is ample support for my statement that the Commission's case against AMA freed physicians to join managed care plans and was one of the factors necessary for the development of such plans" (FTC Special Collections [Steiger to Todd, 28 April 1993]).

Todd's efforts to minimize the importance of *AMA* belie the association's own rhetoric. "By what right," James Sammons asked in 1979, "does the FTC insist that the AMA, and state and local medical societies, play ab-

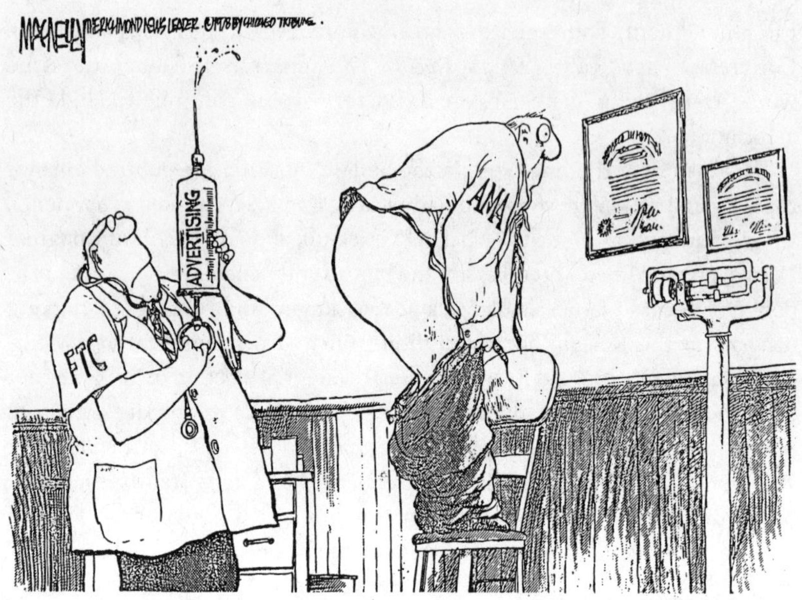

Cartoon by Jeff MacNelly, December 1978.

solutely no role in setting ethical standards for the promotional practices of its members?" (*Proceedings* July 1979:19). "The Federal Trade Commission looks for all the world like it's out to get doctors," warned Richard Peck, the Washington editor of *Medical Economics* (Peck 1979:29). "I think [what the FTC is doing is] unadulterated hogwash," emoted Wallace Mathews, a family practitioner from Minnesota (as quoted in Chapman 1980:23). Mark Gorney, a board member of the American Society of Plastic and Reconstructive Surgeons, complained: "We think we're on the hook because of a profound misunderstanding. What we see as our duty to protect the patient against rip-off artists and charlatans, the FTC interprets as an infringement of First Amendment rights. . . . What we believe is our obligation to maintain the highest possible standards of quality, the FTC views as illegal restraint of trade" (Gorney 1980:34).

Virtually every major medical journal and spokesperson for the profession joined the fray. Arnold Relman, the editor of the *New England Journal of Medicine,* wrote: "If this crucial legal contest should ultimately be resolved fully in favor of the FTC, not only would the commercial solicitation of patients be encouraged but medical societies would no longer be

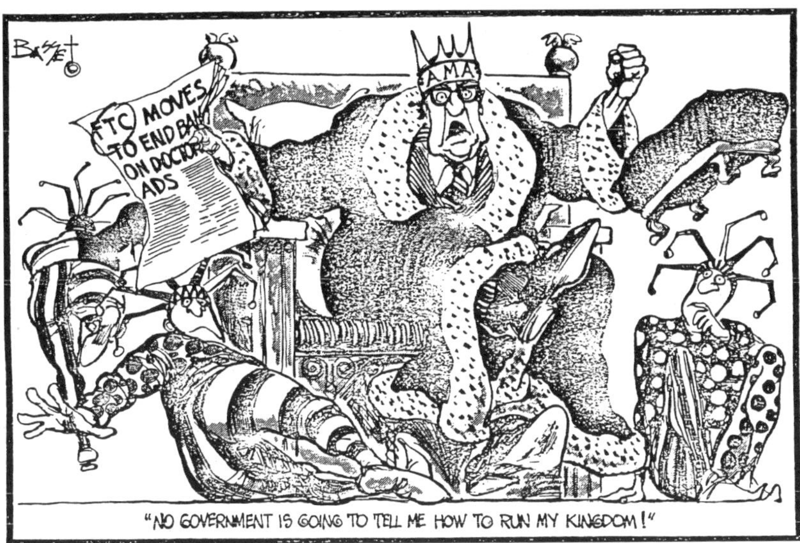

Cartoon by Gene Basset, December 1978. Reproduced by permission of Scripps Howard Newspapers.

allowed to discipline their members for unethical advertising practices. The power to regulate medical advertising would be transferred to governmental authority" (Relman 1978:477). James Snyder, Washington correspondent for *Physician's Management,* observed: "When the Federal Trade Commission filed suit charging that the AMA's code of ethics on advertising violated antitrust laws, it was proof to many doctors that the Carter administration had sided with the bureaucrats" (Snyder 1982:28). Stu Chapman of the journal *Legal Aspects of Medical Practice* exclaimed: "For years, the Federal Trade Commission has flattened just about every medical group that stood in the way of its full-throttle campaign to mow down anticompetitive business practices" (Chapman 1980:22).

The case had become a cause célèbre. Cartoons lampooned the AMA's fate. One showed the FTC administering an injection labeled "advertising" into the AMA's posterior. Another depicted the AMA sitting on a throne, complaining, "No government is going to tell me how to run my kingdom!"

AMA led to much hand-wringing and some introspection among medicine's leaders. Medical ethicist Leon Kass wrote: "Outside the profession, there are various efforts to cut medicine down to size: widespread malpractice litigation, massive government regulation, and various attempts, by consumer groups and others, to redefine medicine as a trade rather than a profession and the physician as a morally neutered technician for hire under contract." But in denouncing medicine's critics, Kass also "acknowledge[d] that organized medicine and its contemporary practitioners may have brought some of these troubles on themselves" (Kass 1983:1305). Kass's statements augured a transitional period marked by inter- and intraorganizational strife and turmoil. An editorial by the AMA's Lester King reflected the sea change that was occurring. "A vast mythology has grown up regarding the unselfish devotion of physicians," King wrote. "The myths, while they do contain grains of truth and, moreover, satisfy ideal cravings, are—perhaps fortunately—gradually disintegrating. The whole concept of a profession, and its relation to trade, has gradually been changing, along with the entire social and economic structure" (King 1985:2709–2710).

Far from being the limiting force that James Todd suggested it was, the *AMA* case had important legal, political, social, and economic implications for the health care industry and for the professional regime in particular. By signaling an end to ethical restraints in the economic realm, the commission cut the ties that bound rank-and-file physicians to their national, state, and local medical societies, thereby undermining the entire disciplinary structure of the medical hierarchy. Stripped of their organizing principles and enforcement mechanisms, medical societies lost the legal and ethical authority to resist the formation of large-scale provider networks and the integration of insurance products and delivery systems. The market regime that *AMA* announced became the standard-bearer for the emerging social and economic order. Competition was the new buzzword. The antitrust laws would ensure that competition took hold and that health plans, hospitals, and individual practitioners (physicians and nonphysicians alike) were free from the restrictions of professional associations.

7 Drawing the Line between Clinical and Business Practices

Viewed in historical context, the early health care agenda of the FTC was bold, even radical, in design. It reflected the preferences of its chief architects, Clark Havighurst and Jim Liebeler, and the prominent position of the FTC in the policy-making community in the mid-1970s. The main focus of the commission's early investigations and prosecutions was on removing barriers to competition in the commercial sphere. These barriers included professional control of insurers and health plans, professional review of reimbursement standards, and ethical restraints on advertising, solicitation, and contract practice.

But there were limits to what the FTC could or should do to advance competition. Before moving against potentially anticompetitive practices, the agency had to consider the practical ramifications. Medicine's dominant role in the standardization of clinical performance and in the production and dissemination of information to consumers was particularly problematic. AMA control of accrediting bodies, such as the Liaison Committee on Medical Education and the Joint Commission on Accreditation of Hospitals, raised legitimate concerns. Should the commission delve into these matters, or should it, for prudential and political reasons, stay away from issues related to scientific and technical endeavors?

PROFESSIONAL ASSOCIATIONS AS BARGAINING AGENTS FOR PHYSICIANS

An important function of organized medicine was as arbiter for physicians in their dealings with the insurance industry in the United States. Medicine allowed only two forms of health insurance to prevail in the private market before the advent of antitrust: commercial indemnity and service benefit.

Indemnity arrangements reimbursed patients, not physicians, for medical expenses. Because patients paid their physicians and then sought reimbursement from their insurers, insurers had little control over the behavior of physicians. Service-benefit plans, on the other hand, paid physicians directly for patient care. Because these plans reimbursed physicians, not patients, there was greater risk of third-party interference. Blue Shield was a form of service-benefit plan (see Starr 1982:290–295).

Medicine's influence over Blue Shield began to decline in the 1960s "as increasing numbers of public representatives were added to the boards of many plans" (Havighurst 1988:251). Some state medical societies, such as Michigan, stopped appointing members to Blue Shield boards as early as 1970 (*In the Matter of Michigan State Medical Society,* 101 F.T.C. 191, 267 [1983] *[MSMS]*), while other state societies continued to select "all or a majority of members" until the late 1970s and early 1980s, when fear of antitrust action curtailed the practice (FTC Special Collections [Bureau of Competition, Staff Report, April 1979:91–124]). In late 1976, the AMA discontinued the appointment of members to serve on the Blue Shield Association Board (*Proceedings* June 1978:184).

With the attenuation of physician control, medical societies became potential adversaries of Blue Shield. Professional associations discovered that "as some Blue plans came to be more independent, . . . the bargaining process between them became more intense." This raised antitrust issues that, though present in prior dealings between associations and plans, did not cause serious concern. "Given the gradualness of the evolution away from strict provider control," Clark Havighurst opined, "it probably never occurred to anyone that providers should be negotiated with only individually and not collectively." Because "there was usually no explicit agreement on actual prices to be charged or paid, the most obvious antitrust concern—price—was not aroused, and it was possible to see other issues, such as cost containment measures, merely as questions of ethics and administrative detail" (Havighurst 1978:382). Other factors also discouraged antitrust scrutiny. These factors included state regulation of insurers, the special exemption from antitrust for insurance under the McCarran-Ferguson Act, and the large size of some Blue Shield plans.

While in residence at the FTC from 1978 to 1979, Havighurst alerted the health shop to a situation brewing in Michigan where he felt "collective bargaining could not be justified" (Havighurst 2003). Problems had surfaced in 1974 when the Michigan State Medical Society formed a "negotiating committee" to address doctors' concerns, including excessive paperwork, the use of regional rather than statewide "screens" for reimbursement purposes, and the failure to update billing histories of participating physicians. Unable to broker an agreement, the committee moved to collect "departicipation proxies" from physicians in an attempt to pressure Blue Cross/Blue Shield. Although this "first proxy solicitation" never occurred (Blue Cross/Blue Shield made several concessions), discord continued when Blue Cross/Blue Shield introduced certain cost-containment initiatives designed to limit physicians' fees (*MSMS,* 101 F.T.C. at 267–271).

One such initiative arose in connection with collective bargaining agreements between the United Auto Workers and the Big Three automakers—Ford, Chrysler, and General Motors. The Vision Care Plan and the Hearing Care Plan that the UAW and the automakers agreed upon restricted or denied payment to nonparticipating physicians, that is, physicians not associated with Blue Cross/Blue Shield (*MSMS,* 101 F.T.C. at 234). The medical society claimed that the new payment arrangements and benefits "interfered with the physician-patient relationship and discriminated against patients of nonparticipating providers" (*MSMS,* 101 F.T.C. at 235). In retaliation, the medical society inaugurated a second proxy solicitation and encouraged doctors to provide "only barely minimal data" on claim forms, thus "increas[ing] both administrative costs and delays in payment of claims" (*MSMS,* 101 F.T.C. at 275).

An FTC investigation of the medical society led to the filing of charges on 27 July 1979. FTC attorneys asserted that the medical society had "engage[d] in concerted action to restrict, regulate, impede or interfere with the health care cost containment or reimbursement policies of [Blue Cross/Blue Shield]" (*MSMS,* 101 F.T.C. at 192). The medical society claimed that its actions had "no effect on fee levels," that its "recommendations to members were merely policy positions," and that "it did not speak for or bind any of its members as a group" (*MSMS,* 101 F.T.C. at 280). None of these assertions proved convincing. Commissioner David Clanton, writing for a unanimous FTC, stated: "Thus, at the outset we find that the very creation of the Division of Negotiations reveals a collective purpose on the part of [the medical society] and its members to go beyond the point of giving advice to third party payers; in fact, it reveals a purpose to organize and empower a full-fledged representative to negotiate and resolve controversies surrounding physician profiles, screens and other similar matters" (*MSMS,* 101 F.T.C. at 285).

Having established that a conspiracy existed, Clanton determined whether the boycott was illegal per se. Opinions differed on this issue. Commissioners Michael Pertschuk and Patricia Bailey found the conduct of the medical society unlawful per se, while Clanton and two other commissioners refused to "close the door on all asserted procompetitive justifications" (*MSMS,* 101 F.T.C. at 291, 310–312). But a closer review under the rule of reason could not save the medical society. "While we are not addressing ethical standards in this case," Clanton wrote, "many of the quality and patient welfare arguments asserted here have a ring similar to those advanced in *AMA*. . . . We find no suggestion among [the medical society's] justifications that the concerted behavior here enhanced competition in any market by injecting new elements or forms of competition, reducing entry barriers, or facilitating or broadening consumer choice" (*MSMS,* 101 F.T.C. at 294–295).

The commission issued an order which modified only slightly that of the administrative law judge who held against the medical society. The FTC's order prohibited the medical society from, among other things, "acting as an agent for any of its members in their dealings with third party payers concerning reimbursement or the acceptance or rejection of any participation agreement" (*MSMS,* 101 F.T.C. at 302). *MSMS* made explicit what, after *Goldfarb,* seemed implicit—that is, medical societies could not act as arbiters or collective bargainers for physicians in their dealings with insurance companies or other third-party payers. Henceforth, professional associations would have to devise alternative means for representing physicians' interests in the economic sphere, or they would have to vacate the field altogether.

THE *MARICOPA* CASE

Long before the FTC's ruling in *MSMS,* professional associations had devised an approach that they hoped would counter the threat of prepaid health care without engaging in the kind of "heavy-handed" tactics that prompted antitrust scrutiny. The approach that they devised involved the formation of society-controlled health plans, or Foundations for Medical Care (FMCs). FMCs adhered to basic principles of fee-for-service and free choice of physician. The general idea was that FMCs would hold down costs of physicians who joined the plan, extend generous benefits to subscribers, and police the quality of medical care. With the cooperation of participating physicians, the plan would undercut the competition. Once market superiority had been achieved, the status quo ante could return (see Brown 1983:43).

Two types of FMCs had made their appearance by the early 1970s: the claims-review FMC and the comprehensive FMC (Egdahl 1973:491). Claims-review FMCs performed peer review for fiscal intermediaries, such as Medicare and Medicaid. Comprehensive FMCs, on the other hand, sponsored prepaid plans in addition to setting standards and ensuring quality health care (Egdahl 1973:491–492). Both types were potential obstacles to HMO development, the former because it had the power to regulate and thus hinder HMO performance, the latter because it could prevent HMOs from entering the market altogether (U.S. Congress, Senate, 1974:1041–1042, 1083 [Statement of Clark C. Havighurst]).

In 1969, the Maricopa County Medical Society formed an FMC (Maricopa County comprises the city of Phoenix, Arizona). The purpose of the FMC was to "promot[e] fee-for-service medicine and to provide the community with a competitive alternative to existing health insurance plans" (*Arizona v. Maricopa County Medical Soc.*, 457 U.S. 332, 339 [1982]). All physicians who were members of the county society could join the foundation for a renewable one-year term. Seventy percent, or 1,750, of the doctors who practiced medicine in Maricopa County became members of the Maricopa FMC. A neighboring medical society in Pima County also established a foundation; 400 physicians joined the Pima FMC (*Maricopa*, 457 U.S. at 339).

Promoters of the Maricopa and Pima foundations adopted maximum fee schedules "to prevent opportunism by doctors" (see Liebeler 1986:1035). "It is obvious that in setting up a prepaid health plan, some type of control of payment to physicians is necessary, and since the comprehensive FMC is dedicated to the fee-for-service principle of reimbursement, no program can be actuarially sound without agreement by physicians on maximum fees," proponents claimed (Egdahl 1973:492). But the adoption of maximum fee schedules did not sit well with Arizona's attorney general. The maximum fee schedules that the FMCs established, the attorney general contended, served to stabilize and increase physicians' fees, leading to higher insurance premiums (*Maricopa*, 457 U.S. at 341–342). In 1978, the state of Arizona (hereafter Arizona) brought an antitrust action against the county medical societies and their respective FMCs. Arizona alleged that the maximum fee schedules constituted illegal price-fixing and asked the federal district court for a preliminary injunction.

The case turned on the proof required to show a violation of section 1 of the Sherman Act. If the maximum fee schedules were illegal per se, then Arizona needed few facts to support its claim; if not, then the rule of reason applied and Arizona would have to demonstrate the untoward effects on competition, a difficult task. The application of the per se rule to the facts of *Maricopa* caused much controversy and debate. Those jurists who favored special treatment for the professions sought to apply the rule of reason. Those who opposed special treatment found the maximum fee schedules to be illegal per se. Footnote 17 of *Goldfarb* resonated once again.

Judge William Copple of the federal district court fell into the former camp. "It has long been recognized that the professions differ fundamentally from ordinary commercial businesses and, consequently, merit more liberal treatment under the antitrust laws," he wrote (*Arizona v. Maricopa County Medical Soc.*, 1979 U.S. Dist. LEXIS 11918, 1979–1 Trade Cas. [CCH] *par.* 62,694 [D. Ariz. 1979]). Likewise Judge Joseph T. Sneed, writing for a three-judge panel of the federal circuit court, held that the rule of reason applied. Drawing from the Supreme Court's decision in *Goldfarb,* Sneed held "that marketing restraints that regulate professional competition may pass muster under the Rule of Reason even though similar restraints on ordinary business competition would not" (*Arizona v. Maricopa County Medical Soc.*, 643 F.2d 553, 560 [9th Cir. 1980]).

The U.S. Supreme Court agreed to review the decisions of the lower federal courts. Very little in the way of pretrial discovery had occurred. Consequently, the record was scant and only the issue of per se illegality was before the Court. Efforts to craft a majority decision followed a tortuous path. The recusals of Justices Blackmun and O'Connor (O'Connor had strong ties to Maricopa County) left only seven justices to decide the case. A bare majority, which included Justices Powell, White, and Rehnquist and Chief Justice Burger, found that the record was inadequate and that the case should be remanded for further proceedings in the district court. Burger asked Powell "to draft a dispositive Per Curiam on this case" (Thurgood Marshall Papers, Box 288, 80–419 [Note from Burger to Powell, 27 November 1981]). The *per curiam* was to be "a short one paragraph [opinion] stating that the action of the District Court [determining] the applicability of the 'per se' rule [on partial summary judgment] was premature" (Thurgood Marshall Papers, Box 288, 80–419 [Note from Rehnquist to Burger, 24 November 1981]).

Upon further reflection, Justice Powell decided that the lower court needed more guidance than a *per curiam* opinion afforded (Thurgood Marshall Papers, Box 288, 80–419 [Powell Memorandum to Conference, 24 February 1982]). He proceeded to draft a detailed memorandum that narrowed the application of the per se rule. Surprised by Powell's attempt to influence the findings of the lower court, Justices Stevens and White staked out an opposing stance. Stevens replied, "[I will] be writing in dissent as soon as I can" (Thurgood Marshall Papers, Box 288, 80–419 [Note from Stevens to Powell, 26 February 1982]); White stated that he would "await [Stevens's] dissent" (Thurgood Marshall Papers, Box 288, 80–419 [Note from White to Powell, 3 March 1982]). This proved fatal for Powell's position. On 26 April 1982, White reversed his conference vote (Thurgood

Marshall Papers, Box 288, 80–419 [Note from White to Powell, 26 April 1982]). Stevens now wrote for a Court majority, while Powell penned a dissent.

Stevens held that the maximum fee schedules were illegal per se. He noted that the FMCs did not claim that the "price restraints," as he called them, enhanced the quality of professional services (*Maricopa*, 457 U.S. at 348–349). Rather, Stevens observed: "The respondents' claim for relief from the per se rule is simply that the doctors' agreement not to charge certain insureds more than the fixed price facilitates the successful marketing of an attractive insurance plan" (*Maricopa*, 457 U.S. at 349). Stevens was unmoved by the argument that maximum fee schedules were necessary to prevent "opportunism by doctors in the insurance plan" (see Liebeler 1986:1035). Indeed, "even if a fee schedule is . . . desirable," Stevens wrote, "it is not necessary that the doctors do the price fixing" (*Maricopa*, 457 U.S. at 352). Insurers could do that just as well, he said.

In a dissenting opinion, Powell challenged the assertion that the maximum fee schedules were "naked" price restraints. "I would give greater weight than the Court to the uniqueness of medical services, and certainly would not invalidate on a *per se* basis a plan that may in fact perform a uniquely useful service," he remarked (*Maricopa*, 457 U.S. at 366 n. 13). But unlike Judges Copple and Sneed of the district and circuit courts, special treatment of the professions was not the central focus of Powell's dissenting opinion. Powell believed that the "novel" arrangement before the Court enhanced consumer welfare and economic efficiency. "The respondents' contention that the 'consumers' of medical services are benefited substantially by the plan is given short shrift," he wrote (*Maricopa*, 457 U.S. at 358–359). "On the record before us, there is no evidence of opposition to the foundation plan by insurance companies—or, for that matter, by members of the public" (*Maricopa*, 457 U.S. at 361). The plan offered certain "transactional efficiencies," Powell suggested (see Liebeler 1986:1021).

Stevens did not see it that way. His concern was not so much with consumer welfare and efficiency as with harm to competition. Stevens believed, as did Clark Havighurst, that the purpose of the antitrust laws was to protect "competition as a process" and not "competitors, efficiency, or consumer welfare as such" (Havighurst, Blumstein, and Brennan 1999:4). Havighurst undoubtedly influenced Stevens's reasoning on this crucial matter. Indeed, Powell related in a draft memorandum that "Justice Stevens apparently finds the views of Professor Havighurst persuasive" (Thurgood Marshall Papers, Box 288, 80–419 [5th Draft from Justice Powell, 16 n. 17]). A "quick look" was all Stevens needed to determine that the FMCs should not prevail. The maximum fees were a "masquerade," the local societies had "substantial" market power, and a less restrictive alternative—price-fixing by insurers—was available. From Stevens's perspective, the record in the case, albeit scant, showed that the scheme violated basic antitrust principles (*Maricopa*, 457 U.S. at 348, 354 nn. 28 and 29). The maximum fee schedules "fit squarely into the horizontal price-fixing mold," he determined (*Maricopa*, 457 U.S. at 357).

Stevens's opinion in *Maricopa* had important implications for the medical profession and for the trajectory of the health care industry (see Herndon and Lopatka 1999). Had the rule of reason applied to comprehensive FMCs, medical societies would have had more influence over the industry's future configuration. *Maricopa*'s principal significance was that it attenuated all remaining vestiges of guild practice following *AMA*. After *Maricopa*, physicians could form group practices or independent practice associations if they satisfied certain requirements, but medical societies invited antitrust scrutiny if they took the lead.

PEER REVIEW AND THE "PATIENT CARE" DEFENSE

In addition to sponsoring health plans, as in *Maricopa*, FMCs performed other functions that required physicians to collaborate, such as peer review. Peer review activities were not the focus of Arizona's attack, and the district court, the Ninth Circuit, and the Supreme Court left them alone. Judge Earl Larson, who dissented from the Ninth Circuit opinion of Judge Sneed, viewed fee-setting activities apart from peer review. Maximum fee schedules, Judge Larson indicated, were illegal per se because they were "wholly commercial" in nature, exhibited "no relation to any public service aspect of the medical profession," and did not seem "to be motivated by a desire to benefit consumers" (*Maricopa*, 643 F.2d at 565). "Eliminating the fee-setting," he stated, "would not inhibit defendants from continuing to perform peer review, quality control, or other permissible functions. These activities are entirely separable" (*Maricopa*, 643 F.2d at 565).

Judge Larson's remarks suggested that medical societies and independent practitioners could collaborate freely in noncommercial activities if "public service" motivated their behavior. This raised an important question: Would efforts to improve patient care exonerate anticompetitive activities? Those who saw no reason to distinguish business from profession for antitrust purposes answered "no." They asserted that "public service" or "proper motives" should not constitute a valid defense to a lawsuit for violation of the Sherman Act, even in the context of peer review. "The law leaves virtually no room for defending a restriction on competition by claiming that it was inspired by pure or public-spirited motives," Clark Havighurst contended (1986:1120).

AMA leaders, not surprisingly, viewed the matter quite differently. They stressed that "public-spirited motives" should protect activities related to quality assurance from antitrust scrutiny, especially peer review. Peer review was important to the profession's quest for quality control. The practice originated on a formal basis in 1918 through the American College of Surgeons and, once established, became integral to the oversight of clinical performance within hospitals and other health care facilities (*Proceedings* June 1976:124). Accrediting bodies, such as the Joint Commission on the Accreditation of Hospitals, afforded peer review broad-based recognition and institutional support. Congress signaled its protection of peer review when it established Professional Standards Review Organizations in 1972 and Peer Review Organizations in 1982 to monitor the quality of care and physician spending under the Medicare program.

Ironically, physicians were among the first to allege in certain instances that peer reviewers of hospitals and medical societies engaged in anticompetitive practices. Indeed, actions by doctors against other doctors comprised the largest percentage of all antitrust cases in the health care industry during the 1980s (*Proceedings* June 1988:225; Sage 2003:102). Most of these cases arose when medical staff denied hospital privileges to poorly performing physicians. Physicians had little to lose by filing lawsuits against peer reviewers. The prospects for settlement were quite high—judges refused to dismiss cases outright if economic motives were properly alleged. Plaintiffs could claim treble (or threefold actual) damages, plus attorneys' fees, under the Clayton and Sherman Acts. In addition, defendants faced high legal expenses, loss of time from their medical practices, and emotional distress.

Some forms of peer review were immune from attack because federal laws applied. Federal legislation establishing the Peer Review Organizations, for instance, exempted reviewers from civil and criminal liability (42 U.S.C. sec. 1320c-6(a) [1982]). Certain state laws also provided protection, but the Supreme Court in *Goldfarb* and in other cases had narrowed the application of the state-action doctrine announced in *Parker v. Brown*. The new test made it more difficult to seek immunity under the doctrine. First, there had to be clear evidence "that the legislature intended to replace competition with regulation in the relevant market" (*Patrick v. Burget*, 800 F.2d 1498, 1505 [9th Cir. 1986]). Second, there had to be proof that state officials "actively supervised" those who carried out the legislative scheme (*Califor-*

nia Retail Liquor Dealers Ass'n v. Midcal Aluminum, Inc., 445 U.S. 97, 105 [1980]).

Physicians' fear of legal liability jeopardized the peer review process. Concerns reached epic proportions in 1984 when a federal district court awarded Timothy Patrick, a doctor from Astoria, Oregon, $2.2 million in treble damages plus attorneys' fees for violations of the Sherman Act. Patrick, a general and vascular surgeon, had an independent practice that competed with physicians who owned and practiced at the Astoria Clinic. From 1972 (the year Patrick established his independent practice) until 1979, he and doctors at the clinic clashed over consultations, patient referrals, and backup coverage. An incident in 1979 led to accusations that Patrick was deficient in patient care. Clinic doctors complained to the state licensing board and, in 1981, took steps to revoke Patrick's privileges at Columbia Memorial, the only hospital in Astoria. Along with hospital personnel, physicians at the clinic prepared charges against Patrick. A clinic physician even chaired the hospital committee that heard the charges. Before the hospital could take action, Patrick resigned and, in 1981, sued the hospital and several clinic doctors (*Patrick*, 800 F.2d at 1502–1505).

The U.S. Court of Appeals for the Ninth Circuit overturned the district court's decision on the grounds that the physicians at Columbia Memorial, as peer reviewers, were immune from civil liability. Though the circuit court found the reviewers' behavior to be "shabby, unprincipled and unprofessional," it invoked the state-action doctrine (*Patrick*, 800 F.2d at 1505, 1509). Patrick appealed, and the Supreme Court reversed the decision of the circuit court. The Court, in an opinion by Justice Thurgood Marshall, held that the doctrine did not apply to the reviewers' activities. State officials did not "actively supervise" hospital committees, Marshall wrote, let alone decisions of the medical staff of Columbia Memorial Hospital (*Patrick v. Burget*, 486 U.S. 94, 101 [1988]).

Seeking relief from the Court's ruling in *Patrick* and from the onslaught of legal actions, physicians lobbied Congress for statutory protection. Their efforts led to passage of the Health Care Quality Improvement Act of 1986. The act's passage, though consequential, was hardly a victory for the AMA. For all practical purposes, its central feature was the imposition of court costs and attorneys' fees for "frivolous" claims. The penalty for filing frivolous suits undoubtedly reduced the caseload, but the act did not alter the rules governing antitrust liability. It provided immunity if reviewers' principal purpose was to further "quality health care," but it did not grant blanket relief or extend the grant of immunity beyond the realm of peer review. The act, law professor Charity Scott concluded, "[fell] short of that heralded by its supporters" (Scott 1991:321). The "procedural handling of peer-review litigation should be the same," she said, "with or without [the act]" (Scott 1991:404).

THE SPECIAL CASE OF CHIROPRACTIC

Before the 1980s, the medical profession often barred psychologists, podiatrists, optometrists, nurse midwives, nurse anesthetists, and chiropractors from health care facilities. The application of the antitrust laws to the learned professions in 1975 made these efforts more tenuous. Physicians could deny access to hospitals for reasons related to quality, but they could not engage in concerted efforts to boycott entire professions. Medical societies, nonetheless, continued their attempts to exclude certain groups from a variety of health care settings. Their principal focus in the 1970s was the chiropractic profession. Chiropractic, according to the AMA, was not a "valid scientific discipline" (*Proceedings* 1975:180–181).

The AMA's campaign against chiropractic, which had escalated in the 1960s, intensified even further in the 1970s. In 1974, the House of Delegates "asked that the Association's anti-quackery activities be intensified" (*Proceedings* 1975:185). Responding to the call, the AMA's Committee on Quackery and Department of Investigation stepped-up their attacks, using the association's trade journals. *Today's Health* featured three articles on "quackery" in 1972, two in 1973, six in 1974, and one in 1975. The *AMA News* contributed forty-three reports and three editorials on chiropractic in 1972, thirty-two reports and two editorials in 1973, and forty-one reports and three editorials from 1974 through the first five months of 1975 (*Proceedings* 1975:185).

Chiropractors turned to the FTC, hoping to gain relief from the AMA's anticompetitive activities. In November 1975, the International Chiropractors Association, comprising about three thousand members, wrote Chair Lewis Engman (FTC Special Collections [Harrison to Engman, 13 November 1975]). Using Congressman John Moss as its intermediary, the chiropractic association provided the commission with "a substantial amount of material," which included private correspondence and AMA files. The "material" allegedly had been "leaked" by a "disaffected staffer" of the AMA who was known as "Sore Throat"—"after Deep Throat of Watergate fame" (Wardwell 1988:175).

Owen Johnson, director of the Bureau of Competition, responded to the chiropractors. He advised: "We are evaluating [the Sore Throat] material to determine whether that matter should be included in this Bureau's health care program, either as a separate inquiry or as part of some larger investigation. Although I suspect that we will not be in a position to take on this matter as a case by itself, we may want to consider it as it may relate to other inquiries that we are making" (FTC Special Collections [Johnson to Harrison, 19 January 1976]). Calling Johnson's letter "non-responsive and non-productive," the chiropractors' attorney, James Harrison, threatened to "pursue the matter through proper channels" should the FTC fail to "provide . . . a candid assessment of Congressman Moss' recommendation" (FTC Special Collections [Harrison to Johnson, 28 January 1976]).

Harrison's letter provoked a terse response from Alfred Dougherty, the deputy director of the Bureau of Competition. After reminding Harrison that the agency acts "in the public interest rather than on behalf of any specific interest group," Dougherty gave Harrison what he asked for—a "candid assessment of this matter as it relates to the Federal Trade Commission" (FTC Special Collections [Dougherty to Harrison, 8 March 1976]). Dougherty wrote:

> Although the information we received involves the issue of control over health care delivery which we are presently examining, we do not believe that the case you present is the best vehicle for exploring that issue. First, the matter you raise involves serious dispute with regard to scientific and medical facts and opinion about which the Commission has no expertise. Second, this dispute has become highly publicized and politicized, which would make it difficult for us to control our own investigation and would hamper a dispassionate examination of the issues. Third, we have reason to question the method by which the documents which we received left the possession of the AMA, which factor would jeopardize any litigation if it were to result from an investigation. Fourth, as the memorandum which accompanied the documents pointed out, there are legal questions involved which would complicate, although not necessarily defeat, any antitrust litigation resulting from an investigation. (FTC Special Collections [Dougherty to Harrison, 8 March 1976])

Dougherty suggested to Harrison that private remedies might be in order. "The Commission's evaluation criteria are far different than those of a private plaintiff," Dougherty observed—"a private suit" might still "succeed" (FTC Special Collections [Dougherty to Harrison, 8 March 1976]).

Though Dougherty signaled the end of FTC involvement, the health care shop kept chiropractic on its agenda. Flush with resources, Alan Palmer asked Jonathan Gaines to explore "new investigations" (FTC Special Collections [Gaines Memorandum to Evaluation Committee, 21 September 1976:1]). After completing his preliminary analysis, Gaines recommended that the commission open a "separate investigation" into the problem of chiropractic (FTC, Gaines Memorandum:12). Gaines proposed that the investigation focus on Principle 3 of the Code of Medical Ethics. Principle 3 stated that "a physician should practice a method of healing founded on a scientific basis; and he should not voluntarily professionally associate with anyone who violates this principle" (AMA Code of Medical Ethics [1957]).

Rather than offer any new facts, Gaines provided an alternative perspective to that contained in Dougherty's letter to Harrison. Gaines observed, for instance, that Principle 3 furnished "a 'neutral' basis for proceeding against [the AMA] that does not depend on the medical merits of chiropractic" (FTC, Gaines Memorandum:12). The "public interest" in containing the "cost of medical care," he asserted, favored "lower-cost providers. . . . Chiropractors not only constitute[d] additional suppliers of health care, but they charge[d] less than doctors" (FTC, Gaines Memorandum:15). Gaines also countered Dougherty's "remaining objections"—the "highly politicized" nature of the dispute and the fact that the documents, sent anonymously to the commission, might have been stolen (FTC, Gaines Memorandum:11). As to the stolen, or Sore Throat, documents, Gaines professed that their use would not be improper. The commission had not "solicited" them, he noted, and they were "directly relevant" to the investigation (FTC, Gaines Memorandum:16).

Despite Gaines's recommendation, the commission failed to open a "separate investigation" concerning chiropractic (see FTC, Gaines Memorandum:16). FTC attorneys discussed the possibility of adding the chiropractors' allegations to the *AMA* case, which was in litigation at the time, but Barry Costilo and his team of lawyers objected. In the opinion of Costilo, efforts to include chiropractic would have "spread" the case "too thin" (Costilo 2003).

Rebuffed, chiropractors sued the AMA in Pennsylvania, New Jersey, and Illinois. In the Illinois case, *Wilk v. American Medical Ass'n* (671 F. Supp. 1465 [N.D. Ill. 1987]), chiropractors claimed that the AMA and several other defendants, including the Joint Commission on the Accreditation of Hospitals, had conspired to destroy their profession. *Wilk,* which began in 1976 and lasted over eleven years, focused on Principle 3. In addition, chiropractors doggedly pursued a judicial ruling that their profession was a "valid, efficacious, even scientific health care service."

Judge Susan Getzendanner, who heard the Illinois case, declined to "pronounce chiropractic valid or invalid on anecdotal evidence." Nonetheless, she found that the AMA, the American College of Radiology, and the American Academy of Orthopaedic Surgeons had conspired to "contain and eliminate the chiropractic profession." By way of relief, Getzendanner enjoined defendants from further antitrust violations. To comply with the injunction, the AMA had to publish the court's order in *JAMA,* mail it to each of the AMA's members, and revise the current opinions of the Judicial Council. The United States Court of Appeals for the Seventh Circuit affirmed Getzendanner's ruling and upheld the injunction (*Wilk v. American Medical Ass'n,* 895 F.2d 352 [7th Cir. 1990]). A century-long struggle between physicians and chiropractors ceased, in large part because of the application of the antitrust laws to the learned professions.

PHYSICIAN EDUCATION AND TRAINING

The dispute over chiropractic raised important questions about the scope of FTC authority. Citing scientific and technical facts "about which the Commission has no expertise," FTC attorneys refused to be drawn into the conflict between physicians and chiropractors. But was "lack of expertise" a proper reason for failing to proceed or a convenient excuse for avoiding a problematic investigation? In point of fact, Judge Getzendanner resolved all pertinent legal issues without delving into the scientific basis for chiropractic. What other anticompetitive practices might be off-limits because they involved professional regulation of scientific and technical endeavors? Were organized medicine's efforts to require conformance with standards for the education, training, and credentialing of physicians and for the accreditation of medical schools and hospitals also circumscribed? There was nothing wrong with the development of standards and the labeling of products "as conforming to standards," but organizations arguably violated the antitrust laws if they conspired to suppress the production of "nonstandard" products (see Havighurst and King 1983b:308).

The FTC first raised concerns about professional self-regulation in the context of a perceived doctor shortage. This matter, which Jim Liebeler brought to the commission's attention, implicated the Liaison Committee on Medical Education, a private organization that, under the auspices of the U.S. Office of Education, accredited schools of medical education. The FTC postponed action in January 1976 pending a report from the task force for occupational licensure (FTC Special Collections [Schwartz Memorandum to Evaluation Committee, 6 June 1975:21]). In April 1976, the commission authorized a formal investigation under Dan Schwartz's direction (FTC Special Collections [Zeitlin Memorandum to FTC, 8 November 1976]). A report by H. E. Frech, an economist from the University of California, Santa Barbara, was a contributing factor in the decision to commence a formal investigation. Timothy Muris had engaged Frech to examine the FTC's current activities and to consider further initiatives. According to Frech, Muris "wanted the FTC to become more active in the health care arena" (2003).

Frech's report, entitled "Expanding the FTC Health Care Program," emphasized the AMA's control over professional education, licensing, and medical standards (FTC Special Collections [Report of H. E. Frech, III, January 1976]). Frech drew support from the work of Reuben Kessel, who believed that "the AMA should be stripped of its power to control the output of physicians" (Frech 2003; Kessel 1970:283). Kessel wrote:

> It is important to remember that, whatever the times, the AMA has an inevitable conflict of interest. It has presumed simultaneously to represent (1) the public, in maintaining standards for the production of physicians and in determining the quantity to be produced, and (2) the medical profession, the purveyors of medical services. In other words, the AMA represents both the buyers and the sellers of physician services in determining the output of physicians. Given this anomalous position, it is difficult to believe that the AMA will ever permit the number of physicians to be produced that the public is willing to support with its patronage. Consequently its power to determine output via the rating of medical schools should be withdrawn and graduation from an AMA-approved medical school should not be a condition for admission to licensure examinations. (1970:282)

Based in part on Kessel's findings, Frech urged the commission to challenge the association's role in physician education and training (FTC Special Collections [Report of H. E. Frech, III, January 1976:CA52]).

On paper, the AMA's influence over the Liaison Committee appeared extensive. The association appointed six of the committee's fifteen board members, provided 50 percent of its operational funds, and directly administered the committee every other year. Acting in its administrative capacity, the AMA selected survey teams for medical school on-site visits (FTC Special Collections [Schwartz to Aguirre, 11 November 1976]). Claiming a conflict of interest, Schwartz challenged the status of the Liaison Committee as the sole accrediting body for medical schools in the United States. He recommended that the Office of Education select "a new group to accredit medical schools" or require the committee to undergo "substantial restructuring" (FTC Special Collections [Statement of Daniel C. Schwartz before the Advisory Committee on Accreditation and Institutional Eligibility, 24 March 1977:18, 31]).

Though the commission persisted for over three years in claiming "that a broader community of interests should be recognized by the [Liaison

Committee]" (FTC Special Collections [Dougherty to Profitt, 18 April 1980:6]), the Office of Education, in the end, declined to take substantive action. A principal reason why the office failed to act was insufficient evidence of a doctor shortage in 1977, the ostensible reason for the FTC's challenge. Financial support of the federal government for medical education, which began in the 1960s, had averted a potential shortfall, more than doubling the number of medical school graduates by the mid-1980s (Ginzberg 1990:141). It appeared that federal funding had more to do with physician supply than medicine's control of the Liaison Committee.

THE MARKET FOR MEDICAL INFORMATION

By attacking the AMA's role on the Liaison Committee, the FTC ventured into a sensitive area. It was one thing to challenge anticompetitive practices in the commercial arena; it was quite another to scrutinize the role of organized medicine in the education and training of physicians. "In taking its position," AMA biographer Frank Campion contended, "the commission struck at the traditional responsibility a profession has for the educational standards of its future members" (Campion 1984:351).

Clark Havighurst, who was a consultant to the FTC from 1978 to 1979, was solidly behind the commission's initiative (Havighurst 2003). But AMA efforts to restrict the supply of physicians were not the central basis for Havighurst's objection. Rather, Havighurst linked the training and socialization of physicians to the guild aspects of medical practice. As he explained in a letter to the Office of Education, written together with Gaylord Cummings, a business professor at Tulane University,

> The power to define how a doctor is educated is the power to define what a doctor is, and this is more than a straightforward, technical undertaking which can be entrusted to organized professional interests. We attempt to demonstrate in this statement the existence of a substantial danger that the [Liaison Committee], by reason of its control by organized medicine and the medical education establishment, imposes on medical education, a particular professional ideology, deeply rooted in a particular perception of the physician's role in society and antagonistic to educational endeavors premised on different perceptions. (FTC Special Collections [Havighurst and Cummings to Office of Education, 9 March 1977])

It was at this point that Havighurst and the FTC parted company. Indeed, the commission "explicitly disassociated" itself from Havighurst's more "radical" agenda (see FTC Special Collections [Grimmer Memorandum to

Winslow, 9 November 1978]). The ascendancy of Chicago school philosophy had much to do with the commission's reluctance. Chicagoans' "conservatism," Havighurst insisted, "meant that my ideas about, say, policing the profession's monopoly on standard setting, information, and opinion did not have much chance of attracting attention" (2006). Writing in the *New England Journal of Medicine,* Barry Costilo signaled that there were limits to what the FTC could or should do to police professional regulation of scientific and technical matters. "Ethical rules and self-regulation are desirable in the field of medicine if they are tailored to the special medical concern involved and if care is exercised that they do not unreasonably impinge on competition," Costilo indicated. "Certification by medical-specialty boards is an example of self-regulation that can promote quality and is permissible under the antitrust laws as long as the system is not abused" (Costilo 1981:1102). Costilo seemed to be saying that the FTC would stay out of the doctor's workplace if medicine left the marketplace alone.

Havighurst undoubtedly understood the agency's position, including the legal and political difficulties it faced in pursuing the role of professional associations in setting standards. But this did not stop him from attempting to make his case and from admonishing the commission for not going further (Havighurst and King 1983a:184–185). In certain articles and letters published in 1983, Havighurst and his colleague Nancy King endeavored to extend antitrust analysis from one market to another, from the market for health care services to the market for health care information. Unless this occurred, they believed, the health care revolution would falter.

Havighurst and King grounded their argument in economic theory. In order to make prudent and cost-effective purchasing decisions, economists said, consumers needed access to a wide variety of products and information. Havighurst and King sought to advance this proposition. "The ideal market," they envisioned, "would offer consumers a variety of health care options that differ not just in price and amenities but in more fundamental ways. It should, for example, enable consumers to locate providers who share their particular philosophy about how drugs and other technology should be used or about how aggressively disease should be treated. Choices should be influenced, too, by differing price tags, in order that the strength of consumer preferences for more costly styles of care may be tested" (Havighurst and King 1983b:295).

Havighurst and King contended that antitrust law had a role to play in targeting restraints on the supply of information. They maintained that the type of information available to health care consumers was "essentially uniform" in nature, that it reflected the values and "ideology" of the medical profession to the exclusion of all competing preferences. Among the areas that Havighurst and King targeted for investigation were certification of physicians for specialty practice and accreditation of hospitals for purposes of state licensure and federal reimbursement. Certain specialty boards (those recognized by the American Board of Medical Specialties), they claimed, had agreed to divide the market, a per se violation. "By mutually agreeing on the precise definition and limits of each specialty, the . . . boards have effectively agreed that each will publish only a certain type of information, . . . thus ensuring that the public will hear only one authoritative opinion" (Havighurst and King 1984:461). Havighurst and King also asserted that the Joint Commission on the Accreditation of Hospitals was "so large and powerful as to be an unlawful combination" (1984:461). The four sponsors of the Joint Commission (the AMA, the American Hospital Association, the American College of Surgeons, and the American College of Physicians) "have agreed among themselves not to express their separate views for the benefit of consumers" (Havighurst and King 1983b:323).

Those opposed to the position of Havighurst and King did not agree with their major premise—that boards and commissions controlled by the profession curbed "competitive diversity" and suppressed the flow of information (Rankin and Hubbard 1984:190). Opponents stressed the "voluntary" nature of the undertaking on the part of the physicians involved and that accrediting and certifying bodies were nonprofit entities. Such organizations were not "engaged in commercial activity"; what they did was for "the protection of the public," attorneys James Rankin and Bruce Hubbard contended (1984:191, 193–194). Rankin and Hubbard dismissed the need for institutions that promoted alternative values and preferences. "It is difficult to see any purpose in competing systems, other than diffusion of legitimacy, increased costs, and confusion among those who rely on accreditation," they stated (1984:195).

To one degree or another, most justices on the Supreme Court subscribed to the views of Rankin and Hubbard. Supreme Court justices, law professor Philip Kissam observed, have endeavored to distinguish between professional regulation of "the economic aspect of professional services" and that involving "technical quality" (Kissam 1983:21–23). According to Kissam, the Court's oft-repeated statement in *OSMS* that "forms of competition usual in the business world may be demoralizing to the ethical standards of a profession" still resonated. In *Professional Engineers,* for instance, Kissam pointed out that the Court recognized professional regulation of technical quality if the "main purpose" was to protect public safety (1983:22–23). And in *Maricopa,* Kissam noted, the Court "implied" tolerance of professional regulation that enhanced the "quality" of professional services (1983:23). Kissam might have added that footnote 17 of *Goldfarb* also supported "judicial deference to the regulation of technical services" (1983:21).

Notwithstanding the FTC's decision to curtail its investigation of medicine's "ideological and informational monopoly," physicians' grip over hospital governance loosened in the 1980s. One reason for this was a new system for paying hospitals that the federal government introduced in 1983. Under "prospective payment," as it was called, the Medicare and Medicaid programs paid hospitals in advance based on a flat rate per patient rather than retrospectively for costs incurred. Length of hospital stay and complexity of treatment based on diagnostic related groups, or DRGs, determined the preestablished rate for purposes of program administration.

By placing hospitals at financial risk for doctors' inefficient performance, prospective payment "drove a wedge" between hospital administration and staff physicians (*Proceedings* 1984:144). So did court rulings that made hospitals vicariously liable for provider negligence in the hospital setting (see *Darling v. Charlestown Community Memorial Hosp.*, 211 N.E.2d 253 [Ill. 1965]; *Thompson v. Nason Hosp.*, 591 A.2d 703 [Pa. 1991]). In the *Darling* case, an Illinois court held that a hospital was liable for failing to supervise a negligent physician. *Darling* and cases like it prompted hospital administrators and governing boards to scrutinize medical staff more carefully (compare Kissam et al. 1982:602–603).

CONCLUSION

By the time Arthur Lerner returned to the health care shop in 1981, the shop was pursuing a narrower agenda—"more state and locally focused" (Lerner 2003). The FTC had conquered the medical monopoly and had laid the groundwork for managed care. "When we started the program," Lerner noted, "we were looking at national problems. Look at who we sued—we sued the AMA, we sued the American Dental Association, we were investigating the Joint Commission on Accreditation of Hospitals, we were investigating Blue Shield plans all across the country" (2003). But from 1982 to 1985, with Lerner in charge, the shop litigated what Lerner called "clean-up cases." Professional associations, he said, had begun to "appreciate the constraining role of the antitrust laws on the traditional guild aspects of the health care professions." These "clean-up cases" Lerner declared, "were not driven by organized medicine" (2003).

Havighurst may have inspired the FTC's early case selection, but his attempts to extend antitrust analysis from the commercial to the clinical realm encountered stiff resistance. In the late 1970s, the FTC seemed on board with Havighurst's auspicious agenda. But the commission soon faced political and ideological retrenchment. A new dynamic—more conservative, certainly less adventurous—took hold after Ronald Reagan became president and selected James Miller to chair the commission. The commission's low standing in Congress, as reflected in the jurisdiction-stripping battle of 1982, engendered much caution and circumspection (Muris 2003).

The failure to apply antitrust principles to the monopolistic practices of organized medicine in the production of information and in the generation of standards circumscribed treatment options when new forms of health care finance and delivery emerged in the 1980s and 1990s. Despite the AMA's forced retreat from the commercial sphere, it retained, and in some instances tightened, its authority over the schooling of physicians and the dissemination of medical data. Physician education, residency training, licensing and discipline, peer review, privileging and credentialing, specialty certification, institutional accreditation, standard setting, and technology assessment remained under its control or influence.

8 The Quest for Antitrust Relief

The application of the antitrust laws to the medical profession spurred a structural transformation of the health care industry. New forms of finance and delivery emerged that medical societies previously had prohibited. Equally important, moreover, was the effect on physicians' practices. By preventing independent practitioners from joining together through their professional associations or ad hoc to enhance their bargaining power, the antitrust laws encouraged doctors to form group practices or become salaried employees of large corporate entities. This did not bode well for organized medicine. Physicians who chose corporate practice had less need for professional associations that perpetuated the old ways. Their loyalties split between the organization they worked for and the profession they belonged to, corporate doctors and those who joined large group practices were less inclined than self-employed physicians to support the AMA and its component state and local medical societies.

Because independent practitioners were the association's primary constituency, efforts to preserve independent, fee-for-service practice became the principal goal of organized medicine in the 1980s and 1990s. A quid pro quo developed. The AMA would help self-employed physicians in their battles with hospitals and corporate health plans, and independent practitioners, in turn, would support the AMA.

As the theoretical insights of political scientists Mark Blyth, Paul Sabatier, and Hank Jenkins-Smith predict, the AMA formed an "advocacy coalition" to promote independent, fee-for-service practice. A primary purpose of this coalition—comprising state and county medical societies, specialty societies, and certain professions, such as dentistry—was to roll back and circumvent the antitrust laws. Managed care organizations, insurers, and the federal antitrust agencies—the FTC and the Department of

Justice—resisted the AMA's efforts. The struggles between the AMA-led and the managed care–led coalitions strongly influenced the course of health policy in the United States.

THE EVOLUTION OF THE HEALTH CARE INDUSTRY

The health care industry evolved across three dimensions in the decades following *Goldfarb.* First, insurers diversified into HMO and PPO (preferred provider organization) products, merged and consolidated their operations and, in several instances, converted from nonprofit to for-profit status. Second, hospitals diversified to include not only inpatient but outpatient services and clinics, formed national chains and alliances, and often purchased doctors' practices, nursing homes, and other entities to establish regional systems. Third, physicians joined other physicians in small, medium, and large group practices, organized loose networks or independent practice associations, sold their practices to management firms, and increasingly became salaried employees of hospitals and other corporate entities.

The trend among managed care organizations was toward large, for-profit firms. For-profit ownership of HMOs increased from fewer than 20 plans in the mid-1970s to 382 (two-thirds of all plans) in 1992 (*Proceedings* June 1995:251). By 1994, the top five HMO firms (Blue Cross/Blue Shield, Kaiser, United Healthcare, PruCare/Prudential, and U.S. Healthcare) had a combined market share of about 43 percent (Feldman, Wholey, and Christianson 1999:99). By 1997, the top five firms (Blue Cross/Blue Shield, Kaiser, United Healthcare, Aetna, and Cigna) had a combined market share of almost 50 percent (Feldman, Wholey, and Christianson 1999:99).

Blue Cross/Blue Shield followed the merger stampede. In 1990, there were more than eighty separate Blue Cross/Blue Shield plans; by 2000, there were forty-seven (Jacob 2000:21). The largest Blue Cross/Blue Shield plans in 2000 were Wellpoint (comprising Blue Cross of California and Blue Cross/Blue Shield of Georgia), Anthem (comprising Blue Cross/Blue Shield of Colorado, Connecticut, Indiana, Kentucky, Maine, Nevada, New Hampshire, and Ohio), and Health Care Service Corporation (comprising Blue Cross/Blue Shield of Illinois, New Mexico, and Texas) (Jacob 2000:21). In addition, the Blues capitalized on the shift that occurred in the 1990s from HMOs to PPOs. Consumers often preferred the enhanced choice and flexibility of the PPO option, and the Blues made it available to them. According to health analysts Robert Hurley, Bradley Strunk, and Justin White, "The Blues [were] uniquely positioned to offer attractive PPO options because in most local markets they [had] the broadest provider networks and often enjoy[ed] superior discounts, given the negotiating leverage they [had] accumulated with providers through their broad product portfolios" (Hurley, Strunk, and White 2004:62).

Like insurers, hospitals also merged with other health care entities, forming national chains and regional systems. Reasons for consolidation included market competition, economies of scale, and financial pressures from reductions in government reimbursements and prospective payment. Mergers occurred at the relatively meager "rate of between eight and [thirty] per year during the 1980s" but escalated during the 1990s (*Proceedings* December 1992:36). Hospital mergers peaked at 197 in 1997 then steadily declined to 38 in 2003 (Kaiser Family Foundation 2004). Many hospitals also shut down entirely because of financial difficulties. From 1987 to 2002, there were 486 hospital closings in the United States alone (Cook 2002:20; see also Stevens 1989:321–341).

Physicians often took part, in some fashion, in hospital mergers. Data from a 1993 AMA survey found that 56 percent of 137 hospitals formed Physician Hospital Organizations, or PHOs (*Proceedings* June 1995:248). In the typical situation, hospitals financed and exercised control of PHOs while individual physicians or physicians' groups acted as limited partners. Hospitals adopted the PHO strategy to ensure a steady flow of patients, yet the results often failed to meet expectations. According to economist David Dranove, "Most PHOs are struggling to hold down costs, and many suffer from bitter divisions among [primary care providers], specialists, and the hospital" (Dranove 2000:133). One of the first areas that Columbia/HCA, a Nashville-based company, chose to cut when it faced financial difficulties in 1997 was doctors' practices (Jacob 1999:13).

Despite legal and economic incentives to become employees or to merge their practices, the majority of doctors (61 percent) remained self-employed in 2001, many of them in independent or small-group arrangements (Casalino 2004:873). As Lawrence Casalino observed, "Most physicians still work for themselves [and] of the [39] percent of physicians who were employed in 2001, more were employed by physician-owned medical groups than by private hospitals, academic medical centers, or staff model HMOs" (2004:873–874). Physician practice management firms, which had purchased 8 percent of all doctors' practices in the United States by 1997 (Benedict and Feorene 1997:14), faltered, in part because physicians resisted the efforts of such firms to dictate their clinical behavior (Barnett 1998:17).

BUREAUCRACY AND PROFESSIONAL AUTONOMY

Medical sociologists, such as David Mechanic (1969), Eliot Freidson (1973), Jeffrey Berlant (1975), and Paul Starr (1982), warned that government and corporate bureaucracy posed a threat to the medical profession. Bureaucracy, for instance, was incompatible with fee-for-service practice, the only form of payment that did not require centralized administration (see Weller 1984). Because the ideas that underlay professional authority and market competition occupied polar ends of the same philosophical spectrum, confrontations were inevitable and occurred along several dimensions. These dimensions included the following:

Collegiality versus Hierarchy Hierarchy imposes a process of decision making that flows up and down a chain of command. Although most organizations, including professional associations, employ hierarchical controls in their administrative apparatus, professionals typically reach decisions in a collegial fashion. This is true of medical societies, hospital medical staffs, state licensing boards, peer review organizations, and most other professional bodies. Such organizations typically do not view efficiency as their overriding concern. Achieving consensus is more important.

Cooperation versus Competition The goals of professionalism and market competition are essentially the same (efficiency, innovation, and quality), but the means for achieving them are quite different. Whereas the market model relies on competition to promote efficiency, innovation, and quality, the professional model depends on cooperation among physicians to advance similar ends. These differences in approach reflect profound differences in underlying premises. While those who promote the market model believe that individuals act in their own self-interest (see Downs 1985; Stigler 1988; Feldstein 1988), those who support the professional model argue that professionals act in the "service of others and of some higher [calling]" (Kass 1983:1305).

Self-Regulation versus Bureaucratic Oversight Self-regulation reflects the belief that those best able to judge the work of professionals are professionals themselves. State-supported institutions of self-regulation include licensing boards, accrediting bodies, and peer review organizations. These institutions control entry to the medical profession, the organization and structure of medical work, and many of the policies and practices of hospitals and other health care organizations. Managed care, as it developed, threatened self-regulation. HMOs, PPOs, and other corporate forms and arrangements engaged administrators to devise clinical standards and to oversee physicians' work.

Autonomy versus Standardization Autonomy ensured that physicians could exercise their best judgment in the diagnosis and treatment of disease. Physicians opposed the standardization of medical practice and the limitations on their discretion that "cookbook medicine" imposed (Freidson 2001:217). Proponents of managed care supported a model of medicine that rested on "systemic, replicable, statistical research" rather than "internalized, intuitive, professional judgments" (Marone and Belkin 1996:3). Science-based medicine, they claimed, aided in differentiating among health plans and physicians. It also supported a corporate culture that regulated physicians' performance. Practice guidelines, treatment protocols, outcomes research, continuous quality improvement, and utilization review were tools of managed care.

These four distinct differences in approach and philosophy underlay the struggle between professional associations and market reformers throughout the 1980s and 1990s. To members of Congress and other politicians, the health care revolution was about controls on health care spending. But to individual and small-group practitioners, the revolution was about professional norms and values. These were the AMA's constituents, not physicians who worked for HMOs or belonged to large group practices (see *Proceedings* December 1986:110–111). If the AMA was to remain viable, it had to cater to these interests. According to an AMA spokesperson: "The AMA first reflects those who belong to it, which continues to be, to a great extent, physicians in individual practices, the small practice of medicine, small businessmen . . . who have little ability to take on heavy regulatory burdens, to make quick technological changes, and who have a firm belief that autonomy and their professional training are what's necessary to see that their patients are well taken care of" (Rubin 2003).

TURBULENT TIMES AT THE AMA

In 1990, James Todd, a Harvard-educated surgeon, became the AMA's fourth chief executive, replacing James Sammons. Todd assumed leadership of the AMA at a particularly divisive and tumultuous time. The Board of Trustees had forced Sammons to resign because of financial improprieties (McCormick 1997:25). Sammons had approved, without the board's knowledge, a transfer of AMA funds to cover stock market losses of the association's chief operating officer. In addition, Sammons authorized a loan, again without the board's knowledge, to another AMA official. On 20 November 1989, the board instituted financial controls and curtailed Sammons's authority (*Proceedings* December 1989:154). Days later, Sammons resigned his position.

In his first speech before the House of Delegates as the AMA's new executive vice president, Todd announced the need to "move forward on all fronts." "If there was ever a time for divisiveness, that time has passed," Todd said. "If there was ever a time for recrimination, that time has passed. If there was ever a time for regret, that time has passed. There are far too many forces arrayed against us, too many challenges left unmet, too many frontiers yet to be crossed for us to engage in centrifugal and deunifying pursuits" (*Proceedings* June 1990:12). Todd would face several challenges during his six-year tenure as executive vice president.

Membership in the AMA slipped from 44.7 to 35.9 percent between 1985 and 1995, almost ten percentage points (AMA Special Collections [Historical Membership]). State and county medical societies experienced similar declines. Between 1977 and 1997, membership in state societies decreased from 73 to 47 percent, while membership in county medical societies decreased from 67 to 43 percent (Karlin 1998:20). Demographic factors dampened the association's chances for a turnaround. Those entering the profession in the 1980s and 1990s, many of them women, were less likely than their predecessors to join the AMA and its component state and local societies (*Proceedings* June 1986:144, 150; June 1985:150). In 1984, the Board of Trustees announced the AMA Women in Medicine Project and, in 1986, the establishment of the Assembly of Young Physicians. These projects achieved some success, but they did not alter declining trends (*Proceedings* June 2001:150–152).

Reduced numbers of physicians joining "geographic" societies (local, state, and national) did not mean doctors lacked interest in professional pursuits. Many young physicians joined specialty societies instead (Karlin 1998:20). Yet the AMA did not agree until 1977 to accept representatives of specialty societies into the House of Delegates and then only reluctantly, refusing to grant specialty societies proportional voting rights until 2000 (Campion 1984:83; Krieger 1998:19). Though recognition of specialty societies was, as Frank Campion suggested, "a change of major dimensions," the AMA's action was grudging and meager, a reaction to external events (1984:88).

In addition to specialization, new practice patterns, employment arrangements, and lifestyle changes created segmentation. Physicians became corporate managers, medical directors, hospitalists, and salaried workers. They drafted standards, established performance objectives, and engaged in various types of supervisory control. For much of the twentieth century, differences among physicians reflected types and degrees of specialization (see Stevens 1971). After 1985, diverse characteristics associated with patterns and practices of employment entered the mix. "On both analytic and pragmatic grounds," sociologist Eliot Freidson observed, "growing divisions between the managers and the managed, the judges and the judged, the employers and the employees, and the standard-setters and the standard followers are emerging to be a good deal more important than specialty in the segmentation of the profession" (Freidson 1986:221–222).

Todd recognized these growing divisions, albeit in an effort to bolster the AMA. "The potential for civil war within the profession has never been greater," he reported in 1992 (*Proceedings* June 1992:10). "More than anything else," he said, "the loss of collegiality" is damaging the profession (*Proceedings* December 1995:7). We "are succumbing to a sort of internal self-sabotage. If allowed to continue . . . this trend is going to destroy our profession [and] make us look like a quarreling batch of nonprofessionals" (*Proceedings* December 1995:7).

Medicine's internal strife mirrored its declining public image. Surveys showed a decreasing lack "of public confidence dating back to the early 1970s" (Schlesinger 2002:189). Economist Mark Schlesinger attributed medicine's image problem to "concerns about medical efficacy, the failure of physicians to preserve their altruistic image treating the poor, and a lack of trust in the political involvements of the medical profession" (2002:224). In his 1985 inaugural address, President Harrison Rogers acknowledged, "The public's perception of us is slipping, particularly with respect to the cost of our service and whether we are more concerned with making money or with taking care of them" (*Proceedings* June 1985:22).

HEALTH ACCESS AMERICA AND THE CLINTON HEALTH PLAN

For the first time in over a decade, health care rose to the top of the nation's agenda in the early 1990s. America paid more for health services than other industrialized nations yet counted thirty-seven million of its citizens, or 15 percent of the population, as uninsured. Middle-class Americans fretted because a recession, coupled with corporate downsizing, jeopardized not only their jobs but also their health and pension benefits. Politicians were quick to pounce on the health care "crisis," particularly with a presidential election only a year or two away. Presidential contenders Bob Kerry and

Paul Tsongas were among the first to announce their plans for comprehensive health care reform. Governor Bill Clinton was not far behind (Johnson and Broder 1996:61–78).

The prospect of a national debate on health care provided an opening, and potential leverage, for the AMA. Determined to be a player in the impending debate, the association developed its own health plan, known as Health Access America. First announced in 1990, the initiative included a minimum benefit package, a "phased-in requirement of employment coverage," and other features intended to expand access to care (*Proceedings* June 1992:103). Health Access America incorporated "six fundamental principles and [sixteen] key points" (Todd et al. 1991:2503). Embedded in the six principles were medicine's core values and beliefs: self-regulation, autonomy, and free choice of physician.

Accompanying Health Access America was a proposal for antitrust reform. Whatever form the president's proposal took, the AMA wanted antitrust to be included. Its Technical Advisory Committee on Health Care Reform articulated the association's position: "The AMA is not seeking modifications that would allow physicians to engage in anticompetitive conspiracies to fix prices or otherwise stifle competition. That would be counter to the AMA's market based approach to health system reform. However, the AMA is seeking [legislation that would give] independent physicians [the ability] to approach large, financially powerful payors with group proposals" (*Proceedings* December 1992:44).

Only months from the presidential election in 1992, the association used every means available to promote Health Access America, including television and radio advertising, media commentary, congressional testimony, promotional videos, and journal articles (*Proceedings* June 1992:104). These efforts failed, however, to produce the desired results. Five days after taking office, President Clinton announced the formation of a Task Force on National Health Reform with the first lady, Hillary Rodham Clinton, as its chair. Although the task force eventually embodied over 630 members, it did not include the AMA (Johnson and Broder 1996:96–112). Physicians were chafed. One group of doctors sued, claiming noncompliance with the open meetings laws (*Ass'n of American Physicians and Surgeons v. Clinton,* 997 F.2d 898 [D.C. Cir. 1993]). James Todd vented his frustration, albeit in a less confrontational manner. In his June 1993 report to the Board of Trustees, he wrote:

> Since January [1993], the AMA has engaged the new Administration and 103rd Congress in a carefully constructed campaign of advocacy on behalf of physicians and patients. . . . Our early contacts with the

> Clinton transition team suggested that the input of medicine would be welcome. But it quickly became obvious that the White House was organizing a special task force to revamp the nation's health care system without the expertise of practicing physicians. . . . After the AMA protested the exclusion of physicians, public opinion and editorial support helped persuade the Administration to pay attention to organized medicine's point of view. (*Proceedings* June 1993:23)*

On 10 September 1993, the AMA received a "leaked" copy of President Clinton's plan (Painter, Bristow, and Todd 1994:786). Known as the Health Security Act, the Clinton plan incorporated important features of "managed competition." Managed competition originated with Stanford business professor Alain Enthoven and the so-called Jackson Hole Group. The idea was to rationalize the forces of supply and demand. Health insurance purchasing cooperatives—comprising business, labor unions, and consumer groups—would negotiate with health plans and providers to furnish health care. Government's role would be limited to organizing the purchasing cooperatives and to establishing a minimum level of benefits.

The Clinton plan, however, envisioned a more prominent role for Congress and federal agencies than Enthoven's idea of managed competition. There would be a single alliance in each region rather than a "mulitiplicity of voluntary purchasing cooperatives" (Robinson 1999:46). A national health board would determine the benefits that regional alliances provided. Congress, moreover, could establish a global budget that all would have to meet. "The regional alliances would have to live within these externally determined budgets in the same sense that the provincial health insurance programs in Canada live within their tax-based budgets," economist James Robinson observed (1999:46). "If competition among health plans in any particular region did not hold premium inflation to a rate compatible with the centrally determined budget, the federal authorities were empowered to impose regulatory controls on the alliances, the health plans, and on health care providers" (Robinson 1999:46).

James Todd and other AMA leaders "were both encouraged and dismayed" (Painter, Bristow, and Todd 1994:786). They supported the president's plan and certain of its key features—universal coverage, a "prevention-

*Todd claimed that the AMA did not "seek a seat on the Task Force." He also noted that AMA leaders gained access to Ira Magaziner, the president's senior domestic policy advisor, and testified before the Task Force and some of its working groups (*Proceedings* June 1993:23). Nonetheless, the overall content and tone of Todd's report reveals discontent with the new administration for the AMA's lack of a more central role in policy development.

oriented benefit package modeled on the AMA's own recommendations," and a "fee-for-service option." But "the degree of centralized administration" that the proposal called for dampened their enthusiasm. The plan, they said, deviated too far from the "market-based approach" of managed competition because it used premium caps, or global budgeting, "as a 'backstop' to competition" (1994:786). Of further concern was the creation of a national health board to oversee administration of each region's purchasing alliance. Besides determining minimum benefits, the board's responsibilities included information control, cost containment, and quality assurance, activities that could encroach on medicine's traditional domain. Threatened by the extent of the board's potential authority under the Clinton plan, the AMA proposed a "national commission that [was] advisory in nature," was more limited in scope, and included a representative from the association (*Proceedings* December 1993:192).

Those against the president's proposal, special interests and persons philosophically opposed to greater government control, contributed to its defeat in 1994. By incorporating selected features of competing philosophies—market theory, government "command and control," and professionalism—to achieve universal coverage, the Clinton plan upset many. The creation of a national health board to regulate benefits, costs, and quality threatened professional autonomy; global budgets went against market competition; and the use of purchasing cooperatives concerned members of Congress who favored a single-payer system. Contemporaneous accounts of the plan's demise gave the AMA little more than passing reference (see Johnson and Broder 1996; Skocpol 1996). Most likely this was because the association's role was ambivalent at best. Doctors sought expanded access to care but feared government intervention. Initially, the AMA joined big labor and the American Association of Retired Persons in a series of advertisements to promote universal coverage but soon abandoned the effort under pressure from Republican members of Congress and its own rank and file (Skocpol 1996:161–162; Weissert and Weissert 1996:136).

PHYSICIAN JOINT VENTURES

Though the AMA was unable to obtain a special exemption from FTC jurisdiction, relief from the antitrust laws remained a high priority. Many physicians felt that the playing field was uneven, that the consolidation of hospitals and insurers in the 1980s and 1990s had led to disparities in bargaining power. Self-employed physicians, who comprised the bulk of the AMA's membership, sought ways to enhance their negotiating position. Because the antitrust laws prohibited independent practitioners from collaborating in certain instances to enhance their competitive positions, as in the case of collective bargaining with insurers over price, doctors sought legal means to gain leverage with managed care organizations. Physicians' options essentially were twofold: they could integrate their practices, as in the formation of partnerships or group practices, and thereby negotiate as a single unit, or they could become managers or employees of hospitals and corporate health plans.

The first option, integration, was not without danger. Justice Stevens's decision in the *Maricopa* case reproached foundations for medical care or other loose forms of integration. "The foundations are not analogous to partnerships or other joint arrangements in which persons who would otherwise be competitors pool their capital and share the risks of loss as well as the opportunities for profit," Stevens offered. "In such joint ventures, the partnership is regarded as a single firm competing with other sellers in the market" (*Maricopa*, 457 U.S. at 356).

The FTC vigorously applied the criteria that Justice Stevens established for the formation of joint ventures—"pooled capital" and "shared risk." Only doctors who merged their practices and shared risk through capitation, or "fee withholds," met the commission's criteria. Physicians felt they should be given more leeway to show that their activities had procompetitive effects under the rule of reason, but the FTC applied the per se test. In *Southbank IPA, Inc.* (114 F.T.C. 783 [1991] [consent order]), for instance, the FTC charged twenty-three obstetrician/gynecologists in Jacksonville, Florida, with illegal price-fixing. Though the physicians had used a discounted fee schedule and had engaged in quality assurance and utilization review, this was not enough, the agency said, to meet the definition of an "integrated" joint venture. "Physicians," the FTC admonished, "[must] pool their capital to finance the venture . . . and share substantial risks of adverse financial results" (114 F.T.C. at 792–793).

The AMA roundly criticized the FTC's position in *Southbank*. Of particular concern was the degree of integration required to satisfy the commission. "Under the *Southbank* definition," Edward Hirshfeld, the AMA's chief legal counsel, wrote, "an [independent practice association] will not qualify as an 'integrated joint venture' if it accepts payment on a fee-for-service basis" (AMA Special Collections [Hirshfeld Paper, "Physician Negotiations with Third Party Payers: Proposals for Antitrust Reform," March 1993:21]). The FTC's approach, he protested, "fails to recognize that [independent practice associations] can offer significant efficiencies even without financial risk-sharing." The type of "efficiencies" Hirshfeld had in mind were "joint billing, utilization review, quality assurance, adherence to practice guidelines, and the like" (Hirshfeld Paper, March 1993:21–22).

But the commission was not yet ready to accept Hirshfeld's more expansive definition. Rather than loosen its criteria for physician integration, the FTC dug in its heels. In 1993 and 1994, the FTC and the Department of Justice issued guidelines for physician joint ventures. The guidelines stated: "The Agencies will not challenge, absent extraordinary circumstances, an exclusive physician joint venture comprising 20 percent or less of the physicians in each physician specialty with active hospital staff privileges who practice in the relevant geographic market and share substantial financial risk. . . . The Agencies will not challenge, absent extraordinary circumstances, a non-exclusive physician network joint venture comprising 30 percent or less of the physicians in each physician specialty with active hospital privileges who practice in the relevant geographic market and share substantial financial risk" (U.S. Department of Justice and FTC Joint Statement 1994:68–69).

The 1994 guidelines codified the *Southbank* ruling. From Hirshfeld's perspective, the commission's position was unrealistic. According to Hirshfeld, most physician joint ventures comprised over 40 percent of the doctors in a particular market (Hirshfeld 1994:16). In addition, the commission's criteria for "substantial risk sharing" were difficult to implement. Many networks, Hirshfeld contended, "relied on discounted fees," while others accepted "capitation from some payers, fee withhold arrangements from others, and discounted fee arrangements from still other payers" (1994:16).

Physicians who wished to form joint ventures required extensive (and often expensive) legal advice. Seeking to protect their clients from allegations of price-fixing, lawyers contrived the "messenger model," a rather "cumbersome" device. "Messengers" under the model acted as liaisons between network physicians and managed care organizations. To escape antitrust scrutiny, physicians could not discuss fees among themselves, but they could communicate on an individual basis their "fee range" to their appointed messenger. Messengers then aggregated the fee range information and, without discussing the data with network doctors, used it to solicit and, if authorized, accept offers from third parties. Physicians abhorred the design. "These convoluted structures," Hirshfeld complained, "not only add costs and inefficiencies to the operation of a partially integrated network, they also place physicians at a disadvantage in the development and control of health care delivery networks in comparison to insurers, hospital holding companies, and other institutions" (1994:17–18).

Even Clark Havighurst came to physicians' aid. Asserting that the antitrust agencies had "adopt[ed] a rule of thumb when they should have applied the rule of reason," Havighurst decried the agencies' "doctrinal" stance. He believed, as did Hirshfeld, that the market for health care services had changed. "Although competition has not yet come to every local market," Havighurst observed, "concerted action by physicians is no longer an obstacle to its emergence." "*Maricopa*," he wrote, "involved a market very different from most of those one finds today" (Havighurst 1996:79, 78, and 84).

In an effort to gain relief for independent practitioners, the AMA employed a two-pronged strategy. While asking Congress to pass favorable legislation, it pressed the FTC and the Department of Justice for more lenient rules concerning physician joint ventures. Few at the AMA believed that Congress would loosen antitrust restructions. The association's gambit was intended to mollify its members and to put pressure on the antitrust agencies to change their enforcement posture. Admitting as much in a report concerning the Antitrust Health Care Advancement Act of 1996, a bill that required the antitrust agencies to apply the rule of reason to physician joint ventures, the Board of Trustees stated: "It is not realistic to expect that the antitrust laws or the federal labor laws to be changed by Congress or the courts to allow independent physicians to engage in collective bargaining. The nation is preoccupied with controlling the cost of health care, and allowing physicians to engage in collective bargaining is perceived to be inflationary. In addition, the public does not perceive physicians to be working under the kind of hardships that would warrant extending collective bargaining rights to them" (*Proceedings* December 1996:91).

In hearings before Congress on the 1996 act, AMA leaders unabashedly invoked Havighurst's name in support of the bill. Nancy Dickey, chair of the AMA Board of Trustees, testified, "Professor Havighurst strongly advocates applying the 'rule of reason' to legitimate physician networks" (AMA Special Collections [Statement of Nancy W. Dickey, 28 February 1996]). James Todd wrote Congressman Henry Hyde, professing Havighurst's endorsement of more relaxed standards (AMA Special Collections [Todd to Hyde, 8 March 1996]). P. John Seward, James Todd's successor, included Havighurst's forthcoming article on physician networks in a letter to President Clinton (AMA Special Collections [Seward to Clinton, 31 July 1996]).

The tactic worked. In August 1996, under pressure from members of Congress, the Department of Justice and the FTC issued more lenient criteria for the formation of physician joint ventures. "In accord with general antitrust principles," the guidelines said, "physician network joint ventures will be analyzed under the rule of reason, and will not be viewed as per se illegal, if the physicians' integration through the network is likely to produce efficiencies that benefit consumers" (U.S. Department of Justice and FTC Joint Statement 1996:71). The agencies agreed "in all cases [to] focus on substance, rather than form, in assessing a network's likelihood of producing significant efficiencies" (Joint Statement 1996:73). "Noncapitated," or fee-for-service, networks and various forms of clinical integration (practice parameters, utilization review, quality assurance programs, etc.) could suffice.

The AMA called the 1996 guidelines a "major victory" while taking credit for the final result. An editorial in *AMA News* boasted: "There *is* one thing that we can say right now and for certain: These landmark reforms are the direct result of a diligent five-year campaign by the AMA. No other organization could have taken on this fight anywhere near as effectively" (Antitrust Relief 1996). The association also credited Clark Havighurst and Robert Pitofsky, whom President Clinton had appointed to chair the commission. Chair Pitofsky's "openness to change," the association indicated, "provided a fresh break from the FTC's past" (Antitrust Relief 1996).

PHYSICIAN UNIONS AND THE CAMPBELL BILL

Another approach the AMA pursued on behalf of its membership was a special exemption from the antitrust laws for collective bargaining purposes. While the antitrust laws allowed employees to form unions and engage in collective bargaining, the exemption did not cover "independent contractors." Self-employed physicians could join unions, but collective bargaining remained illegal.

Physician unions first appeared in the early 1970s, principally in response to the formation of HMOs and the diminishing power of medical staff vis-à-vis hospital administration (Budrys 1997:9–17). The AMA moved to curtail these early voices of discontent within its own ranks. In 1973, it issued a report showing the disjuncture between professional goals and union principles. In the words of the report, "The union movement's traditional emphasis on collective action through strict majority rule [was] ill-suited to professional values of individualism and autonomy" (*Proceedings* December 1984:47).

Unions and foundations for medical care appeared about the same time. This was not a coincidence. While each attempted to counter the development of HMOs, each was also a reaction to the other. Physicians who joined unions often perceived that medical societies moved too slowly to confront the development of prepaid health care; professional associations, for their part, used FMCs to stem the union tide. In its 1975 Plan, the AMA sought to expand the role of state and national professional societies in negotiations on behalf of doctors with third parties. According to the 1975 Plan:

> The issue of third-party interference in the physician-patient relationship extends to the local level as well. As more and more controls have been imposed, a need has developed for a direct form of representation for physicians at the local level. Component societies are increasingly being put in the position of having to act as negotiating agents with local hospitals, insurance plans, and governmental bodies. Few local societies are in a position to perform this function, and as this activity increases and becomes more sophisticated in the future they will need support from the state and national levels of organized medicine. As the need for this type of negotiating activity has increased, various non-medical organizations have entered the health care industry to perform the negotiation function on behalf of local physician groups. This function is a legitimate responsibility of organized medicine and AMA thus faces a leadership challenge. (*Proceedings* 1975:54–55)

As this passage makes clear, the AMA recognized that its role in collective negotiations might be key to attracting future members. But once the Supreme Court applied the antitrust laws to the "learned professions" in *Goldfarb,* collective bargaining among independent doctors over business practices became illegal. Although state and local societies continued to skirt the antitrust laws in the late 1970s and early 1980s, they met their waterloo in the case of *Michigan State Medical Society.*

Despite the FTC's issuance of favorable guidelines in 1996 on physician joint ventures, the AMA, at the urging of its rank and file, continued to press Congress for a broader exemption (*Proceedings* December 1999:4–5, 29–36). In successive years—1998, 1999, and 2000—Representative Thomas Campbell of California (ironically, the head of the FTC's Bureau of Competition from 1981 to 1983) introduced the Quality Health-Care Coalition Act (otherwise known as the Campbell bill). The Campbell bill sought to exempt independent practitioners from the antitrust laws for collective bargaining purposes. Though modeled in part on the antitrust exemption for organized labor, the Campbell bill differed in several respects. First, it targeted self-employed providers, not employed practitioners. This was a dramatic departure from the labor exemption, which applied only in the employment context. Second, the exemption was limited to the bargaining unit. Individual providers could come together to negotiate with a particular plan but not with multiple firms, as in the case of organized labor. Third, the National

Labor Relations Act would not apply; there would be no government oversight of the collective bargaining process (U.S. Congress, House, 1999:19–20, 45, 55–59).

Just as the 1982 battle to remove FTC jurisdiction over the professions occurred when the political capital of the FTC was at its lowest, so the AMA pursued an exemption for collective bargaining when the backlash against managed care, discussed in the next chapter, was at its highest. There was no media campaign against the Campbell bill, as had occurred in 1982. Significantly, House Democrats supported the bill, believing that it checked the growing power of HMOs and other corporate arrangements. According to Representative John Conyers of Michigan: "We are responding to two alarming consumer trends . . . the ever-increasing level of concentration among health insurers and the exclusionary contracting practices by health insurance companies" (U.S. Congress, House, 1999:5 [Statement of John Conyers, Jr.]). Efforts of physicians to gain support of consumers, however, were unsuccessful. Consumer groups, for the most part, stayed on the sidelines, leaving it to the two big "power groups" (professional associations and health plans) to work out their differences (Kinder 2000; Court 2000).

The FTC strenuously objected to an antitrust exemption, just as it did in 1982. In the words of commission chair Robert Pitofsky: "The bill, while appealing in its apparent simplicity, threatens to cause serious harm to consumers, to employers, and to federal, state, and local governments" (U.S. Congress, House, 1999:16 [Statement of Robert Pitofsky]). Joining the FTC in opposition to the bill were the Department of Justice, the Health Insurance Association of America, the American Association of Health Plans, the U.S. Chamber of Commerce, and the Antitrust Coalition for Consumer Choice and Health Care. Nurse anesthetists and nurse midwives initially opposed the bill but relented when Democrats amended it to their satisfaction (U.S. Congress, House, 2000:5).

The House Judiciary Committee voted 26 to 2 in favor of the Campbell bill on 30 March 2000. Committee amendments to the proposed legislation included a three-year sunset provision and a prohibition on concerted action by physicians against other provider groups (U.S. Congress, House, 2000:4–5). Factoring in the sunset provision, the Congressional Budget Office projected modest losses and expenditures for government agencies and private insurance companies if the bill became law (U.S. Congress, House, 2000:19–28). The bill passed by a vote of 276 to 136 on the House floor but gained no sponsors in the Senate during an election year (Pear 2000).

While Congress debated the Campbell bill, another significant event occurred. In 1999, the AMA House of Delegates approved the formation of a collective bargaining unit over the Board of Trustees' objections. Support for the collective bargaining unit primarily came from medical students, residents, young doctors, female physicians, and international medical graduates (Klein 1999b). The need to increase the association's membership among these groups was a key factor in the House vote. Some doctors believed that "if the AMA can provide an organized and collective voice for physicians, it might be able to stem its declining membership" (Foubister 1998). Another important consideration was the message that AMA support for unions sent to state legislatures and HMOs. "Knowing that the AMA supports physician unions helps get antitrust bills passed at the state level, because lobbying groups are able to tell state legislatures that the AMA felt strongly enough about the issue to create a union," promoters said (Albert and Robeznieks 2002). Finally, an AMA-affiliated union gave doctors an outlet for their concerns—"an ethical alternative to more traditional labor organizations"—an editorial in the *AMA News* declared (The Right Approach for Doctors 2000).

The Board of Trustees named the new bargaining unit PRN, thus conveying to physicians that "the organization will only be used as needed" (Klein 1999a). PRN was to operate as an unincorporated association located at AMA headquarters in Chicago yet separate from the founding association. It would differ from a traditional union in several respects—no striking or honoring of picket lines, no union membership rules, and no ties to other labor groups. The AMA would select the board of directors of PRN and would require PRN to work with state and local medical societies (Klein 1999a). PRN would depend on the AMA, at least initially, for funding to cover its start-up and operating expenses.

But the AMA's experiment with unionization quickly fizzled. Plagued by financial difficulties, PRN severed its relationship with the AMA in 2003. In 2004, PRN combined forces with two other doctors' unions, the Committee of Interns and Residents and the Doctors Council, under the auspices of the Service Employees International Union, the largest health care union in the United States (www.seiu.org). The lesson of PRN was that professional associations and unions were not a good fit. PRN's inability to strike was only a small part of the rift. Dissimilar organizational structures, leadership styles, decision-making processes, and member composition marked the divide. Medical societies, with their numerous committees and detailed reports, were designed for collegial deliberation; unions were more dynamic, confrontational, and top-down. Professional associations and unions were products of unique experiences, contexts, and historical trends. Their founders designed them to perform certain tasks. Collective bargaining on behalf of employed physicians was not an optimum endeavor for the AMA or any of its divisions.

CONCLUSION

After its failed attempt in 1982 to obtain an exemption from FTC jurisdiction, the AMA began a decades-long struggle to modify the commission's rules and regulations. Although the FTC and the Department of Justice relaxed their rules on the formation of physician joint ventures, Congress did not pass a more comprehensive exemption. Still, legislative efforts like the Antitrust Health Care Advancement Act of 1996 and the Campbell bill put pressure on the FTC and the Department of Justice to accommodate the medical profession.

Though public opinion turned against managed care, as the next chapter relates in more detail, the political, social, and economic conditions that prompted a decline in professional power and authority persisted. Among these conditions were federal subsidization of health care and corresponding efforts to contain costs, expanded liability on the part of physicians and hospitals for medical injury, the growth of commercial enterprise, and the inclusion of public interest groups in the legislative process. Further trends pointed to public discontent with the medical profession over excessive fees and inadequate self-discipline, an aversion to professional monopolies, and congressional support for market competition.

Physicians failed in their efforts at so-called countervailing power, which the Campbell bill promoted, mainly because the trajectory of the health care industry fostered, rather than hindered, the emerging corporate model. Neither the federal government nor consumer groups saw a direct benefit to their interests if organized medicine succeeded. Indeed, the federal government enlisted managed care organizations beginning in the 1980s to stem costs in the Medicare program (Patel and Rushefsky 1999:173–174). Antitrust relief, if excessive, could undermine government policy (see Krause 1996:20–25, 29–49). Consumers, for their part, favored attempts to strengthen patient autonomy, not the pecuniary interests of physicians that bills like Campbell embodied.

9 The Demonization of Managed Care

Rolling back the antitrust laws as they applied to physicians proved to be a difficult undertaking. A special exemption for collective bargaining or the relaxation of enforcement standards for physician joint ventures required the acquiescence of Congress or the federal antitrust agencies. The health care revolution had altered an important dynamic: Before the revolution, insurers and health plans were allies of physicians. After the revolution, insurers and health plans were allies of government and employers in the quest for cost containment (see Fox 2006; Krause 1996). Protecting physicians from the full force of the antitrust laws threatened this shift in allegiance. If physicians regained their leverage over insurers, then the interests of government and employers might suffer.

Under the circumstances, how could the AMA achieve its objectives? How could it act on behalf of its main constituents, solo and small-group practitioners, in the absence of an antitrust rollback? The answer was simple but the strategy complex. Rather than seek "countervailing power," which was highly problematic for philosophical and logistical reasons, why not ask state legislatures and state courts to regulate the managed care industry? Indeed, the FTC could do little to prevent this occurrence. Professional associations, for instance, could lobby state legislatures for laws that were anticompetitive. In addition, they could encourage doctors to sue corporate health plans and then provide the necessary financial aid and legal assistance.

This chapter traces the efforts of the AMA and its component state and local societies to alter the rules of engagement between physicians and health plans. The core beliefs of the medical profession—self-regulation, clinical autonomy, and free choice of physician—framed the AMA's agenda. These core beliefs would determine the content of so-called patient protection legislation that the AMA and its allies, consumer groups among them, pursued in the mid- to late 1990s. Key to medicine's success in advancing these initiatives was the unpopularity of managed care, which surfaced in the early 1990s and grew throughout the decade. To be sure, poor treatment of consumers in many instances furthered managed care's downfall, but the AMA and its component state and local medical societies hastened its demise through state legislation, public relations, and various other tactics (Jacobson 2003; Havighurst 2002a:74–77).

THE AMA EMBARKS ON A NEW COURSE OF ACTION

The AMA had to come to terms with corporate medicine and physicians' role in it. Anachronistic policies and attitudes involving nontraditional practice patterns and arrangements had held medicine back, but so had declining membership, internal scandals, and ideological rift. James Todd endeavored to prepare the association for the transition to a market-oriented and competitive environment. His task would not be easy. As early as 1992, Todd attended a conference for leaders of corporate health plans at which he "formally acknowledged the equal legitimacy of prepaid and fee-for-service practice" (Millenson 1997:188). Outraged with Todd's acknowledgment, AMA members deluged the association with letters calling for his ouster (Millenson 1997:188).

Fortunately for Todd, the AMA employed a capable staff of lawyers and legislative analysts who were eager to move the association forward. Among the most innovative were Edward Hirshfeld and Ross Rubin. Hirshfeld joined the AMA in 1988 after gaining recognition as a specialist in antitrust law with a Chicago-based firm. A "tireless advocate for physicians," Hirshfeld "commanded universal respect" (Jaklevic 1998). Upon his untimely death in 1998 at age forty-eight, the FTC issued the following statement: "Ed Hirshfeld worked with many at the FTC over the years and was highly regarded by all who dealt with him for his intellect and professionalism" (as quoted in Jaklevic 1998). Ross Rubin, a contemporary of Hirshfeld, began his career with the AMA in 1976, three years after obtaining his law degree from the University of Illinois. A consummate strategist, Rubin helped to formulate and implement the association's legislative agenda as vice president of legislative affairs from 1990 to 2005. When he retired in 2005, the AMA recognized Rubin as "one of [its] most popular and adept executives" (Japsen 2005).

Hirshfeld and Rubin combined their energies to develop a blueprint for overcoming features of managed care that physicians opposed. They understood that the environment had changed, that the so-called iron triangles, or policy subsystems, that medicine once dominated had given way to more fluid networks comprised of many individuals and groups, including journalists, academics, and policy analysts. Political scientists Carol and William Weissert explained the transition: "The interest group world [had] come full circle: from tightly knit, closely coordinated, closed, and impervious to atomistic, uncoordinated, and highly permeable" (Weissert and Weissert 1996:113). For the AMA to wield power in this "free-floating" environment, it had to become more proactive. It had to use all the tools available to special interest groups, including legislation, litigation, and private sector advocacy. It had to form loose coalitions with other professional associations, consumer organizations, and former adversaries to advance mutual interests. Finally, it had to refine its message to stress values common to doctors and their patients.

State-action immunity and the *Noerr* doctrine underlay Hirshfeld and Rubin's sophisticated strategy. The *Noerr* doctrine, announced by the U.S. Supreme Court in *Eastern R.R. Presidents Conf. v. Noerr Motor Freight, Inc.* (365 U.S. 127 [1961]), limited the Sherman Act to the regulation of marketplace, not political, behavior. Thus, the Court's decision in *Noerr* allowed professional associations to seek passage of anticompetitive state laws that, because of state-action immunity, would be enforceable. Though there were limits to the *Noerr* doctrine—bogus or sham transactions, for instance—medical societies had much room to maneuver. They could pressure Congress and state legislatures to regulate managed care; they could lobby the FTC and the Department of Justice to relax enforcement criteria; they could sue managed care organizations on behalf of individual physicians; and they could instigate complaints and dissension to foster favorable rules of competition.

To be sure, Hirshfeld and Rubin's multipronged approach reflected earlier efforts. The AMA's attempt to pressure Congress in 1982 to restrict the FTC's jurisdictional authority was a prime example. But under the leadership of Hirshfeld and Rubin, the AMA did not pursue a zero-sum game. Although the association advanced certain initiatives, such as an antitrust exemption for collective bargaining purposes, there was always a backup plan that was more realistic and negotiable. In addition, the AMA emphasized core values, such as the doctor-patient relationship, to entice consumers. Medical societies no longer stood alone. They had allies, such as public interest groups, that also favored confidentiality and autonomy and were willing to fight for choice and independence.

For several months in 1994, senior executives of the AMA and its member councils engaged in strategic planning. At the association's annual meeting in June, Todd announced the AMA's revised goals and corporate mission. Henceforth, the AMA would "[do] fewer things [and do] them better"; it would "exemplify and promote professionalism within the medical profession and to the public"; it would "demonstrate leadership . . . on important issues of public health, professionalism and physician/patient advocacy"; and it would "be perceived as a friend to those we serve—both physician members as well as the public whose health we promote" (*Proceedings* June 1994:11).

In May 1994, the association launched the Patient Protection Act, its flagship initiative (*Proceedings* June 1994:12 and December 1994:13–26). Future legislative proposals (both federal and state), the AMA said, should include the following "elements":

> First, . . . any managed care health plan [would have to provide patients]: *a list of* covered services . . . *a list of* exclusions . . . directions on *who to call before a physician can treat them*. . . . And information about *how other patients feel about the health plan*. . . . In addition, all patients would have *three options of plans*—an HMO or PPO; a traditional insurance plan (without copays and deductibles); and a benefit payment schedule—the exact dollar amount the plan would pay for any medical service. . . . And *for those who choose the HMO option*—a point-of-service plan must be available—meaning, *the chance to buy an additional plan to see an outside doctor[.]*
>
> [Second], to *keep the plans honest and allow physicians to give patients the care they need*, the following would be required: The managed care *plans must allow physicians a voice for their patients in medical policy-making[.] And, no physician could be kicked out of a plan for giving patients all the care they need[.]*
>
> Finally, to keep the big insurance companies from stacking the deck against practicing physicians, *further safeguards would be put in place: Physicians* along with the plan *would develop practice parameters*—measures *by which patient care is judged* by the plan[.] And, *the managed care plan would have to disclose to physicians just who is reviewing their work*. (AMA Special Collections [Patient Protection Act Elements, 18 May 1994, emphasis in original])

Todd created an action group called Health Policy Advocacy to promote the new proposal (*Proceedings* December 1994:11). In 1995, the action group formed the Litigation Center and the Private Sector Advocacy and Support Team to assist in the endeavor. The AMA's goals in forming the Litigation Center and the Private Sector Advocacy team were twofold: (1) to maintain doctors' independence and loyalty to the profession, and (2) to achieve a level playing field between physicians and health plans. Efforts to undermine managed care and to overcome the antitrust laws furthered these two objectives.

THE QUALITY-CARE STRATEGY

In advancing legislation and in pursuing litigation, the profession's leaders emphasized the threat to quality that they asserted managed care posed. The AMA's entire strategy encompassed this one important notion—insurers could not be trusted to look out for patients' best interests; only physicians could. The strategy played to consumers' fears, as well as those of policy makers and politicians. Almost every piece of legislation that the AMA introduced in the 1980s and 1990s contained a reference to "quality" in its title—the Health Care Quality Improvement Act, the Patient Protection Act, the Quality Health-Care Coalition Act, and others. Organized medicine sought to create the false impression that managed care and quality care were inimical. The only concern of corporate health plans, the AMA both claimed and inferred, was to generate a profit.

But the evidence did not support the AMA's assertions. Most studies showed that allegations of poor quality were anecdotal and, for the most part, unfounded (see Peterson 1999:881–882). Contrary to the views of many observers, profitability and quality were positively correlated. "Our findings suggest that plans may not be making a choice between profits and quality but, rather, that plans need to generate profits to enable quality," researchers Patricia Born and Carol Simon determined (2001:173). More important, corporate medicine advanced several quality measures (best practices and outcomes data), reduced variance (clinical guidelines and protocols), and eliminated unnecessary treatments (see Agrawal and Veit 2002:41–43). Innovations such as these could not have occurred under the former, atomistic delivery system. Lost in all the rhetoric, moreover, was the role that managed care had played in checking health care spending. During the early to mid-1990s, national health expenditures "slowed dramatically," increasing only 4.4 percent in 1996, "the slowest growth recorded since 1960" (Levit, Lazenby, and Braden 1998:35–36).

Though managed care had rationalized the delivery system, lowered costs, and introduced quality measures, the market regime faltered, in part because health plans did not incur the trust of consumers. Many plans failed to integrate providers, to respond to patient complaints, and to accept legal accountability for erroneous decisions (see Havighurst 2002a:74–77).

"Consumers could not see HMOs' vaunted accomplishments," Clark Havighurst related, because "reported cost savings . . . appeared to accrue only to employers, plan shareholders, or well-paid CEOs" (2002a:75). Law professor Peter Jacobson agreed with Havighurst's assessment. "Through self-inflicted wounds, the industry self-destructed," he suggested (Jacobson 2003:394). "Some health plans have needlessly antagonized physicians in their cost control efforts rather than try to find ways to win their cooperation. . . . Many have done a poor job of recognizing and responding to reasonable and legitimate consumer and patient concerns. Although this behavior is not true of all health plans and not always true of any of them, such resistance, lack of responsiveness, and antagonistic behavior reflect negatively on the industry" (Jacobson 2003:390).

To be sure, health plan administrators were poor communicators, but the AMA fostered consumer dissent. Known as Medicine in Transition, the association's "managed care initiative" ostensibly professed "education of physicians" when first announced in 1992 (*Proceedings* June 1993:217). The initiative included a television series, a multimedia subscription series called "Doctor's Resource Service," and a speakers' bureau. Nationally recognized experts in managed care prepared several white papers for medical societies, large group practices, medical faculty practice plans, physician networks, and other physician-driven organizations (*Proceedings* June 1993:218–221).

In 1995, the AMA's Judicial Council issued a report setting forth certain "ethical dilemmas" that arose when corporate health plans came between doctors and their patients. These ethical dilemmas included the use of financial incentives to limit referrals, diagnostic tests, and other medical services and instructions to physicians, by contract or otherwise, to withhold information about unauthorized medical procedures. Seeking to remedy these ethical dilemmas, the Judicial Council made several recommendations, including a medical staff structure similar to that of hospitals for HMOs and other managed care entities, full disclosure to patients of treatment options and financial incentives, and the right of patients to appeal adverse decisions of health plans on medical coverage (AMA Council on Ethical and Judicial Affairs 1995:330–335).

In an abrupt change from just a few years earlier, speeches of AMA presidents were highly confrontational. President Daniel Johnson's remarks in 1996 before the House of Delegates reflected this new stance. He declared:

> Since June, I have been on the road a lot, crisscrossing the country, meeting every kind of doctor in every kind of setting, taking the pulse of our profession. I've heard it all. The good, the bad and the ugly. Literally. And it's left me with a need to pick up my discussion with

> you where I left off in Chicago last June. Near the end of my inaugural remarks I talked about my pride in being a physician. But what I'm seeing and hearing in my travels is that my beloved profession is being decimated. Degraded. Debased. I see a dumbing down of medicine. And I've become very angry and disgusted with what I see. It's like that country and western song: A lot of health plans are getting the gold mine, but patients and their physicians are getting the shaft. Outside forces that do not necessarily have our patients' best interests at heart are driving a stake in our hearts. Our collegiality is being destroyed. The patient-physician relationship is literally being plowed under. Patients are being herded like cattle. Primary care physicians are being pitted against those not in primary care. Physicians are being forced out of current delivery settings and required to choose up sides, often no longer speaking to other physicians. (*Proceedings* December 1996:4)

Rhetoric such as this encouraged aggressive action by AMA staff. During 1995, the health law division gathered information on the alleged abuses of managed care (*Proceedings* December 1996). AMA attorneys contacted hundreds of physicians and their office managers, obtaining over two hundred contracts between doctors and health plans in the process. The division's findings became grist for the mill. Several contracts, it turned out, contained so-called gag clauses that, the association's attorneys claimed, prevented doctors from fully disclosing information about proper medical treatments to their patients. For example, a 1994 managed care contract of U.S. Healthcare contained the following provision:

> Physician shall agree not to take any action or make any communication which undermines or could undermine the confidence of enrollees, potential enrollees, their employers, their unions, or the public in U.S. Healthcare or the quality of U.S. Healthcare coverage.
>
> Each physician must be supportive of the philosophy and concept of U.S. Healthcare.
>
> Physician shall keep the Proprietary Information [payment rates, utilization review procedures etc.] and This Agreement strictly confidential. (AMA Special Collections [U.S Healthcare 1994 Physician Contract; brackets in original])

Health plans removed provisions like these from managed care contracts once the AMA brought the matter to light (AMA Special Collections [Statement of Robert McAfee, 30 May 1996]), but plans could not avoid the bad publicity their early actions generated. AMA spokespersons asserted in press releases and interviews with the media that gag clauses impeded the legal and ethical duties of doctors to provide informed consent (*Proceedings*

December 1996:120). Several newspapers with broad national circulation, such as the *New York Times,* the *Boston Globe,* and the *Philadelphia Inquirer,* trumpeted doctors' and patients' adverse reactions to gag clause restrictions. So did magazines such as *Time, Newsweek,* and *U.S. News and World Report.* A headline from the *Los Angeles Times* read: "Unmuzzling HMO Physicians: State and Federal Bills Aim at Treatment Option 'Gag Rules'" (2 July 1996); a *Washington Post* headline—"MAMSI Gives an Ultimatum to Doctors on Referral Limits"—targeted the largest health plan in Washington, D.C. (22 July 1996). Health and trade publications, including *Money, Modern Healthcare,* and *Medical Economics,* touted the AMA's perspective. Many of the major television networks and cable stations—CNN, ABC, NBC, and PBS—criticized managed care (*Proceedings* December 1996:120–121; see also Brodie, Brady, and Altman 1998).

Public opinion surveys showed decreasing support for the managed care industry. According to a Louis Harris poll, consumer dissatisfaction with HMOs increased from 39 percent to 58 percent between 1995 and 1998 (Jacobs and Shapiro 1999:1024). Several other surveys, including those conducted by *Time*/CNN, Princeton Survey Research Associates, and ABC/*Washington Post,* showed similar results (Jacobs and Shapiro 1999:1024–1026). Common complaints were that health plans denied coverage, limited referrals to specialists, and decreased the time physicians spent with their patients (Berger, Weissman, and Surrusco 2000:1). Physicians and nurses admitted they exaggerated medical findings to obtain insurance coverage for consumers (*USA Today* 24 September 1999). Political scientists Lawrence Jacobs and Robert Shapiro remarked: "The negative turn in the public's evaluation toward the quality of treatment under managed care as it has expanded is striking; as striking, though, is the erosion in public perception of the efficacy of managed care" (1999:1025).

REWRITING THE CONTRACT BETWEEN PHYSICIANS AND HEALTH PLANS

Media criticism of managed care fueled legislative action. The AMA targeted limitations on specialty referrals and emergency care, "deselection" of doctors, and payment denials. During a four-year period, from 1994 to 1998, states passed nine hundred laws that regulated health plans (Page 1999b). These laws loosened managed care's restrictions by providing direct access to ob-gyns, establishing prudent layperson standards for emergency room use, incorporating independent review of plan decisions, requiring that plans disclose restrictive formularies, furthering continuity of care (retention of doctor for a certain period after changing plans), and compelling minimum hospital stays for mastectomies (Page 1999a).

In addition, several states enacted "any-willing-provider" or "freedom of choice" laws that covered physician services (Ohsfeldt et al. 1998:1540). Under any-willing-provider, health plans had to include on their panels all physicians that were willing to accept the price terms of managed care contracts; under freedom of choice, subscribers could receive care from any licensed provider, subject to larger co-payments or price differentials. Because all physicians who signed a contract received the same payment under any-willing-provider, no physician could hope to increase patient volume through a price reduction. Thus, health plans could not reward price-cutters with an assurance of more business.

Representatives Greg Ganske and Ed Markey introduced a bill in Congress in 1996 that declared all gag clauses null and void. Though the AMA testified in favor of the bill, wrote letters, and formed the Patient Advocacy Alliance, the initiative floundered (AMA Special Collections [Seward to Boss, 20 August 1996]). The U.S. General Accounting Office (GAO) found, at the time of its review in 1997, that no such clauses existed (GAO 1997). Yet the GAO's findings did not deter state legislatures nor alter public opinion. Before 1997 drew to a close, thirty-four states had enacted antigag legislation and Congress had outlawed similar provisions in the Medicare and Medicaid programs (AMA Special Collections [Seward to Gingrich, 8 October 1997]).

As shown in table 3, state legislative enactments in the mid- to late 1990s, collectively known as patient protection legislation, closely tracked the core beliefs of the medical profession. Any-willing-provider and point-of-service options, for instance, addressed free choice of physician; restrictions on preauthorization and utilization review dovetailed with clinical autonomy; the initiation of grievance procedures, including the right of patients to appeal treatment denials to a body independent of their health plans, bolstered professional self-regulation.

The AMA's Litigation Center sought to expand, defend, and enforce the new legislation and to alter the managed care contract even further. In 1998, a group of Florida doctors, the Florida Physicians Association, and the Florida Medical Association sued Prudential Health Care Plan, Inc., for alleged improper claim denials and other claims-handling violations (Klein 1998). Over the next several years, the Litigation Center paid attorneys' fees, offered legal advice, and filed *amicus* briefs in lawsuits in Pennsylvania (*Pennsylvania Psychiatric Society v. Green Spring Health Services*, 280 F.3d 278 [3rd Cir. 2002]), New York (*American Medical Ass'n v. United Health-*

TABLE 3. *Core Beliefs of the Medical Profession and Related Legislative Initiatives*

Core Belief	*Related Legislation*
1. Free choice of physician	Any-willing-provider laws
	Freedom of choice initiatives
	Access to specialists
	Point-of-service options
	Continuity of care requirements
2. Clinical autonomy	Restrictions on preauthorization and utilization review
	Continuity of care requirements
	Information disclosure
	Access to emergency services (prudent layperson standard)
	Gag clause prohibitions
	Confidentiality of medical records
	Disclosure or bar of financial incentives
	Mandated benefits
	Noninterference rules
	Minimum hospital stays
	Clinical trials or experimental treatment
3. Self-regulation	Grievance procedures (independent, external review of denials of care and other treatment decisions)

care [S.D.N.Y.]), Georgia (*Medical Ass'n of Georgia v. Blue Cross and Blue Shield of Georgia,* 536 S.E.2d 184 [Ga. App. 2000]), and Florida (*In re Managed Care Litigation,* 209 F.R.D. 678 [2002]). "Physicians are getting over their collective case of liticaphobia (that's fear of lawsuits)," an editorial in the *AMA News* duly noted (Medicine's Legal Offensive 2001).

The AMA also backed legal actions that attacked certain features of managed care contracts. These included "hold harmless" clauses, "all products" clauses, and "deselection" provisions. The case of *Potvin v. Metropolitan Life Ins. Co.* (997 P.2d 1153 [Cal. 2000]) concerned physician deselection. In 1992, the Metropolitan Life Insurance Company (MetLife) terminated Dr. Potvin "without cause" from its preferred provider panel. Other health plans as well as independent practice associations "became suspicious." They too dropped Potvin (Klein 2000). When pressed to disclose the reason for its action, Metlife noted that Potvin had been sued on four separate occasions for medical malpractice, one of which resulted in a settlement for $713,000. Despite his past history, Potvin sued MetLife, claiming that he had a right to "fair procedure" before his termination.

California's highest court agreed with Potvin, holding that the termination clause in MetLife's contract had limited Potvin's right to fair procedure (*Potvin*, 997 P.2d at 1162). The decision recognized a "public interest" exception to the law on "at-will" employment. Health plans, in the view of the court majority, were "private entities affecting the public interest" and, as such, had "obligations to the public" that were separate and "apart from and in some cases despite the existence of a contract" (*Potvin*, 997 P.2d at 1159). The court's ruling was a coup for the AMA, which had paid a portion of Potvin's attorneys' fees and filed a brief on his behalf. Commenting on the decision, Jack Bierig said, "A case like this that sets forth the public policy reasons for affording due process is very useful in designing legislation and advocating for that legislation" (Klein 2000:4). Though rulings of federal and state courts following *Potvin* "varied," legislation in Colorado, California, and other states constrained the ability of corporate health plans to terminate physicians (Furrow et al. 2004:835–836).

Court pronouncements, such as *Potvin*, and legislative enactments, such as any-willing-provider laws, had a cumulative effect. Economist James Robinson warned that "myriad small rules, requirements, and judicial precedents designed to protect the purportedly helpless consumer" would undermine corporate medicine (Robinson 1999:235). Law professor David Hyman claimed that costs would rise and that efforts to increase access to care would suffer. "In a voluntary insurance market," Hyman insisted, "cost-increasing consumer protections (which are what has emerged to date) will predictably price some people out of the market" (Hyman 1999:1062–1063). The observations of Robinson and Hyman proved to be prophetic. Though the reasons health care costs began to rise again in 1996 were multipronged and complex, it was difficult to ignore that this rise coincided with the passage of anti–managed care legislation. "Prior to 1996 . . . managed care had succeeded in lowering annual cost increases to around two percent," law professor Robert Rich and his colleague Christopher Erb observed (Rich and Erb 2005:248). But "between 1996 and 2002," they noted, "annual cost increases rebounded to around ten percent, essentially in parallel with the rise in state anti–managed care laws" (2005:248).

The relationship between the rising costs of health care and the passage of patient protection legislation in all fifty states and the District of Columbia was more than coincidental. Anti–managed care laws targeted certain principles of market competition, among them the ability of health plans to select low-cost providers and to monitor the cost and quality of their services. Any-willing-provider and freedom of choice provisions, for instance, made it virtually impossible for insurers to restrict provider panels for economic reasons. The *Potvin* case exacerbated the situation still further by constraining the dismissal of poorly performing physicians. Dissenting in *Potvin,* Judge Janice Brown highlighted the key fallacy in the court's reasoning: "What I am saying," she wrote, "is that this court has made doctors a protected class. Until the economy turned around, one could hardly open a newspaper without reading of yet another company that had laid off thousands of employees. However, no one has suggested that textile workers or bank employees, for example, had a right to a hearing before losing their jobs" (*Potvin,* 997 P.2d at 1165). The antitrust laws protected competition as a process, not doctors from competition. Any-willing-provider laws, freedom of choice provisions, and the *Potvin* decision perverted this important distinction.

ERISA, CONGRESS, AND THE U.S. SUPREME COURT

The list of provisions struck from contracts between doctors and health plans was becoming quite long. It included gag clauses, hold harmless clauses, deselection clauses, and "all-products" provisions. But success at the state level did not alter the AMA's quest for patient protection legislation at the national level. Congressional action, members of the association believed, was necessary to overcome the Employee Retirement Income Security Act (ERISA) of 1974 that, in an effort to streamline and make uniform the administration of employee benefit plans, preempted inconsistent state laws and regulations.

ERISA was of no concern to physicians at the time it passed—the health care revolution had yet to occur, few contemplated corporate liability for medical malpractice, and pension and welfare funds, not health care benefits, were the law's main targets. ERISA, moreover, contained an exception for state laws that regulated insurance; health insurance presumably fell within the exception (see Havighurst, Blumstein, and Brennan 1998:66–67). But the exception only applied to companies that were in the business of selling or underwriting insurance (see *Pilot Life Ins. Co. v. Dedeaux,* 481 U.S. 41, 45 [1987]). Thus companies that self-insured could avoid burdensome state regulations, including state taxes on health insurance premiums. Avoidance of state regulations and state taxes proved to be a strong inducement, particularly for large companies with several hundred employees. By 1998, approximately 70 percent of Americans with employer-sponsored health insurance were in self-insured plans (Havighurst, Blumstein, and Brennan 1998:67).

The AMA's problems with ERISA began in the 1980s. In 1988, the House of Delegates expressed concern over the growth of self-insured plans. A House resolution questioned the "adequacy of [federal] controls or national voluntary standards to which self-insured companies may be subject." Federal regulation was "minimal," AMA leaders said (*Proceedings* December 1989:204). Proposed legislation to "repeal or amend ERISA" accompanied the association's Health Access America plan in 1992. The reason for repealing or amending ERISA, the association claimed, was "to allow for more rational and competitive regulation of self-insured health benefit plans" (*Proceedings* June 1992:103).

Efforts to override ERISA gained momentum in 1993 following a decision by the U.S. Court of Appeals for the Fifth Circuit in *Corcoran v. United Healthcare, Inc.* (965 F.2d 1321 [5th Cir. 1992]). At issue was the decision of United Healthcare to pay for home nursing care but not hospitalization during Mrs. Corcoran's high-risk pregnancy. Tragically, Mrs. Corcoran's unborn child died when she was at home and no nurse was on duty (965 F.2d at 1324). Asserting a connection between the failure to hospitalize and the death of their unborn child, the Corcorans sued United Healthcare under Louisiana's wrongful death statute. The case turned on the application of ERISA. If the federal law preempted Louisiana's wrongful death action, then the Corcorans' cause of action against United Healthcare for compensatory and punitive damages would vanish. ERISA only provided contractual, not tort, damages.

The federal courts sought to determine whether United Healthcare's refusal to cover the costs of hospitalization was a "medical" or an "eligibility" decision. If a medical decision, then the wrongful death claim could proceed; if an administrative or eligibility decision, then ERISA applied. The Corcorans asserted that United Healthcare's failure to cover the costs of hospitalization was an "erroneous medical decision" and, as such, was "not merely an administrative determination" (965 F.2d at 1330). In response, United Healthcare claimed that its decision was administrative in nature, that, in the words of the statute, it "related to" Mrs. Corcoran's employee benefit plan (965 F.2d at 1329).

A federal district court ruled in favor of United Healthcare, and the Fifth Circuit affirmed. "In our view," the circuit court held, "United makes medical decisions as part and parcel of its mandate to decide what benefits are available under [Mrs. Corcoran's] plan" (965 F.2d at 1332). Despite ruling for United Healthcare as she felt compelled to do, Judge Carolyn Dineen King (the author of the court's opinion) expressed her displeasure with the ERISA preemption: "The result ERISA compels us to reach means that the Corcorans have no remedy, state or federal, for what may have been a serious mistake. While we are confidant that the result we have reached is faithful to Congress's intent . . . , the world of employee benefit plans has hardly remained static since 1974. Fundamental changes such as the widespread institution of utilization review would seem to warrant a reevaluation of ERISA" (965 F.2d at 1338).

Corcoran and cases like it caused an outcry among patients and physicians for legislative action (see Jacobson 2003; Havighurst 2002a). Coincident with the passage of patient protection legislation, federal courts began to "chip away" at the ERISA preemption. Efforts to circumscribe the ERISA preemption started in the mid-1990s when courts observed that it was often difficult to separate medical from administrative decisions. Cases in which HMOs hired and retained poor physicians or delayed treatment so that patients would have access to plan-eligible providers, for instance, contained elements of each. Such "mixed" treatment and eligibility decisions, courts held, escaped ERISA's preemption (see *Dukes v. U.S. Healthcare, Inc.*, 57 F. 3d 350 [3rd Cir. 1995]; *Pegram v. Herdrich*, 530 U.S. 211 [2000]). The result was a "litigation explosion against managed care," law professor Barry Furrow and others indicated (Furrow et al. 2004:671).

The AMA asked Congress to go a step further by overriding ERISA altogether. On at least four separate occasions during the months of July and August 1998, E. Radcliff Anderson, the association's executive vice president, and Nancy Dickey, its president, wrote House speaker Newt Gingrich, imploring him to strike the preemption. In one letter, Dickey wrote: "The rhetoric on the HMO liability issue fails to address our sole motivation. Our objective is to restore fairness and basic principles. . . . No organization should be granted special legal protections for negligent acts that result in permanent injury" (AMA Special Collections [Dickey to Gingrich, 10 August 1998]). But Republicans, who controlled the House of Representatives, resisted. "Our goal is not to create more lawsuits," Speaker Gingrich said. "Our goal is to get the patient to the right doctor with the right knowledge to get the right care as rapidly as possible" (Aston 1998).

Despite congressional inaction, the Supreme Court continued to circumscribe the ERISA preemption. In the cases of *Rush Prudential HMO v. Moran* (536 U.S. 355 [2002]) and *Kentucky Ass'n of Health Plans v. Miller* (538 U.S. 329 [2003]), the Court curtailed ERISA's preemption of patient protection legislation. *Rush Prudential* upheld an Illinois law on external review, while *Miller* sustained a Kentucky law on any-willing-provider. Elated, a prominent AMA official stated: First "we [had] patient protection acts in forty-eight states. And now we have *Rush Prudential* and *Miller*. The U.S. Supreme Court said that, even in self-insured plans, administrators have to comply with state laws. It took fifteen years . . . [but] we knew it was going to happen. We saw the writing on the walls. So what we did was, we lined up the states. Sure, we pushed this national agenda. People say the AMA lost. I say we won. It will take a long time for them to realize that" (Rubin 2003).

Rush Prudential and *Miller* destroyed any pretense of a uniform, national health policy. Though the AMA suffered a setback in 2004 when the Court held that ERISA preempted a Texas law making health plans liable for their coverage decisions,* *Rush Prudential* and *Miller* significantly advanced the association's agenda. "In short, the Supreme Court has sounded an ERISA 'all-clear' for state regulation of plans' management practices," health policy experts Gregg Bloche and David Studdert maintained (Bloche and Studdert 2004:35). Even HMOs that administered self-insured plans, the Court indicated, would have to comply with state rules and regulations (*Miller*, 538 U.S. at 336 n. 1).

FOOTNOTE 17 REVISITED

By upholding laws on any-willing-provider and external review of treatment denials, Supreme Court rulings in *Rush Prudential* and *Miller* bolstered professional beliefs in clinical autonomy and free choice of physician. In *California Dental Ass'n v. F.T.C.* (526 U.S. 756 [1999]), the Court also expanded professional self-regulation by making it more difficult for the FTC to police ethical restraints on business practices. The sentiments expressed in footnote 17 of *Goldfarb* loomed large in *California Dental.*

California Dental involved ethical restrictions on discount pricing and quality-based advertising. The defendant dental association claimed that its actions protected consumers from the dissemination of information that

---

*In the consolidated cases of *Aetna v. Davila* and *Cigna v. Calad* (542 U.S. 200 [2004]), the Court distinguished between "plans that are owned and operated by treating physicians or provide care through their own employed physicians, and plans that merely impose coverage constraints on independent providers through coverage rules or decisions" (Jost 2004:w423–w424). "The former," law professor Timothy Jost wrote, "are subject to direct and vicarious liability under state malpractice law; the latter are protected from state tort liability under ERISA" (2004:w424).

was false and deceptive. But there was nothing inherently false or deceptive about the type of advertising that the association restricted. The case seemed a logical extension of the FTC's ruling in the *AMA* case. Indeed, the FTC found the restrictions illegal per se, and the United States Court of Appeals for the Ninth Circuit affirmed, using a "quick-look," rule of reason analysis. Yet in a 5–4 decision, the Supreme Court reversed. Justice David Souter, writing for the majority, found that the restrictions might have "a net procompetitive effect, or possibly no effect at all" (*California Dental*, 526 U.S at 771). Souter's reasoning on this key point invoked footnote 17 of *Goldfarb* (526 U.S at 771 n. 10). As Souter explained: "The [Ninth Circuit] assumed . . . that some dental quality claims may escape justifiable censure, because they are both verifiable and true. But its implicit assumption fails to explain why it gave no weight to the countervailing, and at least equally plausible, suggestion that restricting difficult-to-verify claims about quality or patient comfort would have a procompetitive effect by preventing misleading or false claims that distort the market. It is, indeed, entirely possible to understand the [dental association's] restrictions on unverifiable quality and comfort advertising as nothing more than a procompetitive ban on puffery" (526 U.S. at 777–778).

Justice Stephen Breyer, writing in dissent, seemed dumbfounded. He thought that the "anticompetitive tendencies" of the dental association's limitations on advertising "were obvious." Breyer wrote: "An agreement not to advertise that a fee is reasonable, that service is inexpensive, or that a customer will receive a discount makes it more difficult for a dentist to inform customers that he charges a lower price. If the customer does not know about a lower price, he will find it more difficult to buy lower price service. That fact, in turn, makes it less likely that a dentist will obtain more customers by offering lower prices. And that likelihood means that dentists will prove less likely to offer lower prices. But why should I have to spell out the obvious?" (526 U.S. at 784).

The Court's decision reopened the door to professional self-regulation in the commercial sphere, a matter that many believed had been put to rest in *Professional Engineers.* The Court said, in effect, that professional associations might restrain competition if necessary to overcome market failure. "It is not easy," Clark Havighurst wrote, "to reconcile the Court's reasoning in [*California Dental*] or the higher burden of proof it imposed on the FTC with what had previously appeared to be a strong trend in antitrust law away . . . from the seemingly permissive dictum in *Goldfarb*'s footnote 17" (Havighurst 2001:950). "Some attorneys," Thomas Greaney noted, "believe that the *California Dental* opinion leaves a wide opening for professionals to assert that a broader inquiry is almost always required because quality claims can be broadly made" (Greaney 2002:190). Why did the Court rule the way it did? Was the decision an anomaly, the result of doctrinal confusion, or did it indicate a change in the Court's composition and accompanying philosophy?

To be sure, the decision reflected a shift in court composition (see Muris 2000:286). Many of the justices who had decided the *Goldfarb, Professional Engineers,* and *AMA* cases were gone at the time of the ruling in *California Dental,* and new appointees had taken their place. As the opinion in *California Dental* suggests, Justices Scalia, Souter, and Thomas joined Justices Rehnquist and O'Connor to bolster the "professional camp," while Justices Breyer, Ginsburg, and Kennedy joined Stevens to support the "antitrust camp." By the slim margin of one vote, the former minority became the new majority.

More was involved than a simple switch in votes, however. Federal courts after *Professional Engineers* found it increasingly difficult to rule out all noneconomic justifications for the behavior of nonprofit organizations that operated in the commercial sector. In *N.C.A.A. v. Board of Regents of the Univ. of Oklahoma* (468 U.S. 85 [1984]), for instance, the Supreme Court determined that the NCAA's exclusive television contracts with ABC, CBS, and Turner Broadcasting and its restrictions on the number of appearances by any one team violated the Sherman Act. Although the Court held against the NCAA, it relied on noneconomic considerations—education and amateurism—to determine whether the rule of reason should apply to the situation (Kirby and Weymouth 1985:51). In *United States v. Brown Univ.* (5 F.3d 658 [3rd Cir. 1993]), moreover, the U.S. Court of Appeals for the Third Circuit reversed a ruling against the Massachusetts Institute of Technology (one of the defendants in the case) on the grounds that MIT's noneconomic justifications for sharing information with other universities in parceling out financial aid—limited funds, socioeconomic diversity, and need-blind admissions—enhanced consumer welfare and were procompetitive (*Brown Univ.,* 5 F.3d at 677).

Recognition of noneconomic justifications in support of competition, as occurred in the *N.C.A.A.* and *Brown Univ.* cases, may explain the ruling in *California Dental.* At issue in *California Dental* was the amount of proof needed to show that the restraints on discount pricing and quality-based advertising that the dental association imposed were unreasonable. In certain cases involving professional restraints, including *Maricopa,* the Court had used a "quick look" rule of reason analysis, often in deference to professional values (see also *F.T.C. v. Indiana Federation of Dentists,* 476 U.S. 447 [1986]). Yet the Court rarely saw any need for a detailed inquiry in those cases. *California Dental* reversed the trend. By extending the application of footnote 17 further than had occurred previously, the Court in *California Dental* demanded more careful scrutiny. In so doing, the Court made it more difficult for the FTC and other enforcement agencies to pursue the anticompetitive practices of professional associations.

THE AMA EXTENDS ITS INFLUENCE OVER THE CLINICAL ARENA

Medicine's success in the commercial realm accompanied its achievements in the clinical arena. The antitrust agencies of the federal government, as indicated in chapter 7, declined to apply the antitrust laws to the market for medical information. This meant that the AMA was free to extend its influence over private entities that accredited HMOs and other new and emerging forms of health care finance and delivery. Health plans sought accreditation to gain contracts with large employers (many large employers refused to engage the services of unaccredited plans) and to avoid the need for separate state surveys and reviews (many states determined that accreditation satisfied regulatory requirements). Compliance with a uniform set of standards became the touchstone for HMOs and other managed care organizations.

Several entities, including the Joint Commission, the Utilization Review Accreditation Commission, and the National Committee for Quality Assurance, began to accredit health plans in the early 1990s. In each instance, the AMA sought to maintain and extend its influence over the setting of performance standards. The Joint Commission, which changed its name to the Joint Commission on Accreditation of Healthcare Organizations (JCAHO) in 1987, operated five programs of accreditation for health care facilities by 1990. These included ambulatory care (including managed care), home care, hospital care, long-term care, and mental health. Just as the AMA oversaw hospital accreditation, so too it guided the development of standards for the accreditation of managed care organizations. Indeed, a 1991 report of the AMA Board of Trustees boasted of the association's broad command of the process:

> Since the 1983 Annual Meeting, the House of Delegates has taken 56 separate actions that have been transmitted to the Joint Commission. Thirty-nine of these requested specific actions by the Joint Commission, usually in the form of amendments to the standards. The remaining 17 actions were the transmittal of AMA policy for the information of the

> Joint Commission. Of the 39 requests for Joint Commission action, 18 have resulted in standards or actions consistent with AMA policy and only six were acted on unfavorably. Nine actions transmitted after the 1990 Annual and Interim Meetings are still pending. (*Proceedings* June 1991:104)

The AMA's high rate of success stemmed from the close and overlapping connections between the association and the Joint Commission. Seven of JCAHO's twenty-four commissioners in the early 1990s were AMA appointees; of these seven, all were on the association's Board of Trustees (*Proceedings* December 1991:176). As of December 1991, JCAHO had twenty-four commissioners, allocated as follows: AMA (seven), American Hospital Association (seven), American College of Physicians (three), American College of Surgeons (three), American Dental Association (one), and public (three) (*Proceedings* December 1991:175). As of 2005, JCAHO had twenty-nine commissioners. The AMA still had seven seats, with additional seats allocated to the public and to the American Society of Internal Medicine.

It was not until 1997 that the AMA appointed nontrustees to three-year terms as JCAHO commissioners (*Proceedings* December 2004:137). Until then, the AMA was "the only corporate member organization [of JCAHO] that consistently appoint[ed] its Board members exclusively to serve as Commissioners" (*Proceedings* June 1996:127). Appointment of board members to serve as JCAHO commissioners, the association reported, "ensured that AMA policy was consistently represented and that the information and decision-making requirements of the [AMA] were met" (*Proceedings* December 1991:176). While AMA leaders recognized that "it [was] not possible to 'win' every issue," they won in most instances (*Proceedings* December 1991:176).

The AMA's role in the development of JCAHO standards was as follows: After each meeting of the House of Delegates, AMA staff communicated relevant "policy resolutions" to the association's JCAHO commissioners (*Proceedings* June 1991:103). The JCAHO board then referred the association's policy resolutions to the appropriate Professional and Technical Advisory Committee (PTAC). Following due consideration, PTAC advised the Standards and Survey Procedures (SSP) Committee of the Joint Commission and, after further review, SSP "[made its] recommendations directly to the [full commission]" (*Proceedings* June 1991:176). AMA commissioners served on and often controlled both PTAC and SSP. In effect, "the AMA was . . . advising itself," the association acknowledged (*Proceedings* December 1991:177).

As in the case of hospitals and HMOs, the AMA influenced accrediting bodies in generating standards for utilization review organizations. Comprising providers, consumers, employers, and regulators, the Utilization Review Accreditation Commission (URAC) carried substantial weight in the health care community. During the 1990s, URAC adopted AMA positions on external review of managed care decisions and certain "core quality standards" (*Proceedings* June 2000:167). These "core quality standards" concerned "clinical leadership, protection of confidential health information, internal quality management, complaint and grievance handling, operational policies and procedures, and oversight of delegated functions" (*Proceedings* June 2000:167). According to a 1998 report of the AMA: "Membership in URAC continues to be an effective advocacy forum for the AMA because of our continued success in incorporating our policies into standards. Accreditation is an increasingly important option to regulation in response to consumer concerns about managed care. When regulatory efforts are sought, URAC accreditation has the effect of law if mandated or deemed sufficient to satisfy state regulations. At the time this report was prepared, 22 states and the District of Columbia had incorporated one or more sets of URAC standards into their regulatory processes" (*Proceedings* December 1998:126).

Bringing AMA influence to bear on the National Committee on Quality Assurance (NCQA) was a more difficult undertaking. Formed in 1990, NCQA had ties to the Robert Wood Johnson Foundation, large employers, and the managed care industry (www.ncqa.org/about/timeline.htm). In 1992, NCQA assumed responsibility for the Health Plan Employer Data and Information Set and became the lead accrediting organization of health plans in the private sector. NCQA's sudden emergence threatened to derail medicine's strategy for maintaining and expanding its authority over the setting of standards.

The association's initial response to NCQA was confrontational. A resolution of the House of Delegates "asked that the AMA: (a) adopt as policy the position that the NCQA is not an appropriate organization to determine criteria for physician credentialing; and (b) develop its own national physician credentialing criteria" (*Proceedings* December 1997:16). But the AMA had done little to promote specific guidelines for clinical practice before the mid-1990s. Its delay had encouraged others, such as NCQA, to undertake the process (Rewarding Quality Care 2003:19).

In 1997, the association launched the American Medical Accreditation Program (AMAP) to counter NCQA. Although many doctors opposed AMAP (specialty boards feared that AMAP would "replace or diminish board certification"), the AMA promoted it with great fanfare (Krieger 1997:23). Dr. Gary Krieger, vice chair of the Organized Medical Staff Section of the AMA, wrote: "AMAP is no gimmick. It is arguably the single largest project that the AMA has embarked upon in many years. It is designed to bring the profession together and establish quality standards in the delivery of health care" (Krieger 1997:23). Michael Millenson, a former reporter for the *Chicago Tribune* and a longtime observer of the AMA, extolled AMAP. He believed that AMAP signaled a reversal of medicine's long-standing opposition to guidelines for clinical practice. "While skepticism about the AMA's latest effort is justified," Millenson said, "so, too, is a degree of optimism. The AMA stamp of approval on a guideline or a doctor's office practice may or may not guarantee medical excellence, but it most certainly signals the legitimization of guidelines and of performance review" (1997:191).

Using AMAP as a springboard, the AMA gained ties to NCQA. Members of the Board of Trustees and AMA staff met several times with NCQA representatives (*Proceedings* December 1997:17). Matters discussed included "the actions of the House of Delegates; possible joint activities related to development and testing of physician performance measures . . . ; certification and approval of credentials verification organizations; and mutual acceptance of each organization's accreditation decisions" (*Proceedings* December 1997:17). Among the "joint activities" to emerge was the formation of the Performance Measurement Coordinating Council. Launched in 1998, the Coordinating Council set out to develop and implement performance measures with the assistance of the AMA (*Proceedings* June 1998:207). Indeed, the council comprised fifteen members, five from each of the sponsoring organizations—AMAP, the Joint Commission, and NCQA. In addition, AMAP and NCQA collaborated on physician credentialing, site visits, and the review of medical records (*Proceedings* June 1998:208–209).

Although the AMA discontinued AMAP in 2000—it had become a financial drain on the organization (Prager 2000:8, 10)—the endeavor achieved its main purpose: the inclusion of doctors in clinical practice and staffing decisions. NCQA standards, as proposed in 1999, required that a health plan's physicians be "involved in or have responsibility for: (a) quality improvement, (b) clinical practice guidelines, (c) development, adoption and application of criteria . . . , (d) credentialing and recredentialing, and (e) utilization management" (*Proceedings* June 1998:209). Even after AMAP dissolved, the AMA remained active in the Coordinating Council. In addition, NCQA continued to invite comment from the AMA on revisions to its accreditation standards (*Proceedings* June 2000:169).

CONCLUSION

Before the health care revolution, the traditional role of medical societies was that of arbiters of health care services and of the information that insurers and consumers possessed. Efforts of the FTC to apply antitrust concepts to the health care industry changed medical societies from arbiters to advocates in most instances.

The new "rules of the game" that the FTC had helped to establish augured the formation of health plans that sought to alter physicians' behavior. Before the enactment of patient protection legislation, health plans successfully challenged the manner in which doctors performed their work—the patients they saw, the tests they ordered, the drugs they prescribed, and the referrals they made. Patient protection legislation effectively countered these cost-saving measures. Designed to promote patient choice, to protect the doctor/patient relationship, and to maintain professional autonomy, patient protection legislation undercut important tools of managerial competition—selective contracting, closed panels, and the intervention of corporate agents.

AMA strategists understood that medicine needed consumers to advance doctors' agendas and that the support of consumers rested on the nature and framing of proposed legislation. Consumers backed physicians when strategists emphasized patient care and the doctor/patient relationship, not when they sought an exemption from FTC jurisdiction or from the antitrust laws for collective bargaining purposes. Laws that gave consumers greater choice in the selection of physicians and more treatment options satisfied patients while benefiting doctors. Unable to negotiate directly on behalf of physicians, the AMA successfully pressed courts, agencies, and legislatures to alter the terms of the managed care contract.

Medicine's tactics in the commercial realm accompanied those in the clinical arena, where accrediting bodies under the control or influence of the AMA regulated managed care organizations. Performance standards developed by accrediting bodies meshed with state laws on free choice, clinical autonomy, and self-regulation. State laws concerning utilization review and continuity of care, for instance, bolstered NCQA requirements for quality management.

The health care revolution joined two distinct movements: one supported free and unfettered markets, the other backed consumer protection. The professional monopoly broken, the tie between the two movements unraveled as consumer groups, alongside physicians, pursued market regulation to correct perceived market failures. The result was confusion and disarray in policy circles. Citing high costs and rising numbers of uninsured in the United States, critics stressed the need for federal intervention, that is, a government-run or government-financed health care system. Advocates of economic theory, on the other hand, argued that government regulation was the problem, not the solution. They claimed that excessive regulation had prevented the health care market from reaching its full potential.

The debate between proponents of free markets and proponents of government systems has escalated in the early years of the twenty-first century. The conclusion to this book places this debate in a broader context; it considers the past and future trajectory of the health care industry against the backdrop of conflicting regimes and their accompanying ideologies.

Conclusion

The 1890 Sherman Act became America's gospel of free enterprise, its "second constitution." On initial inspection, the act appeared to embody the principles of laissez faire, the policy of relying on competitive markets to guide economic development and to protect consumer interests. But, like the equal protection clause or the due process clause of the U.S. Constitution, the Sherman Act's prohibition on "every contract, combination . . . or conspiracy, in restraint of trade" called for interpretation.

In the first half of the twentieth century, progressive ideas set the tone for the development of the medical profession. Progressives, such as Louis Brandeis, favored cooperation over "ruthless" competition and small over large producers. Progressive ideas bolstered the belief that physicians were not engaged in business or commerce and that most efforts of the medical profession to regulate the health care industry were in the public interest. The AMA's ten principles, or rules for the formation of insurance plans, ostensibly protected consumers. From about the 1940s to the 1970s, federal agencies, such as the FTC, embraced the populist, or "industrial organization," school of antitrust enforcement. This school of thought, which disdained big corporations and market concentration, accommodated professional interests.

In an attempt to revive a sputtering economy in the late 1970s, the federal government implemented the ideas of Milton Friedman, George Stigler, and other market theorists. These luminaries of the Chicago school promoted deregulation, privatization, and lower taxes. They based their approach on the economic theory of regulation, which viewed legislative enactments and agency rules as aiding special interests, not the broader public. Following their lead, legal scholars, including Robert Bork and Richard Posner, fused antitrust analysis with neoclassical economic theory. The

Sherman Act, Robert Bork contended, stood for consumer welfare and economic efficiency; it did not encompass noneconomic values and beliefs, such as the protection of small producers.

Application of the antitrust laws to the "learned professions" signaled the end of the medical monopoly. Building upon the work of law professor Clark Havighurst, the Federal Trade Commission commenced several probes, investigations, and enforcement actions. The agency's flagship case against the AMA greatly diminished the authority of organized medicine to dominate the health care industry. Absent the ability to police the commercial realm, medical societies could not enforce professional norms, prevent the formation of HMOs and other innovative health plans, or exclude "unorthodox" providers. After the ruling in *AMA*, medical societies lacked the means to preserve "professional order."

U.S. Supreme Court decisions in the health care field from Group Health to *California Dental* display wide-ranging values, outcomes, and case dispositions. Professional values were at their zenith in the 1950s when the Court decided the case of *United States v. Oregon State Medical Society;* but after market theory took hold, the Court dismissed any distinction between business and profession in the case of *National Society of Professional Engineers v. United States*. Disparities in the application of antitrust principles to the guild aspects of medical practice demonstrate the importance of historical context and political ideology. "Doubtless much of the changes taking place in the organization and direction of professional work today are economically inspired," sociologist Eliot Freidson has written. "But it is politics," he said, "that advances and protects such change, and in politics ideology is a critical factor" (Freidson 2001:197).

WHY MARKET COMPETITION AND NOT GOVERNMENT REGULATION?

When Congress passed legislation in 1974 to encourage health planning, many observers believed that some form of national health insurance was in the offing (Dranove 2000:55–56). Indeed, Clark Havighurst opined: "The odds are beginning to seem good that sometime in the next several years Congress will enact some kind of improved health insurance system emphasizing subsidization of the purchasing power of disadvantaged consumers" (Havighurst 1974b:251). But continuing economic turmoil in the 1970s diverted politicians from their original objective. An important debate ensued concerning how best to deal with the rapid escalation of health care spending. "Never before or since," Havighurst observed, "were minds so open" to a frank discussion of the advantages and disadvantages of government regulation versus market competition (Havighurst 2003). Once Congress defeated President Carter's effort to cap hospital costs in 1979, it seemed that policy makers had made their selection. A market-based policy sealed the fate (at least for the foreseeable future) of a government-run or government-financed health care system.

Based on research from primary sources, this book calls upon scholars to reexamine an old but still vibrant question: Why has the United States failed to enact a program of universal health care like all other Western industrialized nations? Though the answer to this question is beyond the scope of this book, the role of the antitrust laws in the shift from a professional to a market regime in the 1970s provides fresh insight into the choice between government regulation and market competition. Few scholars have considered to any appreciable extent the contribution of federal antitrust policy to the current configuration of the health care industry. The perceived complexities of the antitrust laws may account for some of this indifference. But the fact that many legal scholars and economists have made antitrust law the centerpiece of their analysis suggests that political scientists and historians should review their work more closely.

Those who have sought to explain the lack of universal health care in the United States often adhere to either "popular choice" or "power group" theories (Navarro 1994). Scholars who favor popular choice theories point to Americans' deep-seated distrust of big government, coupled with their penchant for free enterprise (see Ginzberg 1977; Fuchs 1986; Fein 1986). Scholars who advance power group theories argue that a fragmented political system in the United States enables powerful special interests, such as hospitals, insurance companies, and the medical profession, to block a government-run system (see Starr 1982; Marmor 1994; Peterson 2005; Funigiello 2005). Still others implicate a weak labor movement (see Navarro 1994; Gottschalk 2005), a market ideology that produces racial and class inequalities (see Stone 2005; Schlesinger 2005), or "policy legacies" based on "critical junctures" and "path dependencies" (see Mayes 2004:5). Recent accounts provide fresh insights yet build, for the most part, on earlier approaches to show why "incremental" strategies rather than comprehensive reform persists (see Weissert and Weissert 1996; Derickson 2005; Quadagno 2005).

Many scholars pin their analysis on certain watershed events—the enactment of Social Security and Medicare or the defeat of national health care during the administrations of Presidents Truman and Clinton. Because such accounts predominantly relate policy struggles between presidents and Congress, they often ignore other important government institutions, such as courts and agencies, or other key actors, particularly those in the academic community. In addition, by concentrating on discrete events, scholars frequently disregard "paradigmatic shifts," intellectual revolutions that have influenced the ideological context for policy making in America.

Scholars of the popular choice school typically view the lack of a government program of national health insurance as the expression of popular will embodied in certain hegemonic values, such as individualism, free choice, and limited government (see Navarro 1994:172). While these values predominate in the United States more so than in other countries, their influence is complex and subtle. The shift from a professional to a market regime in the 1970s, for instance, was not simply the expression of popular choice. For one thing, the institutions at the center of the shift—courts and agencies—were among the least democratic in American society. For another, the values and beliefs that framed the policy discussion were principally those of doctors and market reformers. Physicians, moreover, were not of one mind on the matter. Some favored government intervention; most opposed the commercialization of medical practice. Market reformers succeeded in large part because certain institutions and legal mechanisms were in place to further their objectives.

This last point bears repeating because, in addition to being the only Western industrialized nation that lacks a government-run or government-financed health care system, the United States is also unique in its enduring adherence to an antitrust tradition. Such a tradition was a significant factor in the decision of policy makers to pursue markets rather than budgets to contain costs and to allocate scarce resources. This is not to say that other countries have failed to employ private markets to supplement government programs or market principles to improve the performance of these programs. It is to say, however, that the United States' antitrust tradition and the legal machinery that accompanied it gave policy makers the tools to counter the medical monopoly and to address rising costs through market competition.

European nations and Canada have differed markedly from the United States in their selection, application, and interpretation of antitrust rules and principles (Wells 2002:210–212; Freyer 1992:278–279; Kintner and Joelson 1974:6). Though Canada enacted antitrust legislation in 1889, one year before Congress passed the Sherman Act, Canadian laws were "entirely criminal" in nature, contained "no provisions for the awarding of civil damages, treble or otherwise," and, according to attorneys Earl Kintner and Mark Joelson, fell "considerably short of the impact of American laws in similar situations" (1974:246–247). Great Britain and most other Western democracies did not even embrace antitrust theory and practice until after World War II (Wells 2002:210–212). Antitrust laws, when finally adopted by European nations, were different in composition and character. European nations, moreover, employed the antitrust laws much less often (Freyer 1992:278–279). From 1962 to 2005, for instance, European judges considered only sixty antitrust cases (Jacoby 2005). By comparison, Americans filed 752 antitrust actions in 2004 alone (Jacoby 2005).

Lack of an antitrust policy in the years before World War II affected the trajectory of European economies. According to historian Wyatt Wells: "Business developed differently. . . . European firms often cooperated in cartels that set prices and allocated markets, and governments frequently supported these efforts. In time, many cartels reached across national borders. By setting minimum prices, they protected small firms against larger competitors, and by stabilizing markets, they kept the overall economy stable. More broadly, their supporters contended that cartels, by replacing 'every man for himself' competition with cooperation for the common good, raised economic life to a higher moral plane" (2002:1–2).

Searching for answers to deflation and mass unemployment in the 1920s and 1930s, Presidents Hoover and Roosevelt pursued European-style cartelization. But Roosevelt abandoned the effort and resumed enforcement of the antitrust laws when policies favoring cartels proved ineffective. The appointment of Thurman Arnold to head the Antitrust Division of the Department of Justice, coupled with the department's lawsuit against the American Medical Association for leading a boycott of Group Health, signaled the restoration of competition theory. Guild practices of medical societies continued after the Supreme Court's decision in Group Health only because the interstate commerce requirement and the de facto learned professions exemption barred relief in most instances.

Despite the overall acceptance of antitrust principles after World War II, many European nations resisted the approach of lawyers and economists of the Chicago school to antitrust enforcement. According to historian Tony Freyer: "During the 1970s and 1980s British and American economic theories remained distinct. In the United States, from the early 1970s on the tension between the approaches represented by [Robert] Bork and [Donald] Turner shaped court decisions and government antitrust enforcement, limiting horizontal but facilitating conglomerate mergers. For the first time in nearly a century, however, the republican values defended by [Louis] Brandeis were of minimal importance. In Britain, the emphasis was also upon efficiency but competition theory was influenced little if at all by the Chicago School's law and economics movement" (1992:278–279).

Europe's rejection of the economic theory of regulation reflected the ascendancy of welfare-state programs and its predilection for centralized administration. Acceptance of the economic theory of regulation in the United States, on the other hand, signaled opposition to big government and a preference for decentralization. From the perspective of many economists and politicians in America in the late 1970s, the market was more efficient and consumer enhancing than government in the allocation of goods and services. Efforts of Congress to deregulate airlines, trucking, and telecommunications paved the way for the emergence of new firms in those industries.

Deregulatory policy also influenced the course of action in the health care arena, where medicine's long-time dominance had established and enforced a preindustrial mode of finance and delivery. This preindustrial configuration, consisting of independent, fee-for-service practitioners, community-based hospitals, and other stand-alone facilities, made it difficult for reformers to implement a market-based policy. First, decision makers had to overcome the anticompetitive practices of the medical profession; second, they had to stimulate market competition.

Medicine's ability to block legislation that threatened its interests was formidable. But Congress did not have to pass legislation to deregulate health care finance and delivery. Medicine was a private monopoly, not government-based, as in the airlines, trucking, and telecommunications industries. Instead, Congress signaled, indeed prodded, the Federal Trade Commission to take action. Hearings before the Senate Subcommittee on Antitrust and Monopoly in 1974 started the ball rolling. The hearings produced a wide array of data showing that medical societies had engaged in anticompetitive practices, that "interlocking relationships between providers of health care services," in the words of Senator Edward Kennedy, predominated (U.S. Congress, Senate, 1974:1561). Congress increased funding to the FTC in the 1970s to jump-start new programs; it demanded bold initiatives. In 1975, commissioners allocated substantial resources to combat the medical monopoly. The FTC's health care shop made its debut in 1976; several bright, young, and capable attorneys eagerly participated. Even when Congress and the Reagan administration reduced funding to the agency in the early 1980s, they continued to support the agency's activities involving the medical profession.

Congressional efforts to stimulate market competition in the health care industry were more ambiguous. Lack of a competitive market for health care meant that entrepreneurs had to build an infrastructure capable of achieving cost savings. To be sure, government spending in the 1960s through the Medicare and Medicaid programs induced corporate investment. But HMO legislation passed by Congress in 1973, which contained requirements for community rating and comprehensive benefits, made many arrangements impractical for business purposes. Revisions to the HMO Act in the late 1970s, coupled with the rejection of the cap proposed by President Carter on hospital spending, signaled congressional acceptance of a market-based health policy (see Brown 1983:22).

During the Reagan administration, market theory became entrenched. "In a way that none had before," columnist Holman Jenkins wrote, "Mr. Reagan put economics at the center of his presidency—not the economy, but *economics*" (Jenkins 2004, emphasis in original). Integration of the health care industry proceeded at a rapid pace. Insurers diversified into HMO and PPO products, merged and consolidated their operations, and, in several instances, converted from nonprofit to for-profit status. Hospitals diversified to include not only inpatient but outpatient services and clinics, formed national chains and alliances, and often purchased doctors' practices, nursing homes, and other entities to establish regional systems. Physicians joined other physicians in small, medium, and large group practices, organized loose networks or independent practice associations, sold their practices to management firms, and increasingly became salaried employees of hospitals and other corporate entities.

Though the antitrust tradition in the United States made the transition from medical monopoly to market competition possible, there were limits to what antitrust reformers could accomplish. Policing professional associations to prevent abuses of power in the areas of specialty certification and the accreditation of medical schools and hospitals proved particularly elusive. Reformers also could not overcome a public relations campaign inaugurated by the AMA-led coalition in the 1990s to demonize the managed care industry. State legislatures, enmeshed in anti–managed care rhetoric, passed myriad laws and regulations to curtail cost-containment practices.

THE REVOLT OF THE PHYSICIANS

The health care revolution of the 1970s produced a new political dynamic. Before the revolution commenced, medicine had no powerful competitors. Increased funding for patient care in the 1950s and 1960s attracted investors and entrepreneurs, but the "rules of the game" limited the formation of HMOs and other corporate arrangements. After the revolution, a market regime, based on an entirely new set of principles, slowly but surely emerged. Unlike the period before the revolution, however, neither physicians nor the new corporate plans could dominate the political spectrum.

Paul Ellwood and Alain Enthoven, early pioneers of market reform, had envisioned the integration of finance and delivery, but insurers, seeking to achieve economies of scale and scope, to adjust risk, and to enhance transactional efficiencies, chose a different path (see Robinson 1999). "Carrier HMOs," as Enthoven called them, had few incentives "to build medical infrastructure, . . . to change doctor culture or practice settings" (1999). They used the techniques of managed care to control the behavior of physicians. By failing to integrate their operations, as Ellwood and Enthoven had projected, insurers and physicians became adversaries, locked in perpetual controversy over cost and quality issues.

Medicine's counteroffensive altered the revolution's trajectory. Faced with declining membership, the AMA strengthened its ties to state, local, and specialty societies in the early 1990s. Combining their resources, medical societies pursued legal actions against insurers and lobbied state legislatures and Congress to revise the managed care contract. Any-willing-provider laws, prompt-pay legislation, and joint ventures improved physicians' negotiating position. By 2005, all states and the District of Columbia had enacted some form of patient protection legislation; the courts had undercut ERISA's preemption of state laws for self-insured plans; and professional associations and individual physicians had filed, and in some instances had settled, class-action lawsuits against large insurers (see Fuhrmans 2007).

The result was a stalemate between the two competing coalitions. The AMA coalition and the managed care coalition checked and counterchecked each other. Many health plans lost the ability and the will to reduce their prices or engage in cost-containing practices. A 2006 article from the *Wall Street Journal* summed up the insurers' position: "Insurers found that, instead of playing the bad guy, it was easier to treat surging health costs as an inescapable force of nature—and to make sure price increases stayed ahead of costs as much as possible. Today, operating margins, once 4% to 5% in a good year, average 8% at the country's biggest insurers" (Fuhrmans 2006).

Medicine tightened its authority over the production of knowledge and the dissemination of information, despite the loss of market power. Medical education, residency training, licensing and discipline, peer review, privileging and credentialing, specialty certification, institutional accreditation, and much standards setting remained under the influence or outright control of organized medicine. The AMA preserved its role on accrediting bodies for hospitals and expanded it to include the accreditation of health plans and utilization review organizations.

The current configuration conflates professional goals and values with those of market competition and management theory. One of medicine's core beliefs that patient protection legislation has restored is free choice of physician. Most health plans now offer an array of options to consumers, from HMOs and PPOs to traditional indemnity arrangements. Few physicians work in staff-model HMOs or other types of closed-panel arrangements. Vertical forms of integration, once touted as cost efficient and economically superior, have floundered while joint ventures among doctors and contractual arrangements between doctors and health plans ("virtual" integration) have flourished. Physicians have organized groups, established networks, and developed "strategic alliances across ownership boundaries" to market their services (Savage 2004:666). For the most part, these enterprises have remained small to accommodate doctors' desire for autonomy and independence (Casalino 2004:880).

Under the circumstances, it is not surprising that Ellwood and Enthoven lament the direction the revolution has taken (see also Havighurst 2002b). Given the political dynamics (the cyclical nature of ideas and interests), the opposition of medicine to the market regime was a foreseeable occurrence. The theories and approaches articulated by political scientists Mark Blyth, Paul Sabatier, and Hank Jenkins-Smith inform the current predicament. Once a new regime emerges, they advised, coalitions form and compete within a policy subsystem. Medicine's counteroffensive reflects the tensions among ideas, interests, beliefs, and values in both the clinical and the commercial settings. Profession versus bureaucracy, cooperation versus competition, self-regulation versus bureaucratic oversight, autonomy versus standardization—these are key ingredients in the battle for control of the workplace and the market.

A THEORY OF REGIME CHANGE

As the twenty-first century begins, a market-based system for financing and delivering health care faces increasing attack from certain quarters. Critics stress the large and rising number of uninsured individuals in the United States (see Stone 1999, 2005; Funigiello 2005; Schlesinger 2005; Marone and Jacobs 2005). Others point to the United States' relatively poor life expectancy and infant mortality rates compared to rates for other industrialized nations (Kawachi 2005; Woolfe and Stange 2006). America's health care system, Alain Enthoven and Richard Kronick have observed, is "a paradox of excess and deprivation" (Enthoven and Kronick 1989). The United States spends more per capita on health care than most other industrialized countries yet "has fewer physicians per 1,000 population, physician visits per capita, acute beds per capita, hospital admissions per 1,000 population, and acute care days per capita than the median OECD [Organisation for Economic Co-operation and Development] country" (Anderson et al. 2003). Some people receive too much care while others receive too little (see also Bodenheimer and Grumbach 2005).

The question that many are asking, of course, is whether a change of regimes is imminent, whether a government regime similar to those in Canada or Western European nations eventually will prevail in the United States (White 2003; Reeher 2003; Brown 2003). Forecasters point to current "trends in costs, demographics, and inequalities" (Reeher 2003:356) which show that "the federal budget is on an unsustainable trajectory" and that spending on benefits for health care and retirement "will rise much faster" than projected revenue (Wessel 2005). To be sure, government financing is increasing at a steady rate. Just as the share of private spending on health care is diminishing, so the public share is expanding. In 2002, the federal government reported that combined spending on Medicare, Medicaid, and other public programs reached 44 percent, while combined spending in the private sector stood at 56 percent (GAO 2004:6). Even these percentages, some believe, understate public expenditures. If lost tax revenues and money spent on health care for public employees is included, they say, total public spending would exceed 55 percent (Fox and Fronstin 2000:271).

Despite these trends, those who prophesy an end to the market regime are premature and, more often than not, display wishful thinking. Few of the fundamental precursors of change that occurred in the 1970s are in place today. This book began with a set of questions related to the circumstances under which new regimes arise and the process for shifting power from one regime to another. Several theorists, as mentioned earlier, view ideas as central to such an occurrence (Derthick and Quirk 1985; McDonough 1997; Blyth 2002). John McDonough, for instance, crisply noted that "regulatory schemes are borne out of explosive crises when old ideas no longer work and the status quo no longer meets current [requirements]" (1997:214). Embedded in this statement, I submit, is the notion of adaptability—old ideas give way to new ones when they fail to accommodate changing conditions. The question then, for the market regime, is whether it possesses the flexibility and the capacity to meet the needs of purchasers, providers, and consumers. If it does, then regime change will not transpire.

Analysts typically point to three significant factors—cost, access, and quality—when examining health care policy. By the 1970s, the professional regime had failed in all three categories. Problems of cost and access to care emerged immediately before and during the Great Depression. Yet medicine responded by thwarting contract practice and government assistance and by constraining the supply of physicians. Demand exploded in the years after World War II when medical technology and employer-based coverage developed and expanded. Still, medicine constrained access to care by discouraging the formation of public health centers and by limiting the availability of government and private insurance (Starr 1982). Though the AMA finally lost the battle over government-financed health care in 1965 with the passage of the Medicare and Medicaid programs, the conditions that medicine placed on program implementation—unrestricted choice of provider and fee-for-service—fueled cost inflation. Quality too was a problem, and, here again, medicine failed to adapt to social and cultural changes. The consumer movement, begun in the 1960s, spurred calls for enhanced accountability and greater collaboration between doctor and patient. Rather than embrace change, however, professional associations resisted; they opposed reforms to state medical boards and lobbied state legislatures to curtail liability for medical malpractice (Ameringer 1999).

In shifting to a market regime in the 1980s, a process that was in many respects politically painless, policy makers addressed the most immediate concern: cost containment. Managed care and prospective payment reversed financial incentives to overspend. By the mid-1990s, with managed care in full bloom, growth in expenditures for health care had "slowed dramatically," reaching their lowest level since the 1960s (Levit, Lazenby, and Braden 1998:35–36; Rich and Erb 2005:237). Market competition also had produced several innovations intended to enhance quality. These included evidence-based medicine, clinical pathways, guidelines, protocols, outcomes research, practice profiles, quality report cards, and performance measurement. By uprooting the medical monopoly and thus challenging atomistic practice patterns, those who enforced the antitrust laws encouraged physicians to build infrastructure, rationalize delivery, limit variation, and promote best practices. Yet efforts to expand insurance coverage eluded policy makers. "One promise of managed care—besides that it was better than whatever government would offer—was that if insurers were permitted to exercise the necessary controls on medical expenditures for the insured, they would free up money to insure more of the uninsured. None of that new coverage materialized," political scientist Deborah Stone asserted (Stone 1999:1214).

The number of uninsured individuals in America has escalated since the health care revolution, but that does not mean that a market-based system for health care delivery is causally related (see Robinson 1999:231–232). Rather, the principal reasons for an increase in the number of uninsured individuals in the last quarter of the twentieth century concern the shift from a manufacturing to a service-based economy, coupled with the inability of many small employers to afford insurance coverage (see Bodenheimer and Grumbach 2005:15–17; Gilmer and Kronick 2005:w5–w143). The uninsured are usually young, lack an adequate education, and are members of minority groups (Mayes 2004:152). Typically, they "work in service industries and for smaller companies" that cannot or will not provide health care benefits (Mayes 2004:152). So long as insurance coverage is linked to employment, there will be vacillation. Just as a weak economy will produce job layoffs and other dislocations, so a strong economy may cause employers to add coverage to attract workers. Indeed, the number of uninsured, as a percentage of the population, dropped from 17 percent in 1998 to 16.1 percent in 2000, a period of strong economic performance (Fronstin 2006b:4). Of further significance, the total number of uninsured individuals decreased from 40.7 million in 1998 to 39.6 million in 1999, despite an overall growth in the general population (Fronstin 2006a).

Rising numbers of uninsureds will pressure politicians to advance comprehensive solutions. But this does not mean that regime change is certain. Market advocates have demonstrated their resilience and openness to new ideas and approaches in the wake of patient protection legislation and the resistance of physicians to capitation. Pressed by purchasers of health care (government and large employers), most health plans have pursued several initiatives to enhance quality and cost effectiveness. Pay-for-performance, which refers to financial incentives to improve delivery, is one such initiative (see Colliver 2001). The Medicare program, the Leapfrog Group (a consortium of large corporations and certain government agencies), and the Institute of Medicine, among others, have driven this proposal. As of 2007, over 50 percent of HMOs in the private sector had a pay-for-performance program; this accounted for more than 80 percent of those enrolled in HMOs in America (Epstein 2007:515). In addition, health plans have worked with providers to foster quality assurance. The National Committee for Quality Assurance, of which the managed care industry was a principal founder, has developed and expanded the amount of information that is available to purchasers and consumers. And the Joint Commission has been involved in the setting of standards and the accreditation of hospitals, managed care plans, assisted living facilities, and home health agencies (see Federal Trade Commission and Department of Justice 2004).

Many reformers, moreover, view government as an enabler, a conduit for the collection and distribution of data to enhance the market's performance. A recent proposal by Gail Wilensky, an economist and former administrator of the Health Care Finance Administration, captures this mode of thinking. She recommends that purchasers and payers of health care, both public and private, establish a center for "comparative effectiveness" information in order to increase market capacity (Wilensky 2006). "Comparative effectiveness" refers to the systematic review and assessment of data concerning alternative therapies and technologies. Evaluations of alternative therapies and technologies could be made available, Wilensky suggests, to health plans, physicians, and consumers. The Institute of Medicine convened the Roundtable on Evidence-Based Medicine to explore issues related to Wilensky's proposal. Those affiliated with the Institute of Medicine note ongoing activities of federal and state entities to aggregate and analyze data on the comparative effectiveness of competing interventions (Rowe, Cortese, and McGinnis 2006:w593–w595).

An important feature of pay-for-performance and comparative effectiveness is the move toward centralized administration. In order to simplify performance measures and aid uniformity, many persons associated with the Institute of Medicine support the concept of a national quality coordination board, to be housed in the Department of Health and Human Services (Institute of Medicine 2005). Similarly, those who advance coverage decisions based on assessments of comparative effectiveness data would locate such an enterprise "within a quasi-governmental entity" (Wilensky 2006:584). Governments in several other countries already evaluate and publish findings or recommendations concerning medical technologies and drug formularies (see Wilensky 2006:575–576; Smith and York 2004). Were either proposal to materialize as suggested, members of the health care industry would likely achieve greater consensus on practice parameters, coverage decisions, and reimbursement practices.

For a change in regimes to occur, new ideas would have to emerge to replace those that exist currently. That is not happening. Indeed, most of the fresh ideas concerning access to care are tied to market theory. These include health savings accounts, association health plans, tax exemptions, and deregulation to expand access to low-cost insurance policies. The passage of Medicare Part D in 2004, while expanding the federal role to include prescription drug coverage, injected market incentives. Rather than adopt a "single-payer, single-product model," Congress required consumers to choose among competing health plans for their prescription drug coverage. Many who opposed Medicare Part D predicted that confusion would reign and costs would run rampant. So far, the program has performed better than even its proponents expected. What has transpired, economist Daniel McFadden relates, based on first-year findings, "is that elderly consumers were mostly able to navigate the Part D market and reach reasonable choices, despite its novelty and complexity" (McFadden 2007). Monthly premiums have been lower than anticipated, and a substantial portion of the Medicare population (well over 90 percent) has enrolled in the drug program (McFadden 2007). Rather than contract, the Part D market is expanding; seventeen national plan sponsors have emerged in 2007, an increase of nine over 2006 (Cubanski and Neuman 2007:w10). Still, McFadden urges caution, lest government fail to aggressively supervise market forces. Part D's success, he says, "depends substantially on thoughtful and muscular management of the market" (McFadden 2007). Strenuous government oversight is necessary, in other words, to protect consumers and stem market failure.

The professional regime failed because the system for delivering and financing health care that it fostered could not accommodate the complex problems of a postmodern era. Though many express discontent with the current system, no large-scale rebellion on the part of government, employers, or consumers is present or even imminent. Any new regime must face the problem of limited resources and, with it, the need to ration services. Would consumers, most of whom have health insurance, be prepared to risk the loss of benefits should government budgets dictate future treatments? Can public agencies, employers, providers, and the insurance industry work together to address impending fiscal constraints and lack of access? Unless the answer to this last question is a resounding "no," it is unlikely that a change in regimes will take place, that a government-run or government-financed health care system similar to those in other industrialized nations will transpire. As for physicians, their gradual assimilation into the corporate arena is occurring. More each day become employees of hospital or corporate systems, and those that do not are adjusting to the demands of payers and purchasers. An important advantage of markets over professional guilds and government bureaucracies is their greater flexibility and potential for innovation. While conflicts undoubtedly will persist between the principal players, continuing efforts to contain costs, improve quality, and enhance access to care will bring about new and highly productive forms of collaboration.

References

ARCHIVES

American Medical Association: Special Collections (consists of congressional testimony, membership data, and correspondence). American Medical Association, Chicago (Legislative Affairs Division).

Federal Trade Commission: Special Collections (consists of staff reports, memoranda, and correspondence). Federal Trade Commission, Washington, D.C.

Harry A. Blackmun Papers. Library of Congress, Washington, D.C.

Thurgood Marshall Papers. Library of Congress, Washington, D.C.

PRIMARY AND SECONDARY SOURCES

Agrawal, Gail B., and Howard R. Veit. 2002. Back to the Future: The Managed Care Revolution. *Law and Contemporary Problems* 65(4):11–53.

Albert, Tanya, and Andis Robeznieks. 2002. AMA Delegates Likely to Hear Call for PRN Support. *AMA News*, 3 June.

AMA Plans Appeal of FTC's Ruling on Physician Advertising. 1979. *AMA News*, 2 November.

AMA to Continue FTC Battle. 1980. *AMA News*, 17 October.

AMA Vows to Fight FTC Attempt to End Ban on Ads by Physicians. 1976. *AMA News*, 5 January.

AMA Will Challenge FTC Decision on Ads. 1978. *AMA News*, 8 December.

American Medical Association. *Code of Medical Ethics* (see text reference for applicable year). Chicago: American Medical Association.

———. House of Delegates. *Proceedings* (see text reference for applicable dates and page numbers). Chicago: American Medical Association.

———. *Opinions and Reports of the Judicial Council* (see text reference for applicable year). Chicago: American Medical Association.

———. 1964. Legal Conference for Medical Society Representatives, Chicago, 16–18 April.

———. Council on Ethical and Judicial Affairs. 1995. Ethical Issues in Managed Care. *JAMA* 273(4):330–335.

Ameringer, Carl F. 1999. *State Medical Boards and the Politics of Public Protection.* Baltimore: Johns Hopkins University Press.

Anderson, B. J. 2003. Author interview of the former head of the health law department of the American Medical Association. 12 June.

Anderson, Gerard F., Uwe E. Reinhardt, Peter S. Hussey, and Varduhi Petrosyan. 2003. It's the Prices, Stupid: Why the United States Is So Different from Other Countries. *Health Affairs* 22(3):89–105.

Antitrust Relief. 1996. *AMA News,* 23/30 September.

Appeal Brief of Respondent American Medical Association. 1979. *In the Matter of the American Medical Ass'n,* docket no. 9064, 31 January.

Arrow, Kenneth. 1963. Uncertainty and the Welfare Economics of Medical Care. *The American Economic Review* 53(5):941–973.

Asimow, Michael, Arthur Earl Bonfield, and Ronald M. Levin. 1998. *State and Federal Administrative Law.* 2nd ed. American Casebook Series. St. Paul: West Group.

Aston, Geri. 1998. Zero Hour Near for Patient Bill. *AMA News,* 3 August.

Balogh, Brian. 1991. *Chain Reaction: Expert Debate and Public Participation in American Commercial Nuclear Power, 1945–1975.* Cambridge, UK: Cambridge University Press.

Barnes, Ernest G. 2003. Author interview of the administrative law judge in the *AMA* case. 10 July.

Barnett, Albert E. 1998 Protecting Doctor-Patient Relationship in PPMs Isn't Easy. *AMA News,* 9 February.

Benedict, Gerry, and Brent Feorene. 1997. The PPM Phenomenon. *AMA News,* 13 October.

Berger, Loren, Steve Weissman, and Michael Surrusco. 2000. *Holding Patients Hostage: The Unhealthy Alliance between HMOs and Senate Leaders.* Washington, D.C.: Public Citizen's Congress Watch.

Berlant, Jeffrey. 1975. *Profession and Monopoly: A Study of Medicine in the United States and Great Britain.* Berkeley: University of California Press.

Bernstein, Michael A. 2001. *A Perilous Progress: Economists and Public Purpose in Twentieth-Century America.* Princeton, NJ: Princeton University Press.

Bickel, David R. 1983. The Antitrust Division's Adoption of a Chicago School Economic Policy Calls for Some Reorganization: But Is the Division's New Policy Here to Stay? *Houston Law Review* 20:1083–1127.

Bierig, Jack. 2003. Author interview of the lead attorney for the American Medical Association in the *AMA* case. 30 June.

Bloche, M. Gregg, and David M. Studdert. 2004. A Quiet Revolution: Law as an Agent of Health System Change. *Health Affairs* 23(2):29–42.

Blyth, Mark. 2002. *Great Transformations: Economic Ideas and Institutional Change in the Twentieth Century.* Cambridge, UK: Cambridge University Press.

Bodenheimer, Thomas S., and Kevin Grumbach. 2005. *Understanding Health*

Policy: A Clinical Approach. 4th ed. New York: Lange Medical Books/McGraw Hill.

Bork, Robert H. 1978. *The Antitrust Paradox: A Policy at War with Itself.* New York: Basic Books.

———. 1991. Legislative Intent and the Policy of the Sherman Act. In *The Political Economy of the Sherman Act: The First One Hundred Years,* ed. E. Thomas Sullivan. New York: Oxford University Press.

Born, Patricia H., and Carol J. Simon. 2001. Patients and Profits: The Relationship between HMO and Financial Performance and Quality of Care. *Health Affairs* 20(2):167–174.

Brennan, Jeffrey W., David R. Pender, and Markus H. Meier. 2003. *FTC Antitrust Actions in Health Care Services and Products.* Washington, D.C.: Bureau of Competition, Federal Trade Commission.

Brennan, Troyen A. 1991. *Just Doctoring: Medical Ethics in the Liberal State.* Berkeley: University of California Press.

Brief for the United States. 1939. *United States v. American Medical Ass'n.* In the U.S. Court of Appeals for the District of Columbia, docket no. 7488—special calendar, 10 November.

Brodie, Mollyann, Lee Ann Brady, and Drew Altman. 1998. Media Coverage of Managed Care: Is There a Negative Bias? *Health Affairs* 17(1):9–25.

Brown, Lawrence. 1983. *Politics and Health Care Organizations: HMOs as Federal Policy.* Washington, D.C.: Brookings Institution.

———. 2003. Shadow Governance: The Political Construction of Health Policy Leadership. *Journal of Health Politics, Policy and Law* 28(2–3):517–524.

Budrys, Grace. 1997. *When Doctors Join Unions.* Ithaca, NY: Cornell University Press.

Burnham, John. 1982. American Medicine's Golden Age: What Happened to It? *Science* 215:1476–1478.

Burrow, James G. 1977. *Organized Medicine in the Progressive Era: The Move toward Monopoly.* Baltimore: Johns Hopkins University Press.

Campion, Fred. 1984. *The AMA and U.S. Health Policy since 1940.* Chicago: American Medical Association.

Canon, Bradley C. 1991. Justice John Paul Stevens: The Lone Ranger in a Black Robe. In *The Burger Court: Political and Judicial Profiles,* ed. Charles M. Lamb and Stephen C. Halpern. Urbana: University of Illinois Press.

Carper, Jean. 1977. The Backlash at the FTC. *Washington Post,* 6 February.

Casalino, Lawrence P. 2004. Physicians and Corporations: A Corporate Transformation of American Medicine? *Journal of Health Politics, Policy and Law* 29(4–5):869–883.

Chapman, Stu. 1980. Has the FTC Overplayed Its Hand in Trying to Control Your Fees? *Legal Aspects of Medical Practice* February:21–25.

Chase-Lubitz, Jeffrey F. 1987. The Corporate Practice of Medicine Doctrine: An Anachronism in the Modern Health Care Industry. *Vanderbilt Law Review* 40:445–488.

Chiropractic: Its Cause and Cure. 1942. *Medical Economics* 19:41–43, 72–76.

Clarkson, Kenneth W., and Timothy J. Muris, eds. 1981. *The Federal Trade Commission since 1970: Economic Regulation and Bureaucratic Behavior.* New York: Cambridge University Press.

Clayton Act. U.S. Code 15 (1914), secs. 12–27.

Colliver, Victoria. 2001. Blue Cross Sets New Policy on Doctor Bonuses: Physician Rewards Now Based on Quality of Care. *San Francisco Chronicle,* 11 July.

Congress: The Big Battalions. 1979. *The Economist,* 24 November.

Congress Waits for Carter's Signal. 1977. *Business Week,* 4 April.

Cook, Robert. 2002. Clash of the Titans. *AMA News,* 23/30 December.

Costilo, Barry. 1981. Competition Policy and the Medical Profession. *New England Journal of Medicine* 304(18):1099–1102.

———. 2003. Author interview of the lead attorney for the Federal Trade Commission in the *AMA* case. 8 July.

Court, Jamie. 2000. Author interview of the executive director of the Foundation for Taxpayers and Consumer Rights. 30 June.

Critser, Greg. 2005. *Generation Rx: How Prescription Drugs Are Altering American Lives, Minds, and Bodies.* New York: Houghton Mifflin.

Cubanski, Juliette, and Patricia Neuman. 2006. Status Report on Medicare Part D Enrollment in 2006: Analysis of Plan-Specific Market Share and Coverage. *Health Affairs* 25(6):w1–w12.

Demsetz, Harold. 1999. Henry Manne: Scholar, Academic Entrepreneur, and Friend. *Case Western Reserve Law Review* 50:253–257.

Derickson, Alan. 2005. *Health Security for All: Dreams of Universal Health Care in America.* Baltimore: Johns Hopkins University Press.

Derthick, Martha, and Paul Quirk. 1985. *The Politics of Deregulation.* Washington, D.C.: Brookings Institution.

Dodson, John M. 1919. Report of the Council on Medical Education. *JAMA* 72:1752–1753.

Downs, Anthony. 1985. *An Economic Theory of Democracy.* New York: Harper and Row.

Dranove, David. 2000. *The Economic Evolution of American Health Care: From Marcus Welby to Managed Care.* Princeton, NJ: Princeton University Press.

Easterbrook, Frank H. 1984. Foreword: The Supreme Court and the Economic System. *Harvard Law Review* 98:4–60.

Edsall, Thomas Byrne. 1984. *The New Politics of Inequality.* New York: W. W. Norton and Company.

Egdahl, Richard H. 1973. Foundations for Medical Care. *New England Journal of Medicine* 288(10):491–498.

Eisner, Marc. 1991. *Antitrust and the Triumph of Economics: Institutions, Expertise, and Policy Change.* Chapel Hill: University of North Carolina Press.

Employee Retirement Income Security Act. U.S. Code 29 (as amended 1994), secs. 1001 et seq.

Enthoven, Alain C. 1999. Managed Care: What Went Wrong? Can It Be Fixed?

Donald C. Ozmun and Donald B. Ozmun Family Lecture in Management, Mayo Clinic, Rochester, MN, 29 November.

———, and Richard Kronick. 1989. A Consumer-Choice Health Plan for the 1990s. *New England Journal of Medicine* 320(1):29–37.

Epstein, Arnold M. 2007. Pay for Performance at the Tipping Point. *New England Journal of Medicine* 356(5):515–517.

Federal Trade Commission. 1974. *Annual Report of the Federal Trade Commission for the Fiscal Year.* Washington, D.C.: GPO.

———. 1975. *Annual Report of the Federal Trade Commission for the Fiscal Year.* Washington, D.C.: GPO.

——— and Department of Justice. 2004. *Improving Health Care: A Dose of Competition.* Washington, D.C. Http://www.ftc.gov/reports/healthcare/040723healthcarerpt.pdf.

Federal Trade Commission Act. U.S. Code 15 (1914), secs. 41–57a.

Fein, Rashi. 1986. *Medical Care, Medical Costs: The Search for a Health Insurance Policy.* Cambridge, MA: Harvard University Press.

Feldman, Roger B., Douglas R. Wholey, and Jon B. Christianson. 1999. HMO Consolidations: How National Mergers Affect Local Markets. *Health Affairs* 18(4):96–104.

Feldstein, Paul J. 1988. *The Politics of Health Legislation: An Economic Perspective.* Ann Arbor, MI: Health Administration Press.

———. 1999. *Health Policy Issues: An Economic Perspective on Health Reform.* 2nd ed. Chicago: Health Administration Press.

Fishbein, Morris. 1932. The Committee on the Costs of Medical Care. *JAMA* 99:1950–1952.

———. 1947. *A History of the American Medical Association, 1847 to 1947.* Philadelphia: W. B. Saunders.

Foubister, Vida. 1998. Unions a Difficult Option, Physicians Say. *AMA News,* 20 July.

Fox, Daniel M. 1986. *Health Policies, Health Politics.* Princeton, NJ: Princeton University Press.

———. 2006. Keynote address, Menzies Centre for Health Policy Seminar, Sydney, Australia, 5 April.

———, and Paul Fronstin. 2000. Letter to the editor. *Health Affairs* 19(2):271–273.

Frech, H. E., III. 2003. Author interview of the 1975–1976 economic consultant to the Federal Trade Commission. 13 August.

Freidson, Eliot. 1973. *Profession of Medicine: A Study of the Sociology of Applied Knowledge.* New York: Dodd, Mead & Company.

———. 1986. The Medical Profession in Transition. In *Applications of Social Science to Clinical Medicine and Health Policy,* ed. Linda Aiken and David Mechanic. New Brunswick, NJ: Rutgers University Press.

———. 2001. *Professionalism: The Third Logic.* Chicago: University of Chicago Press.

Freyer, Tony. 1992. *Regulating Big Business: Antitrust in Great Britain and America, 1880–1990*. Cambridge, UK: Cambridge University Press.

Friedman, Milton. 1982. *Capitalism and Freedom*. Chicago: University of Chicago Press.

Fronstin, Paul. 2006a. *Employer Health Benefits 2006 Annual Survey.* Kaiser Family Foundation and Health Research and Educational Trust.

———. 2006b. Sources of Health Insurance and Characteristics of the Uninsured: Analysis of the March 2006 Current Population Survey. *EBRI Issue Brief No. 298.* Employee Benefit Research Institute, October.

FTC's Action Improper, AMA Tells U.S. Court. 1980. *AMA News,* 16 May.

FTC:Watch. (Newsletter.) Arthur L. Amolsch and Mimi Madden, eds. Springfield, VA: Washington Regulatory Reporting Associates.

Fuchs, Victor R. 1986. *The Health Economy.* Cambridge, MA: Harvard University Press.

Fuhrmans, Vanessa. 2006. After Streak of Strong Profits, Health Insurers May See Decline. *Wall Street Journal,* 31 July.

———. 2007. Health Insurers Settle Dispute on Pay with 900,000 Doctors. *Wall Street Journal,* 28–29 April.

Funigiello, Philip J. 2005. *Chronic Politics: Health Security from FDR to George W. Bush.* Lawrence: University of Kansas Press.

Furrow, Barry R., Thomas L. Greaney, Sandra H. Johnson, Timothy Stoltzfus Jost, and Robert L. Schwartz. 2004. *Health Law: Cases, Materials, and Problems.* 5th ed. American Casebook Series. St. Paul: West Group.

Garceau, Oliver. 1941. *The Political Life of the American Medical Association.* Cambridge, MA: Harvard University Press.

Gerhart, Peter M. 1982. The Supreme Court and Antitrust Analysis: The (Near Triumph) of the Chicago School. *Supreme Court Review* 1982:319–349.

Gevitz, Norman. 1988. Osteopathic Medicine: From Deviance to Difference. In *Other Healers: Unorthodox Medicine in America,* ed. Norman Gevitz. Baltimore: Johns Hopkins University Press.

Gilmer, Todd, and Richard Kronick. 2005. It's the Premiums, Stupid: Projections of the Uninsured through 2013. *Health Affairs* 24(Supp. 1):w143–w151.

Ginzberg. Eli. 1977. *The Limits of Health Reform: The Search for Realism.* New York: Basic Books.

———. 1990. *The Medical Triangle: Physicians, Politicians, and the Public.* Cambridge, MA: Harvard University Press.

Goldberg, Lawrence G., and Warren Greenberg. 1977. The Effect of Physician-Controlled Health Insurance: *United States v. Oregon State Medical Society. Journal of Health Politics, Policy and Law* 2:48–78.

Gorney, Mark. 1980. Are We Restraining Competition or Human Misery? *Legal Aspects of Medical Practice* (February):32–35.

Gottschalk, Marie. 2005. Organized Labor's Incredible Shrinking Social Vision. In *Healthy, Wealthy and Fair: Health Care and the Good Society,* ed. James A. Morone and Lawrence R. Jacobs. New York: Oxford University Press.

Greaney, Thomas L. 1989. Quality of Care and Market Failure Defenses in Antitrust Health Care Litigation. *Connecticut Law Review* 21:605–665.

———. 1996. Is Antitrust Anti-autonomy? *Health Matrix* 96(6):129–146.

———. 2002. Whither Antitrust? The Uncertain Future of Competition Law in Health Care. *Health Affairs* 21(2):185–196.

Green, Mark J., Beverly C. Moore, and Bruce Wasserstein. 1972. *The Closed Enterprise System: Ralph Nader's Study Group Report on Antitrust Enforcement.* New York: Grossman.

Gressley, Gene M., ed. 1977. *Voltaire and the Cowboy: The Letters of Thurman Arnold.* Boulder: Colorado Associated University Press.

Gross, Stanley J. 1984. *Of Foxes and Hen Houses: Licensing and the Healing Professions.* Westport, CT: Greenwood.

Grunes, Rodney A. 2003. William J. Brennan, Jr., and Human Dignity. In *Leaders of the Pack: Polls and Case Studies of Great Supreme Court Justices,* ed. William D. Pederson and Norman W. Provizer. New York: Peter Lang.

Gunther, Gerald. 1991. *Constitutional Law.* 12th ed. University Casebook Series. Westbury, NY: Foundation Press.

Gwartney, James D., and Richard L. Stroup. 1990. *Microeconomics: Private and Public Choice.* 5th ed. San Diego: Harcourt, Brace, Jovanovich.

Havighurst, Clark C. 1970. Health Maintenance Organizations and the Market for Health Services. *Law and Contemporary Problems* 35(4):716–795.

———. 1974a. *Motion for Leave to File and Brief of Clark C. Havighurst, Amicus Curiae, in Support of Petition for Writ of Certiorari,* 23 September. In the U.S. Supreme Court, *Goldfarb v. Virginia State Bar,* docket no. 74-70.

———. 1974b. Speculations on the Market's Future in Health Care. In *Regulating Health Facilities Construction: Proceedings of a Conference on Health Planning, Certificates of Need, and Market Entry,* ed. Clark C. Havighurst. Washington, D.C.: American Enterprise Institute.

———. 1975. Federal Regulation of the Health Care Delivery System—a Forward in the Nature of a 'Package Insert.'" *University of Toledo Law Review* 6:577–590.

———.1978. Professional Restraints on Innovation in Health Care Financing. *Duke Law Journal* 1978(2):303–387.

———. 1986. Professional Peer Review and the Antitrust Laws. *Case Western Reserve Law Review* 36(4):1117–1169.

———. 1988. The Questionable Cost-Containment Record of Commercial Health Insurers. In *Health Care in America: The Political Economy of Hospitals and Health Insurance,* ed. H. E. Frech. San Francisco: Pacific Research Institute for Public Policy.

———. 1996. Are the Antitrust Agencies Overregulating Physician Networks? *Loyola Consumer Law Reporter* 8(2):78–97.

———. 2000. American Health Care and the Law—We Need to Talk! *Health Affairs* 19(4):84–106.

———. 2001. Health Care as a (Big) Business: The Antitrust Response. *Journal of Health Politics, Policy and Law* 26(5):939–955.

———. 2002a. How the Health Care Revolution Fell Short. *Law and Contemporary Problems* 65(4):55–101.

———. 2002b. Is the Health Care Revolution Finished?—a Forward. *Law and Contemporary Problems* 65(4):3–9.

———. 2003. Author interview of the William Neal Reynolds Professor of Law, Duke University. 31 October–1 November.

———. 2004. I've Seen Enough! My Life and Times in Health Care Law and Policy. *Health Matrix* 14:107–130.

———. 2006. Author interview, Washington, D.C. 29–30 June.

Havighurst, Clark C., James F. Blumstein, and Troyen A. Brennan. 1998. *Health Care Law and Policy: Readings, Notes, and Questions.* 2nd ed. University Casebook Series. New York: Foundation Press.

———. 1999. *Teacher's Manual for Health Care Law and Policy: Readings, Notes, and Questions.* University Casebook Series. New York: Foundation Press.

Havighurst, Clark C., and Nancy M. P. King. 1983a. Private Credentialing of Health Care Personnel: An Antitrust Perspective (Part 1). *American Journal of Law and Medicine* 9:131–201.

———. 1983b. Private Credentialing of Health Care Personnel: An Antitrust Perspective (Part 2). *American Journal of Law and Medicine* 9:263–334.

———. 1984. Correspondence. *American Journal of Law and Medicine* 10(4):459–461.

Hays, Samuel P. 1987. The Politics of Environmental Administration. In *The New American State: Bureaucracies and Policies since World War II,* ed. Louis Galambos. Baltimore: Johns Hopkins University Press.

Health Care Quality Improvement Act. U.S. Code 42 (1986), secs. 11101–11152.

Herndon, Jill Boylston, and John E. Lopatka. 1999. Managed Care and the Questionable Relevance of Maricopa. *Antitrust Bulletin* 44(1):117–178.

Hirshfeld, Edward. 1994. The Case for Antitrust Reform for Physician Groups. In *Antitrust and Health Care: Antitrust Developments in Changing Health Care Markets.* Chicago: ABA Section of Antitrust Law.

Hofstadter, Richard. 1991. What Happened to the Antitrust Movement? In *The Political Economy of the Sherman Act: The First One hundred Years,* ed. E. Thomas Sullivan. New York: Oxford University Press.

Holsworth, Robert D. 1980. *Public Interest Liberalism and the Crisis of Affluence: Reflections on Nader, Environmentalism, and the Politics of a Sustainable Society.* Boston: G. K. Hall.

Hovenkamp, Herbert. 1985. Antitrust Policy after Chicago. *Michigan Law Review* 84:213–284.

Hurley, Robert E., Bradley C. Strunk, and Justin S. White. 2004. The Puzzling Popularity of the PPO. *Health Affairs* 23(2):56–68.

Huston, Luther A. 1952. A.M.A. Is Potent Force among the Lawmakers: Social Security Switch an Example of Lobby's Ability to Win Votes. *New York Times,* 15 June.

Hyman, David. 1999. Managed Care at the Millennium: Scenes from a Maul. *Journal of Health Politics, Policy and Law* 24(5):1061–1070.

Institute of Medicine. 2005. *Performance Measurement: Accelerating Improvement.* Committee on Redesigning Health Insurance Performance Measures, Payment, and Performance Improvement Programs, 1 December.

Jacob, Julie A. 1999. Columbia/HCA Cuts Physician Practices. *AMA News,* 20 September.

———. 2000. Blues Plans See Strength in Consolidation. *AMA News,* 14 August.

Jacobs, Lawrence R., and Robert Y. Shapiro. 1999. The American Public's Pragmatic Liberalism Meets Its Philosophical Conservatism. *Journal of Health Politics, Policy and Law* 24(5):1021–1031.

Jacobson, Peter D. 2003. Who Killed Managed Care? A Policy Whodunit. *Saint Louis University Law Journal* 47:365–396.

Jacoby, Mary. 2005. European Rush to Courthouse? Antitrust Cops Want Firms to Fight Their Own Battles. *Wall Street Journal,* 6 June.

Jaklevic, Mary Chris. 1998. AMA's Hirshfeld Passes Away at Age 48. *Modern Healthcare,* 31 August 1998.

Japsen, Bruce. 2005. Inside Health Care. *Chicago Tribune,* 20 January.

Jenkins, Holman. 2004. MBA vs. Poli Sci. *Wall Street Journal,* 16 June.

Johnson, Haynes, and David Broder. 1996. *The System: The American Way of Politics at the Breaking Point.* Boston: Little, Brown.

Johnson, James A., and Walter Jones. 1993. *The American Medical Association: A Commentary and Annotated Bibliography.* New York: Garland.

Jost, Timothy Stoltzfus. 2004. The Supreme Court Limits Lawsuits against Managed Care Organizations. *Health Affairs* 23(Supp. 2):w417–w426.

Kaiser Family Foundation. 2004. Trends and Indicators in the Changing Health Care Marketplace. Exhibit 5.12: Health Care Mergers and Acquisitions, 1994–2003. Http://profile.kff.org/insurance.

Karlin, Joel M. 1998. Is There a Future for the Federation of Medicine? *AMA News,* 12 January.

Kass, Leon R. 1983. Professing Ethically: On the Place of Ethics in Defining Medicine. *JAMA* 249(10):1305–1310.

Katzmann, Robert A. 1980. *Regulatory Bureaucracy: The Federal Trade Commission and Antitrust Policy.* Cambridge, MA: Massachusetts Institute of Technology Press.

Kawachi, Ichiro. 2005. Why the United States Is Not Number One in Health. In *Healthy, Wealthy and Fair: Health Care and the Good Society,* ed. James A. Marone and Lawrence R. Jacobs. New York: Oxford University Press.

Kaysen, Carl, and Donald F. Turner. 1991. Antitrust Policy: An Economic and Legal Analysis. In *The Political Economy of the Sherman Act: The First One Hundred Years,* ed. E. Thomas Sullivan. New York: Oxford University Press.

Kessel, Reuben A. 1958. Price Discrimination in Medicine. *Journal of Law and Economics* 1:20–53.

———. 1970. The AMA and the Supply of Physicians. *Law and Contemporary Problems* 35(2):267–283.

Kinder, Lori. 2000. Author interview of the chief advisor on health care legislation for Representative Thomas Campbell. 30 June.

King, Lester S. 1982. The Founding of the American Medical Association. *JAMA* 248(14):1749–1752.

———. 1983. The AMA Gets a New Code of Ethics. *JAMA* 249(10):1338–1342.

———. 1985. Medicine—Trade or Profession? *JAMA* 253(18):2709–2710.

Kingdon, John. 1995. *Agendas, Alternatives, and Public Policies.* 2nd ed. New York: HarperCollins.

Kintner, Earl W., and Mark R. Joelson. 1974. *An International Antitrust Primer: A Businessman's Guide to the International Aspects of United States Antitrust Law and to Key Foreign Antitrust Laws.* New York: Macmillian.

Kirby, Wendy T., and T. Clark Weymouth. 1985. Antitrust and Amateur Sports: The Role of Noneconomic Values. *Indiana Law Journal* 61:31–51.

Kissam, Phillip C. 1983. Antitrust Law and Professional Behavior. *Texas Law Review* 62(1):1–66.

———, William L. Webber, Lawrence Bigus, and John Holzgraefe. 1982. Antitrust and Hospital Privileges: Testing the Conventional Wisdom. *California Law Review* 70:595–685.

Klein, Sarah A. 1998. Florida Class Action Challenges Prudential Claim Payment. *AMA News,* 10 August.

———. 1999a. AMA Negotiating Unit Gets Name, Board. *AMA News,* 27 September.

———. 1999b. Board Details Discomfort with Collective Bargaining. *AMA News,* 21 June.

———. 2000. California Court: Plans Can't Drop Physicians without Reason. *AMA News,* 5 June.

Kovacic, William E. 1982. The Federal Trade Commission and Congressional Oversight of Antitrust Enforcement. *Tulsa Law Journal* 17(4):587–671.

Krause, Elliott. 1996. *Death of the Guilds: Professions, States, and the Advance of Capitalism, 1930 to the Present.* New Haven, CT: Yale University Press.

Krieger, Gary F. 1997. Setting the Record Straight about the AMAP Initiative. *AMA News,* 9 June.

———. 1998. Medicine's House of Delegates—Worthwhile or Not? *AMA News,* 21 September.

Kronenfeld, Jennie Jacobs. 1997. *The Changing Federal Role in U.S. Health Care Policy.* Westport, CT: Praeger.

Leffler, Keith. 1983. Economic and Legal Analysis of Medical Ethics: The Case of Restrictions on Interprofessional Association. *Law and Human Behavior* 7(2–3):183–217.

Lerner, Arthur N. 2003. Author interview of the former assistant director of the Bureau of Competition, Federal Trade Commission. 24 September.

Levit, Katherine R., Helen C. Lazenby, and Bradley R. Braden. 1998. National Health Spending Trends in 1996. *Health Affairs* 17(1):35–51.

Liebeler, Wesley J. 1986. Economic Review of Antitrust Developments: Horizontal Restrictions, Efficiency, and the Per Se Rule. *UCLA Law Review* 33:1019–1062.

Lindsay, Robert. 1978. California Tax Revolt: Lesson for Legislators. *New York Times,* 12 June.

Lowi, Theodore J., and Benjamin Ginsberg. 1994. *American Government: Freedom and Power.* 3rd ed. New York: W. W. Norton and Company.

Marmor, Theodore R., ed. 1994. *Understanding Health Care Reform.* New Haven, CT: Yale University Press.

———, and Rudolf Klein. 1994. Rationing: Painful Prescription, Inadequate Diagnosis. In *Understanding Health Care Reform,* ed. Theodore R. Marmor. New Haven, CT: Yale University Press.

Marone, James, and Lawrence Jacobs, eds. 2005. *Healthy, Wealthy and Fair: Health Care and the Good Society.* New York: Oxford University Press.

———, and Gary Belkin. 1996. The Science Illusion and the Triumph of Medical Capitalism. Paper presented at the annual meeting of the American Political Science Association, Washington, D.C.

Mason, Alpheus T. 1956. *Brandeis: A Free Man's Life.* New York: Viking.

Mayer, Caroline E. 1982. Medical Societies Aided Backers of FTC Curbs. *Washington Post,* 10 June.

Mayes, Rick. 2004. *Universal Coverage: The Elusive Quest for National Health Insurance.* Ann Arbor: University of Michigan Press.

McCarran-Ferguson Act. U.S. Code 15 (1945), secs. 1101–1015.

McChesney, Fred S., and William F. Shughart, II. 1995. *The Causes and Consequences of Antitrust: The Public Choice Perspective.* Chicago: University of Chicago Press.

McCormick, Brian. 1997. AMA Mourns Death of Dr. James Todd. *AMA News,* 7 July.

McCormick, Robert E. 1989. A Review of the Economics of Regulation: The Political Process. In *Regulation and the Reagan Era: Politics, Bureaucracy and the Public Interest,* ed. Roger E. Meiners and Bruce Yandle. New York: Holmes & Meier.

McCraw, Thomas K. 1984. *Prophets of Regulation.* Cambridge, MA: Harvard University Press, Belknap Press.

McDonough, John E. 1997. *Interests, Ideas, and Deregulation: The Fate of Hospital Rate Setting.* Ann Arbor: University of Michigan Press.

McFadden, Daniel L. 2007. Editorial: A Dog's Breakfast. *Wall Street Journal,* 16 February.

Mechanic, David. 1969. The Changing Structure of Medical Practice. In *Medical Progress and the Law,* ed. Clark Havighurst. Dobbs Ferry, NY: Oceana Publications.

———. 1998. The Functions and Limitations of Trust in the Provision of Medical Care. *Journal of Health Politics, Policy and Law* 23(4):661–686.

Medicine's Legal Offensive. 2001. *AMA News,* 23/30 April.

Meier, Kenneth J. 2000. *Politics and the Bureaucracy.* 4th ed. Orlando, FL.: Harcourt College Publishers.

Memorandum of Chairman Pertschuk in Response to Motions for His Recusal in This Proceeding. 1979. *In the Matter of the American Medical Ass'n,* docket no. 9064, 18 April.

Memorandum of Respondent American Medical Association in Reply to Posttrial Brief of Counsel Supporting the Complaint. 1978. *In the Matter of the American Medical Ass'n,* docket no. 9064, 25 August.

Millenson, Michael L. 1997. "Miracle and Wonder": The AMA Embraces Quality Measurement. *Health Affairs* 16(3):183–194.

Miller, James C., III. 1982. Redirect the FTC? Yes. Exempt the Professions? No! *Regulatory Action Network: Washington Watch,* May.

Morris, Edmund. 2002. *Theodore Rex.* New York: Modern Library.

Motion of the American Medical Association for the Recusal or Disqualification of Chairman Michael Pertschuk. 1979. *In the Matter of the American Medical Ass'n,* docket no. 9064, 6 April.

Muris, Timothy J. 2000. *California Dental Association v. Federal Trade Commission:* The Revenge of Footnote 17. *Supreme Court Economics Review* 8:265–310.

———. 2002. Creating a Culture of Competition: The Essential Role of Competition Advocacy. Prepared Remarks before the International Competition Network Panel on Competition Advocacy and Antitrust Authorities. Naples, Italy, 28 September.

———. 2003. Author interview of the chair of the Federal Trade Commission. 10 July.

Navarro, Vicente. 1994. *The Politics of Health Policy: The U.S. Reforms, 1980–1994.* Cambridge, UK: Blackwell Publishers.

O'Brien, David. 1990. *Storm Center: The Supreme Court in American Politics.* 2nd ed. New York: W. W. Norton and Company.

Ohsfeldt, Robert L., Michael A. Morrisey, Leonard Nelson, and Victoria Johnson. 1998. The Spread of State Any Willing Provider Laws. *HSR: Health Services Research* 33:5 (December 1998, Part 2):1537–1562.

Olson, Mancur. 1965. *The Logic of Collective Action: Public Goods and the Theory of Groups.* Cambridge, MA: Harvard University Press.

———, ed. 1982. *A New Approach to the Economics of Health Care.* Washington, D.C.: American Enterprise Institute.

Page, Leigh. 1999a. Managed Care Bill Already Law in Most States. *AMA News,* 16 August.

———. 1999b. States Expected to Take Up Flood of Managed Care Bills. *AMA News,* 25 January.

Painter, Joseph T., Lonnie R. Bristow, and James S. Todd. 1994. Shared Sacrifice: The AMA Leadership Response to the Health Security Act. *JAMA* 271(10):786–788.

Palmer, Alan. 2003. Author interview of the former assistant director for general litigation of the Bureau of Competition, Federal Trade Commission. 23

September.

Parsons, Talcott. 1964. *The Social Structure.* Glencoe, IL: Free Press.

Patel, Kant, and Mark E. Rushefsky. 1999. *Health Care Politics and Policy in America.* 2nd ed. Armonk, NY: M. E. Sharpe.

Patients Will Be the Real Losers. 1978. *AMA News,* 8 December.

Pave, Irene. 1977. The 9% Flaw in Carter's Hospital Plan. *Business Week,* 9 May.

Pear, Robert. 2000. Elated by Antitrust Triumph, Doctors Take Case to Senate. *New York Times,* 1 July.

Peck, Richard. 1979. Why the FTC Has Declared War on Doctors. *Medical Economics* 56(16):29–30, 32, 37–38.

Pertschuk, Michael. 1986. *Giant Killers.* New York: W. W. Norton and Company.

Peterson, Mark A. 1999. Introduction: Politics, Misperception, or Apropos? *Journal of Health Politics, Policy and Law* 24(5):873–886.

———. 2005. The Congressional Graveyard for Health Care Reform. In *Healthy, Wealthy and Fair: Health Care and the Good Society,* ed. James A. Marone and Lawrence R. Jacobs. New York: Oxford University Press.

Pinkham, Charles B. 1921. The Chiropractic Problem. *JAMA* 76(2 April):938.

Pitofsky, Robert. 1979. The Political Content of Antitrust. *University of Pennsylvania Law Review* 127:1051–1075.

Posner, Richard A. 1976. *Antitrust Law: An Economic Perspective.* Chicago: University of Chicago Press.

———. 1991. The Chicago School of Antitrust Analysis. In *The Political Economy of the Sherman Act: The First One Hundred Years,* ed. E. Thomas Sullivan. New York: Oxford University Press.

Prager, Linda O. 2000. AMAP's Demise Leaves Void in Physician Evaluation. *AMA News,* 27 March.

Proposed Findings of Fact and Conclusions of Counsel Supporting the Complaint. 1978. *In the Matter of the American Medical Ass'n,* docket no. 9064, 27 July.

Quadagno, Jill. 2005. *One Nation Uninsured: Why the U.S. Has No National Health Insurance.* New York: Oxford University Press.

Rankin, James W., and Bruce A. Hubbard. 1984. Private Credentialing of Health Care Personnel: A Pragmatic Response to Academic Theory. *American Journal of Law and Medicine* 10:189–200.

Rayack, Elton. 1967. *Professional Power and American Medicine: The Economics of the American Medical Association.* Cleveland: World Publishing Company.

Reder, Melvin W. 1982. Chicago Economics: Permanence and Change. *Journal of Economic Literature* 20(March 1982):1–38.

Reeher, Grant. 2003. Reform and Remembrance: The Place of the Private Sector in the Future of Health Care Policy. *Journal of Health Politics, Policy and Law* 28(2– 3):355–385.

Reigel, Quentin. 1981. The FTC in the 1980's: An Analysis of the FTC Improvements Act of 1980. *The Antitrust Bulletin* Fall:449–486.

Relman, Arnold. 1978. Professional Directories—but Not Commercial Advertising—as a Public Service. *New England Journal of Medicine* 299(9):476–478.

Reply Brief of Counsel Supporting the Complaint. 1978. *In the Matter of the American Medical Ass'n,* docket no. 9064, 25 August.

Rewarding Quality Care. 2003. *AMA News,* 6 January.

Rich, Robert, and Christopher Erb. 2005. The Two Faces of Managed Care Regulation and Policy Making. *Stanford Law and Policy Review* 16:233–276.

The Right Approach for Doctors. 2000. *AMA News,* 11 December.

Robinson, James. 1999. *The Corporate Practice of Medicine: Competition and Innovation in Health Care.* Berkeley: University of California Press.

Rodwin, Marc A. 1993. *Medicine, Money, and Morals: Physicians' Conflicts of Interest.* New York: Oxford University Press.

Rosen, George. 1983. *The Structure of American Medical Practice, 1875–1941.* Philadelphia: University of Pennsylvania Press.

Rowe, John, Denis Cortese, and J. Michael McGinnis. 2006. The Emerging Context for Advances in Comparative Effectiveness Assessment. *Health Affairs* 25(6):w593–w595.

Rubin, Ross. 2003. Author interview of the vice president of legislative affairs of the American Medical Association. 31 July.

Sabatier, Paul, and Hank Jenkins-Smith, eds. 1993. *Policy Change and Learning: An Advocacy Coalition Approach.* Boulder, CO: Westview Press.

———. 1999. The Advocacy Coalition Framework: An Assessment. In *Theories of the Policy Process,* ed. Paul Sabatier. Boulder, CO: Westview Press.

Sage, William M. 2003. Protecting Competition and Consumers: A Conversation with Timothy Muris. *Health Affairs* 22(6):101–110.

Savage, Deborah A. 2004. Professional Sovereignty Revisited: The Network Transformation of American Medicine? *Journal of Health Politics, Policy and Law* 29(4–5):661–677.

Schaller, Michael, and George Rising. 2002. *The Republican Ascendancy: American Politics, 1968–2001.* Wheeling, IL: Harlan Davidson.

Schattschneider, E. E. 1975. *The Semisovereign People: A Realist's View of Democracy in America.* Hinsdale, IL: Dryden Press.

Schlesinger, Mark A. 2002. Loss of Faith: The Sources of Reduced Political Legitimacy for the American Medical Association. *Milbank Quarterly* 80(2):185–235.

———. 2005. The Dangers of a Market Panacea. In *Healthy, Wealthy and Fair: Health Care and the Good Society,* ed. James A. Marone and Lawrence R. Jacobs. New York: Oxford University Press.

Schulman, Bruce J. 2001. *The Seventies: The Great Shift in American Culture, Society, and Politics.* New York: Free Press.

Schwartz, Daniel C. 2003. Author interview of the former deputy director of the Bureau of Competition, Federal Trade Commission. 22 September.

Scott, Charity. 1991. Medical Peer Review, Antitrust, and the Effect of Statutory Reform. *Maryland Law Review* 50:316–407.

Segal, Jeffrey A., and Harold J. Spaeth. 1993. *The Supreme Court and the Attitudinal Model.* Cambridge, UK: Cambridge University Press.

Shadid, Michael A. 1939. *A Doctor for the People: The Autobiography of the Founder of America's First Co-operative Hospital.* New York: Vanguard Press.

Sherman Act. U.S. Code 15 (1890), secs. 1–7.

Skocpol, Theda. 1996. *Boomerang: Clinton's Health Security Effort and the Turn against Government in U.S. Politics.* New York: W. W. Norton and Company.

Smith, Peter, and Nick York. 2004. Quality Incentives: The Case of U.K. General Practitioners. *Health Affairs* 23(3):112–118.

Smith-Cunnien, Susan Lee. 1990. Organized Medicine and Chiropractic: The Role of the Deviation of Chiropractic in the Development of U.S. Medicine, 1908 to 1976. PhD diss., University of Minnesota.

Snyder, James. 1982. Assaults on the Medical Profession. *Physician's Management* 22 September:28–30, 32, 37, 40.

Starr, Paul. 1982. *The Social Transformation of American Medicine.* New York: Basic Books.

Stevens, Rosemary A. 1971. *American Medicine and the Public Interest.* New Haven, CT: Yale University Press.

———. 1989. *In Sickness and in Wealth: American Hospitals in the Twentieth Century.* New York: Basic Books.

———. 2001. Public Roles for the Medical Profession in the United States: Beyond Theories of Decline and Fall. *Milbank Quarterly* 79(3):327–353.

Stigler, George. 1988. The Theory of Economic Regulation. In *Chicago Studies in Political Economy,* ed. George Stigler. Chicago: University of Chicago Press.

Stone, Deborah. 1999. Managed Care and the Second Great Transformation. *Journal of Health Politics, Policy and Law* 24(5):1213–1218.

———. 2005. How Market Inequality Guarantees Racial Inequality. In *Healthy, Wealthy and Fair: Health Care and the Good Society,* ed. James A. Marone and Lawrence R. Jacobs. New York: Oxford University Press.

Strum, Philippa. 1993. *Brandeis: Beyond Progressivism.* Lawrence: University of Kansas Press.

Sullivan, E. Thomas, ed. 1991. *The Political Economy of the Sherman Act: The First One hundred Years.* New York: Oxford University Press.

Todd, James S., Steven V. Seekins, John A. Krichbaum, and Lynn K. Harvey. 1991. Health Access America—Strengthening the US Health Care System. *JAMA* 265(19):2503–2506.

Trial Brief of Respondent American Medical Association. 1977. *In the Matter of the American Medical Ass'n,* docket no. 9064, 22 August.

U.S. Congress. House. 1982a. Committee on Energy and Commerce, Subcommittee on Commerce, Transportation, and Tourism. *Hearings on Federal Trade Commission Reauthorization.* 97th Cong., 2nd sess., 1 and 20 April.

———. 1982b. *Congressional Record.* 97th Cong., 2nd sess. Vol. 128, pt. 19.

———. 1984. Committee on Energy and Commerce, Subcommittee on Oversight and Investigations. *Report Prepared by a Member of the Federal Trade Commission Together with Comments from Other Members of the Commission.* 98th Cong., 2nd sess., 19 September.

———. 1999. Committee on the Judiciary. *Quality Health-Care Coalition Act of 1999.* 106th Cong., 1st sess., 22 June.

———. 2000. Committee on the Judiciary. *Quality Health-Care Coalition Act of 2000: Report Together with Additional Views.* 106th Cong., 2nd sess. Report 106–625.

U.S. Congress. Senate. 1974. Committee on the Judiciary, Subcommittee on Antitrust and Monopoly. 93rd Cong., 2nd sess., 14–15, 17, 29–30 May and 10 July.

———. 1982. *Senate Record Vote Analysis.* 97th Cong., 2nd sess., 17 December. Page S-15080 Temp. Record. Vote No. 428.

U.S. Department of Justice and Federal Trade Commission. 1994. *Statements of Enforcement Policy and Analytical Principles Relating to Health Care and Antitrust.* Trade Reg. Reprint (CCH) 4, *par.* 13,152.

———. 1996. *Statements of Antitrust Enforcement Policy in Health Care.* Trade Reg. Reprint (CCH) 4, *par.* 13,153.

U.S. General Accounting Office (GAO). 1997. *Managed Care: Explicit Gag Clauses Not Found in HMO Contracts, but Physician Concerns Remain.* Pub. no. GAO/HEHS 97–175. Washington, D.C.: U.S. GAO.

———. 2004. *Health Care: Unsustainable Trends Necessitate Comprehensive and Fundamental Reforms to Control Spending and Improve Value.* Pub. no. GAO- 04–793SP. Washington, D.C.: U.S. GAO.

Walt, Richard. 1997. Specialty Participation Reflects Medicine's Changing Face. *AMA News,* 2 June.

Wardwell, Walter I. 1988. Chiropractors: Evolution to Acceptance. In *Other Healers: Unorthodox Medicine in America,* ed. Norman Gevitz. Baltimore: Johns Hopkins University Press.

Weissert, Carol, and William Weissert. 1996. *Governing Health: The Politics of Health Policy.* Baltimore: Johns Hopkins University Press.

Weller, Charles D. 1983. Antitrust Joint Ventures and the End of the AMA's Contract Practice Ethics: New Ways of Thinking about the Health Care Industry. *North Carolina Central Law Journal* 14:3–32.

———. 1984. "Free Choice" as a Restraint of Trade in American Health Care Delivery and Insurance. *Iowa Law Review* 69(July):1351–1389.

Wells, Wyatt. 2002. *Antitrust and the Formation of the Postwar World.* New York: Columbia University Press.

Wessel, David. 2005. Deficit Debate Makes for Strange Bedfellows. *Wall Street Journal,* 20 October.

White, Joseph. 2003. Three Meanings of Capacity, or Why the Federal Government Is Most Likely to Lead on Insurance Access Issues. *Journal of Health Politics, Policy and Law* 28(2–3):217–244.

Wilensky, Gail. 2006. Developing a Center for Comparative Effectiveness Information. *Health Affairs* 25:w572–w585.
Wiley, John Shepard, Jr. 1986. A Capture Theory of Antitrust Federalism. *Harvard Law Review* 99:713–789.
Woolfe, Steven, and Kurt Stange. 2006. A Sense of Priorities for the Health Care Commons. *American Journal of Preventive Medicine* 31(1):99–102.
Wylie, Philip. 1952. The Doctors' Conspiracy of Silence. *Medical Economics* 29:173.
Yale Law Journal. 1954. The American Medical Profession: Power, Purpose, and Politics in Organized Medicine (Comment) 63:937–1022.
Zeitlin, Kim, ed. 1985. *Antitrust, Competition Policy and State Professional Regulation: A Manual for Regulators.* Lexington, KY: Council of State Governments.
Zinn, Howard. 2003. *A People's History of the United States: 1492–Present.* New York: HarperCollins.

REPORTED CASES

Aetna v. Davila, 542 U.S. 200 (2004).
American Medical Ass'n, In the Matter of, 94 F.T.C. 701 (1979).
American Medical Ass'n, United States v., 28 F.Supp. 752 (D.D.C. 1939).
American Medical Ass'n, United States v., 110 F.2d 703 (D.C. Cir. 1940).
American Medical Ass'n, United States v., 317 U.S. 519 (1943).
American Medical Ass'n v. F.T.C., 638 F.2d 443 (2nd Cir. 1980).
American Medical Ass'n v. F.T.C., 455 U.S. 676 (1982).
Arizona v. Maricopa County Medical Soc., 1979 U.S. Dist. LEXIS 11918, 1979-1 Trade Cas. (CCH) *par.* 62,694 (D. Ariz. 1979).
Arizona v. Maricopa County Medical Soc., 643 F.2d 553 (9th Cir. 1980).
Arizona v. Maricopa County Medical Soc., 457 U.S. 332 (1982).
Ass'n of American Physicians and Surgeons v. Clinton, 997 F.2d 898 (D.C. Cir. 1993).
Atlantic Cleaners and Dyers, Inc. v. United States, 286 U.S. 427 (1932).
Bates v. State Bar of Arizona, 433 U.S. 350 (1977).
Brown Univ., United States v., 5 F.3d 658 (3rd Cir. 1993).
California Dental Ass'n v. F.T.C., 526 U.S. 756 (1999).
California Retail Liquor Dealers Ass'n v. Midcal Aluminum, Inc., 445 U.S. 97 (1980).
Chicago Board of Trade v. United States, 246 U.S. 231 (1918).
Cigna v. Calad, 542 U.S. 200 (2004).
Cinderella Career and Finishing Schools, Inc. v. F.T.C., 425 F.2d 583 (D.C. Cir. 1970).
Community Blood Bank of Kansas City Area, Inc. v. F.T.C. 405 F.2d 1011 (8th Cir. 1969).
Corcoran v. United Healthcare, Inc., 965 F.2d 1321 (5th Cir. 1992).

Darling v. Charlestown Community Memorial Hosp., 211 N.E.2d 253 (Ill. 1965).
Dent v. State of West Virginia, 129 U.S. 114 (1888).
Dr. Miles Medical Co. v. John D. Park & Sons Co., 220 U.S. 373 (1911).
Dukes v. U.S. Healthcare, Inc., 57 F.3d 350 (3rd Cir. 1995).
Eastern R.R. Presidents Conf. v. Noerr Motor Freight, Inc., 365 U.S. 127 (1961).
Falcone v. Middlesex County Medical Soc.,170 A.2d 324 (N.J. 1961).
F.T.C. v. Gratz, 253 U.S. 421 (1920).
F.T.C. v. Indiana Federation of Dentists, 476 U.S. 447 (1986).
F.T.C. v. National Commission on Egg Nutrition, 88 F.T.C. 89, *aff'd* 570 F.2d 157 (7th Cir. 1977).
F.T.C. v. Sperry & Hutchinson Co., 405 U.S. 233 (1972).
Goldfarb v. Virginia State Bar, 355 F.Supp. 491 (E.D. Va. 1973).
Goldfarb v. Virginia State Bar, 497 F.2d 1 (4th Cir. 1974).
Goldfarb v. Virginia State Bar, 421 U.S. 773 (1975).
Greisman v. Newcomb Hosp., 192 A.2d 817 (N.J. 1963).
Heart of Atlanta Motel v. United States, 379 U.S. 241 (1964).
Hospital Bldg. Co. v. Trustees of Rex Hospital, 425 U.S. 738 (1976).
In re or *In the Matter of* (see name of party).
Katzenbach v. McClung, 379 U.S. 294 (1964).
Kentucky Ass'n of Health Plans v. Miller, 538 U.S. 329 (2003).
Managed Care Litigation, In re, 209 F.R.D. 678 (2002).
McLain v. Real Estate Bd. of New Orleans, Inc., 444 U.S. 232 (1980).
Medical Ass'n of Georgia v. Blue Cross and Blue Shield of Georgia, 536 S.E.2d 184 (Ga. App. 2000).
Michigan State Medical Society, In the Matter of, 101 F.T.C. 191 (1983).
National Society of Professional Engineers, United States v., 389 F.Supp. 1193 (D.C. 1974).
National Society of Professional Engineers, United States v., 555 F.2d 978 (D.C. Cir. 1977).
National Society of Professional Engineers v. United States, 435 U.S. 679 (1978).
N.C.A.A. v. Board of Regents of the Univ. of Oklahoma, 468 U.S. 85 (1984).
N.L.R.B. v. Jones & Laughlin Steel Corp., 301 U.S. 1 (1937).
Northern Pac. Ry. Co. v. United States, 356 U.S. 1 (1958).
Oregon State Medical Society, United States v., 95 F.Supp. 103 (D. Or. 1950).
Oregon State Medical Society, United States v., 343 U.S. 326 (1952).
Parker v. Board of Dental Examiners, 14 P.2d 67 (Cal. 1932).
Parker v. Brown, 317 U.S. 341 (1943).
Patrick v. Burget, 800 F.2d 1498 (9th Cir. 1986).
Patrick v. Burget, 486 U.S. 94 (1988).
Pegram v. Herdrich, 530 U.S. 211 (2000).
Pennsylvania Psychiatric Society v. Green Spring Health Services, 280 F.3d 278 (3rd Cir. 2002).
People v. United Medical Services, Inc., 200 N.E. 157 (Ill. 1936).

Pilot Life Ins. Co. v. Dedeaux, 481 U.S. 41 (1987).
Potvin v. Metropolitan Life Ins. Co., 997 P.2d 1153 (Cal. 2000).
Rush Prudential HMO v. Moran, 536 U.S. 355 (2002).
Southbank IPA, Inc., 114 F.T.C. 783 (1991) (consent order).
Thompson v. Nason Hosp., 591 A.2d 703 (Pa. 1991).
United States v. ___________ (see opposing party).
Wilk v. American Medical Ass'n, 671 F. Supp. 1465 (N.D. Ill. 1987).
Wilk v. American Medical Ass'n, 895 F.2d 352 (7th Cir. 1990).

Index

Text: 10/13 Aldus
Display: Aldus
Indexer: Sharon Sweeney
Compositor: BookMatters, Berkeley
Printer and binder: Maple-Vail Manufacturing Group